The Encomienda
IN NEW SPAIN

Facsimile of title to an encomienda granted by Francisco de Montejo, Governor of Yucatan, to Antonio de Vergara, May 7, 1544. See the translation in Appendix I.

The Encomienda

IN NEW SPAIN

THE BEGINNING
of Spanish Mexico

BY
LESLEY BYRD SIMPSON

UNIVERSITY OF CALIFORNIA PRESS
BERKELEY, LOS ANGELES, LONDON

UNIVERSITY OF CALIFORNIA PRESS
BERKELEY AND LOS ANGELES, CALIFORNIA

UNIVERSITY OF CALIFORNIA PRESS LIMITED
LONDON, ENGLAND

✲

Revised and Enlarged Edition
Copyright 1950 by the Regents of the University of California
Reprinted 1966 with Added Appendix

✲

FIRST PAPERBACK PRINTING 1982
CALIFORNIA LIBRARY REPRINT SERIES EDITION 1982
ISBN 0-520-04630-7 paper
0-520-04629-3 cloth

PRINTED IN THE UNITED STATES OF AMERICA

1 2 3 4 5 6 7 8 9

Foreword

IT IS A commonplace to say that the transplanting to the New World of European institutions and habits of life is heavy with meaning for our understanding of Latin America. Anthropologists have made us familiar with the stubbornness with which peoples cling to their "culture patterns." The Spaniards who carried out the conquest brought with them the accumulated social habits of centuries and never relaxed in their long effort to impose them upon the indigenous population of America. That process, or acculturation, may be thought of, as modern *indigenistas* are fond of reminding us, as a regrettable revolution which destroyed a rich and ancient way of life, although most indigenistas seem content to get along in the European fashion. From the conquistadores' point of view it was the irresistible march of Catholic civilization brought to the heathen by God's new Chosen People.

In New Spain, as Cortés appropriately named his magnificent conquest, assimilation was considerably aided by the nature of preconquest Mexican society. That society had, through long centuries, developed a stable economy based on maize (Indian corn), the production of which forced the bulk of the population to live in conformity with the immutable calendar of clearing, seeding, growth, and harvest, and the other necessary chores incident to its production and storage. Maize, like cereal crops the world over, induced habits of peace and order among those dependent upon it. At the same time those very habits rendered the farmer less able to resist the incursions of warlike and hungry nomads from the north. Aztec picture records tell us of repeated invasions of the "wild men" (Chichimecs). These wild men, of whom the Aztecs themselves were the last successful group (thirteenth century), overran from time to time the rich maize-growing lands south of the "Chichimec frontier" (roughly, the line formed by the canyons of the Santiago and Moctezuma rivers; see the map), and set themselves up as a new class of overlords, levying tribute in goods and in slaves for the sacrificial stone, forcing their subjects to erect vast public monuments, and, in general, governing them with severity. It was the intense hatred evoked by the Aztecs among their vassal states which made possible the conquest of an empire by a mere handful of Spaniards.

Now, Spain itself had gone through a somewhat similar round of invasion and subjugation a number of times (by Goths, Arabs, and Moors), and was living in a social system erected upon the privileges of conquest. We call it the feudal system, the essence of which was a personal relationship between conqueror and conquered. The conqueror seized the land, defended it (when he could) from his marauding neighbors, levied tribute (feudal dues) on his vassals, protected them after a fashion, forced them to serve him, and permitted no one to bear arms but himself and his retainers. In practice the feudal system became much more complicated than that, but essentially it divided society horizontally into lord and vassal, master and serf. Spanish rule in America, as far as the conquerors could make it do so, followed the familiar feudal pattern, which was accepted as right and proper by Spaniard and Indian alike—not that the Indian was pleased with it, but it was the sort of thing he could understand. He merely suffered a change of masters, as he had often done before, and the Spanish conqueror found himself in the desirable position of having serfs to do his bidding and support him in the pleasant life of a quasi-military parasite. Such, at least, was the ideal. The reality will come out in the course of the following pages.

That personal relationship between white man and Indian became the basis of Spanish colonial society, and, in general, it is that of rural Mexico today. It is true, to be sure, that there has been a great deal of blending of the two races; but patterns of conduct do not necessarily follow changes in complexion. That is, an Indian or *mestizo* landowner is indistinguishable from the white in his treatment of those who serve him, and that attitude has not changed perceptibly since the conquest, nor has it changed, it is fairly safe to assume, since a millennium or so before the conquest, on either side of the Atlantic. Hence the pertinence of the present volume, for that curious institution called the *encomienda* was a vigorous offspring of the feudal system.

Politically, feudalism was moribund in Spain at the time of the conquest of America, and it was quite unthinkable that the Spanish monarchs would tolerate in the New World an institution which would disperse their newly won authority. From the beginning the Crown carefully refrained from giving the conquistadores anything resembling permanent ownership of their encomiendas, with the one immense exception in New Spain of the sprawling estate granted to Hernán Cortés. And even there the Crown soon withdrew the privilege of civil and criminal jurisdiction. The feudal tradition was, however, too deeply set among the conquistadores to be eradicated by royal edict. The King's distant and unruly subjects, while loudly proclaiming their invincible loyalty, tended to usurp all authority, to grab land and treasure, to exploit Indian labor, and, in general, to conduct themselves like conquerors of all times. To bring them within the framework of the new despotism cost the Crown generations of dogged effort, only partly successful. It did, indeed, reduce the encomienda to a kind of pension system for the deserving veterans, but the numerous spawn of the conquistadores and the hungry latecomers occupied vast stretches of "vacant" lands where they set up their haciendas on ancient feudal lines, which still persist in spite of the reforms of the past thirty years.

Since this study first appeared, some twenty years ago, so much fundamental research has been done in the history

of Spanish colonial institutions, especially in the history of
those concerned with the exploitation and administration
of the natives, that its rectification has become imperative.
We know, for example, a great deal more about the extent
of the encomienda, in territory and in the number of people
affected by it. We have a much clearer notion of the philo-
sophical and juridical arguments by which it was justified,
and we know something about its economic and demographic implications. We have also uncovered sufficient new
material to allow us to trace the history of the original ruling
class of New Spain (the conquistadores and their immediate descendants) through the critical years of its long
struggle with the Crown, until the effective reduction of
the encomienda some time after the end of the sixteenth
century. Another interesting aspect of the early history of
Mexico is that, although the Spaniards, like everybody else,
were principally excited about discovering sources of metal-
lic wealth, they were not so foolish as to overlook the possibilities of the vast agricultural empire which was already
functioning and which was theirs for the taking. Before
the great break-through of the middle of the sixteenth century into the silver country north of the Chichimec frontier,
New Spain should, in fact, be thought of mainly as the con-
solidation of the various native states into one vast agricultural complex, the administration of which was divided
pretty equally between the Crown and the encomenderos.

A further change of emphasis is made necessary by our
increased knowledge of the ubiquitous Fray Bartolomé de
las Casas. That old master of excoriation, principally, I suspect, because of the ferocity of his invective and the volume
of his writings, has been for four centuries the most quoted
source for the early history of Spanish-Indian relations. His
influence on many generations of historians is proved and
accepted and need not detain us again. Las Casas was a powerful propagandist, and his value to the Crown in its conflict

with the incipient New World feudalism is manifest; but in
the framing of Indian legislation he was, I think, secondary
in importance to Francisco de Vitoria, the philosopher of
Salamanca, and certainly to the great Dominican cardinal,
Fray García de Loaisa, who, as President of the Council of
the Indies, dominated the thinking of that all-powerful body
during the critical years of 1524–1546, when Indian law was
given its theocratic and humanitarian cast. But neither of
those eminent men left writings as forthright and quotable
as those of Las Casas, and he continues to exercise a certain
fascination for students of the period. In a resolution adopted
by the Congreso de Americanistas at Seville in 1935, for
example, Las Casas was voted "the authentic representative
of the Spanish conscience." That kind of canonization does
no particular harm, but if the resolution implies that the
conscience of the Crown was materially affected by Las
Casas, it is open to question. The result of the Crown's campaign to dominate its empire in the New World was, indeed,
the relief of the Indians from exploitation by the encomenderos *qua* encomenderos, but its conscience-probing did not
carry it to the absurd extreme of destroying the foundation
of its wealth in the Indies, namely, the forced labor of the
Indians. It did eventually substitute for the encomienda an
administrative system controlled by the Crown (the *corregimiento*), as well as various devices for coercing labor,
with, however, no discernible benefit to anyone but itself,
the Church, the miners, the planters, and other users of
labor. In any case, the catastrophic decline of the native
population during the sixteenth and seventeenth centuries
(between eighty and ninety per cent!) doomed the encomienda as a device for procuring cheap labor. The deepening crisis led the Crown to assume a strict control of the
allotment of coerced services and brought about the gradual
emergence of a wage-earning class of skilled mechanics
among the Indians of the mines and Spanish towns, as well

as the universal adoption of contract labor (debt peonage)
for unskilled workers (*gañanes*). There was never enough
labor to go round, and there was certainly not enough of it
to support the encomenderos in unproductive parasitism. In
the light of this knowledge I have revised my estimate of
the continuing importance of the encomienda and am now
satisfied that, although it was not definitely abolished until
the eighteenth century, by the end of the sixteenth it had
ceased to exercise any vital function in colonial life. In its
reduced status the encomienda was allowed to survive, it is
tempting to guess, by the growing indifference of the Crown
to its economic aspects; that is, after the immense possibilities
of revenue from the silver mines had become a reality, the
negligible sums collected by the encomenderos from their
vanishing Indian subjects were no longer of much interest,
and it was the easier and wiser course for the Crown to blink
at the irregularities by which the encomienda continued to
exist.

The significance which I ascribed to the development of
institutions in the Greater Antilles before the conquest of
Mexico has been retained. Without that background the
course of Spanish-Indian relations on the mainland would
not be comprehensible. Virtually all the conquerors of New
Spain were men who had served their apprenticeship in Cuba
and Española, where they had imbibed the prevailing attitude toward the natives and accepted the frightful methods
of exploitation which all but destroyed the island population in a generation. Their attitude has an importance for
the subsequent history of New Spain which it would be
difficult to exaggerate. It was always present behind the
actions of legislators, governors, judges, and colonists alike,
and even the clergy shared the general notion that the Indians (all of them, everywhere) had, by some mysterious
dispensation of Providence, been placed there for the particular glory and profit of the Spaniards. That attitude had

had a long period of incubation in the Antilles before Cortés set out on his remarkable adventure, and, indeed, it is still one of the persistent culture traits of the ruling element of Mexico.

As developed in the Antilles, the encomienda was at first (up to the passage of the New Laws of 1542) the delegation of the royal power to collect the tribute from, *and to use the personal services of*, the King's vassals (the Indians). The encomendero undertook to look after the welfare of his charges and to educate them in proper (Spanish) norms of conduct, as well as to discharge the usual feudal obligation of bearing arms in the King's defense. In reality the encomienda, at least in the first fifty years of its existence, was looked upon by its beneficiaries as a subterfuge for slavery, and it was only after half a century of furious agitation on the part of Las Casas and the reformers, and the active interest of the Crown in suppressing it, that it was shorn of its most profitable and harmful feature, the privilege of using the services of the Indians, and was reduced to some semblance of a social system. Indeed, the metamorphosis of the encomienda, which achieved lasting notoriety for its shocking wastage of labor, into a kind of benevolent paternalism is one of the most curious phenomena of colonial history.

There are, unfortunately, no records extant of the actual operation of an encomienda, if, indeed, records were ever kept. It is not until the middle of the sixteenth century, after a relative stability had been achieved, that the investigator can walk with any assurance among the documents. Beyond that point he has court records and the voluminous tribute and tithe rolls to guide him, as well as some reasonably dispassionate reports submitted by missionaries, civil officials, and royal visitors. Hence a more convincing picture of New Spain can be drawn for the latter half of the century, and it is offered as a new contribution in this study.

New Spain in the sixteenth century was not coterminous with modern Mexico. For our purpose it may be limited to the ancient bishroprics of Tlaxcala (later, Puebla), Mexico, Oaxaca, and Michoacán, all of which were under the immediate jurisdiction of the Audiencia of Mexico. The map in chapter twelve will give a notion of its effective limits. The bishoprics of Guadalajara (New Galicia), Chiapa-Guatemala, and Yucatan lay outside its direct control. I have not hesitated, however, to draw examples from them, because the problems incident to the encomienda were common to all.

Following my early conviction that an ounce of original testimony is worth a pound of exegesis, I have quoted liberally from contemporary documents, some of the most illuminating of which will be found translated in the Appendix.

In the revision of my book I am greatly in the debt of a number of coworkers in the field who will be mentioned as I make use of their findings. I am no less indebted to the John Simon Guggenheim Memorial Foundation, the Rockefeller Foundation, and the University of California for making further research possible. I am especially sensible of the unvarying courtesy of my good friends in the archives of Mexico and Guatemala, without whose help I could have accomplished little during my two years' stay with them. Finally, a considerable part of the Spanish archival material used in chapters eleven and twelve was placed at my disposal by Professor Carl O. Sauer of the University of California, to whom I owe a long and pleasant debt of friendship and encouragement. Dr. Woodrow Borah undertook the painful task of reading proof—for which I thank him.

Contents

As far as the Indians are concerned, there have been so many changes that I have said repeatedly we were going crazy with so many experiments. After sixteen years in this government I could swear that I am more confused about them than at the beginning.—VICEROY ANTONIO DE MENDOZA TO HIS SUCCESSOR, LUIS DE VELASCO, 1551.

The two Republics, of Spaniards and Indians, of which this Kingdom consists are so repugnant to each other . . . that it seems that the conservation of the former always means the oppression and destruction of the latter. The estates, buildings, plantations, mines, and herds, the monasteries and religious orders,—I do not know whether it would be possible to maintain them or improve them without the service and aid of the Indians.—VICEROY LUIS DE VELASCO II TO HIS SUCCESSOR, THE COUNT OF MONTERREY, 1595.

1.

The Indian Legislation of Isabella

WHEN ALEXANDER VI issued his bull of May 4, 1493, assigning the temporal dominion of the newly discovered territories to Castile and Portugal, it was expressly stated that the sole justification for that assignment was the propagation of the Christian religion.[1] The monarchs of Castile and Portugal were, in fact, made spiritual viceroys of the Holy See and held their shaky temporal titles only by virtue of their spiritual obligation. It was this dual and self-contradictory role of the Spanish Crown which accounts for the mass of groping and confused legislation for the government of the Indies during the first century of their occupation. On the one hand the Crown undertook to protect and evangelize the native populations; on the other it was bound to favor the numbers of Spaniards who had conquered the Indies at their own expense and who might reasonably expect some material reward, while the fiscal needs of the Crown itself could not be lost sight of.

The Crown's position was not an enviable one. If the

colonists were allowed to exploit native labor (without which no material wealth could be got), it was brought sharply to task by the Mendicant orders. If the latter should be allowed to have their way and make the native populations entirely free from domination by Spanish laymen, the colonists faced bankruptcy and the Crown the loss of indispensable revenue. There could be but one workable solution: as long as the issue was thus sharply drawn, it will be found that in no case did the Crown sacrifice its material interests, which were identical with those of the colonists, to any otherworldly concept of spiritual duty. It made, indeed, many and apparently sincere efforts to ameliorate the lot of the subject race, and it even succeeded in no small degree, as will appear later; but much of the Utopian legislation was evidently adopted merely to appease the clerical element, as is borne out by the fact that everyone, from the governors down, ignored with impunity all measures that conflicted with the common interests of Crown and colonist.

The rivalry between the civil and religious governments over the manner of ruling the native populations which occupies such a deal of space in the histories of the Indies was, however, quite secondary in importance to the competition between the Crown and the conquerors over: (1) the spoils of conquest; (2) the kind of government, feudal or royal, which was to prevail; and (3)—which in a way summarizes the matter—the right to exploit native labor. Such is the framework of this major phase of the history of the Indies during the extraordinary first century of the Spanish occupation.

Columbus returned to Española in 1495 only to learn that the natives had risen against his lieutenants and that the whole island was in a turmoil. His first duty was to establish order, and so after nine months of campaigning he found the island again under his control and himself with some hundreds of native rebels on his hands. The disposition of these infidel prisoners of war followed ancient usage; they were enslaved and shipped off to Spain with Antonio de Torres, and were offered for sale by Juan de Fonseca, Bishop of Burgos and Badajoz, and minister in charge of Indian affairs.[2]

This ill-considered act of Columbus, coming so soon after his lyrical description of the peaceful and generous character of the natives of Española,[3] seems to have caused the pious Isabella to inquire for the first time into the civil status of her new subjects. In her cédula of April 16, 1495, cited above, she instructed Fonseca to hold up the sale of the Indians whom she had ordered him to dispose of until she should get an opinion from theologians and jurists on the legality of the business. She also wished to learn from Columbus his precise reasons for enslaving them.

Whatever the opinion of the theologians and jurists was, Isabella made no immediate decision one way or the other. Meanwhile, the fate of these first Indian slaves is revealed by a royal letter to Bishop Fonseca: "Reverend Father in Christ, Bishop of Badajoz: In order to man certain galleys which the captain of our fleet, Juan de Lezcano, has in our service, we have agreed to send him fifty Indians, who are to be between twenty and forty years of age. You will take his receipt for them, . . . naming in it all the Indians he receives, so that if the said Indians are to be freed the said Lezcano may return *those who are still alive,* and so that, if they are to be kept as slaves, they may be charged against his salary." [4]

Columbus was evidently planning to establish a regular trade in slaves, in imitation of the Portuguese. In his frequently quoted memorial written to Ferdinand and Isabella during his second voyage he suggested the advantages of enslaving the warlike Caribs, who, he said, were interfering with the peaceful settlement of the islands. Several useful ends, he argued, would thus be served: (1) the peaceful natives would be protected from the cannibals; (2) the latter would be turned from their unlovely appetite for human flesh and be made Christians in Castile; (3) their fate would deter other natives from resisting the Spaniards; (4) the Crown would collect revenue from the slave trade.[5]

Columbus's anticipation of a lucrative slave trade was like to frustrate his plans for a third voyage, according to an anecdote told by Las Casas. His brother Bartolomé, the *adelantado* of Española, had dispatched a number of Indian slaves to Castile by one Peralonso Niño, who arrived at Cadiz late in October, 1496. Niño, obeying an unexplained whim, wrote to Columbus that he was bringing a quantity of gold. Ferdinand and Isabella had already set aside six million *maravedis* to defray the expenses of the third voyage but, needing the money for the defense of Perpignan, they used it there, counting on the "gold" of Peralonso Niño to replace it. Their wrath and disappointment, reported Las Casas, were great upon learning of the imposture, "but," he concludes, "the wrath and pain that the Admiral received from the practical joke and folly of the pilot . . . I well believe were greater." [6]

This unpleasant incident, if true, may well have disgusted the Queen with the Indian slave trade, but she took no active step to suppress it until three years later. The occasion was the arrival of fifteen of the men of the rebellious Roldán with a few Indian slaves they had received in Roldán's settlement with Columbus. Herrera records that the Queen was very angry with Columbus for daring to give her vassals as slaves, and she forthwith ordered that all those holding Indian slaves were to send them back to Española, on pain of death.[7]

Isabella's outburst is not to be taken as meaning that she disapproved of slavery. Her objection may have been owing to Columbus's assumption of sovereignty. However it was, she issued an order shortly thereafter commanding Pedro de Torres to collect the Indians—presumably the same ones—and return them to the islands.[8] Three days later Torres reported that, of the twenty-one Indians, nineteen had been deposited with the majordomo of the Archbishop of Toledo. One of the others was ill, and the last, a girl, had elected to remain in Castile. The tenderness of the Crown for this small group of Indian slaves is difficult to explain. There is certainly no evidence of disapproval of slavery generally. Consider the case of Cristóbal Guerra. Guerra had been sent by his brother in the expedition of Peralonso Niño to the newly discovered Pearl Coast in 1499. Guerra returned with a cargo of slaves in 1501 and sold them in Jerez de la Frontera. Wind of the transaction got round to Court and a cédula was issued to the corregidor of Jerez, ordering the release of the slaves and the arrest of Guerra. It declared that the Indians were "free subjects of the Crown," and forbade their enslavement.[9] But a year and a half later Guerra obtained a royal license to explore the Pearl Coast. One paragraph of his patent leads us to believe that the previous prohibition of Indian slavery was not meant to be general. In it Guerra is given permission "to take Indians, men and women, for slaves—which he is to do as nearly as possible with their consent, without harming them; and in the same manner he may take monsters and animals of any kind, and all the serpents and fishes he may desire; and all this is to belong to him, as has been said, the fourth part being reserved for me." [10] There is also a further clause to the effect that Guerra is to be given the slaves whom he had brought on his earlier voyage, for use on this one. Although the Indians in the new contract are not stipulated as cannibals or rebels, it may have been assumed that the natives of the Pearl Coast were Caribs, who could be counted on to resist the invaders.

This supposition is borne out by a general cédula issued a few weeks later to all expeditions of discovery. It declares that, although the capture and enslavement of Indians has been prohibited, the prohibition does not extend to the cannibals (Caribs) who had resisted the propagation of the Christian religion. The Crown reserves its share in the proceeds of their sale.[11]

The slavers soon learned, however, that the capture of the warlike Caribs involved great hardship and expense. They complained that they could not make a profit if they had to pay the royal tax of a third and that they would have to abandon the business unless it was reduced. The Crown reduced the tax to a fifth.[12]

This discussion of Indian slavery is a necessary introduction to the general topic of the labor supply. Enslavement of the natives was the most ancient and obvious solution for the chronic labor shortage. Owing, however, to the vigorous opposition of the religious elements in the government, it was always hedged about with restrictions. Slaves were early defined as those prisoners taken in rebellion against the Crown, or slaves bought from the Indians themselves (*indios de rescate*). As the pacified territory increased, the legitimate supply of slaves decreased, until eventually slaves could be acquired only by such questionable methods that the scandal of the traffic brought about its abolition, by the New Laws of 1542. Slave taking was allowed thereafter only in specific cases as a punitive measure.[13]

Meanwhile, of far greater importance to the early economy of the Indies than chattel slavery, was the institution of the encomienda, a device by which the colonists assured themselves of a labor supply, while avoiding the penalties of slaving. Its beginnings go back to Española in the days of Columbus.

From the establishment of Columbus's first unlucky

colony in 1492 to the coming of the royal governor, Nicolás de Ovando, in 1502, conditions in Española may best be described as something like absolute chaos. The colonists were such as could be attracted by the prospect of sudden riches, gained in a land where restrictions hardly existed. By all accounts the men who went to Española in the first ten years were the choicest collection of riffraff ever brought together: ex-soldiers, broken noblemen, adventurers, criminals, and convicts. That there were some high-minded men among them does not appreciably alter the general picture, and their presence is only a guess in any case. Such was the reputation of the colony given it by disappointed men returning to Spain that the greatest difficulty was encountered in recruiting Columbus's third expedition. Criminals of almost every type were offered the choice of working out their sentences in the Indies. Sentences of death were commuted into two years' service, and lesser sentences might be canceled with one.[14] Columbus himself looked with disgust upon the rabble in his command. In one of his letters he says: "I take my oath that numbers of men have gone to the Indies who did not deserve water of God or man." [15]

This ill-assorted and generally unfit group faced many difficulties, some of them insuperable. They were caught in a vicious circle. Having infrequent communication with Spain, they had to force the natives to supply them with food. The natives, who were living in a primitive hand-to-mouth economy, were in their turn soon reduced to want. It was a round of starvation, oppression of the Indians, falling production, more starvation, more oppression. Moldy supplies from Spain eased matters from time to time, but the eventual extinction of such an ill-ordered republic was certain on the score of food shortage alone. "Nothing in those days," wrote Las Casas, "gladdened the people here . . . more than to learn that ships were coming with provisions from Castile, because all their troubles were from hunger." [16] In one of the few passages in which Oviedo agrees with Las Casas, he says:

Indeed, I saw many of those who at that time [the third voyage of Columbus] returned to Castile with such faces that, although the King had given me his Indies, were I to become as they, I should not have determined to go thither. And if some of them were reduced to this state, it is not so much to be marvelled at as that any of them escaped alive. . . . And since men were now very scarce and did not cease from returning to Castile, save those who could not, the country was almost ruined and was considered worthless and dangerous by those who remained, and doubtless these also would have been lost if they had not been succored by the caravels that came from Castile. The Admiral had sent them from the Canaries with three hundred men sentenced or exiled to this island. These, . . . together with the few who remained, saved the land from being abandoned. [17]

Along with the necessity of obtaining food went the hardly less pressing urge to mine gold. In both these activities laborers in large numbers were required, for the Spanish colonists, whatever their status may have been at home, were extraordinarily averse to working with their hands. Were they not all *hidalgos?* Slaves were expensive and there were never enough of them. So, upon one pretext or another, the natives were forced to work for their conquerors. Such were the conditions out of which evolved the much debated encomienda system. Its first adumbration was a petition of Columbus to the Crown begging that the colonists be permitted to use the labor of the natives for a year or two until the colony should be able to support itself. He had, indeed, already invoked the same principle, after the rebellion of 1494, when in some cases he commuted into personal service the tribute laid upon the native towns. So in his later action he was in all probability seeking the legal recognition of an existing situation, because the Spaniards could not have lived without the forced labor of

the Indians. In the allotment of the lands of Española to
the Spaniards Columbus permitted them to compel the
cacique and the people of each plot to work it for the
owners' benefit.[18]

To put an end to the confusion which prevailed in the
Indies under the rule of the Columbus family, Isabella
appointed a royal governor, Frey Nicolás de Ovando,
Comendador Mayor of the military order of Alcántara, a
man experienced in the government of the conquered provinces of Granada. His instructions are the first thoughtful
attempt to regulate Spanish-Indian relations. They contain
several principles which were later incorporated into the
structure of the Laws of the Indies.

It was laid down as a sacred formula that the governor's
chief duty was the indoctrination of the Indians in the Holy
Catholic Faith; they were to be lovingly taught by the religious. They were to be allowed to go about the island in
entire freedom and protected from robbery and abuse. The
governor was to inform the caciques that it was their sovereign's will that they should be well treated, as good subjects and vassals of the Crown, and that anyone harming
them was to be so punished that he would not dare to repeat the offense. The wives and daughters of Indians who
had been taken without consent were to be returned. Any
Spaniards desiring to marry native women might do so only
with the consent of the parties and not by force. The Indians were to pay tribute, like other subjects, according to
the value of their land, and its amount was to be established
after consultation with the caciques, who were to be given
to understand that it was not unjust.[19]

In the matter of forced labor Ovando's instructions laid
down a principle which was never abandoned, or even
modified, a kind of eminent domain principle applied to
labor: "Since it will be necessary, in order to mine gold and
to carry out the other works which we have ordered, to

make use of the services of the Indians, you will compel them to work in our service, paying them the wage which you think it is just they should have." This principle became the basis for the *mita,* or *repartimiento,* system of forced labor, by which works defined as necessary for the good of the commonwealth were carried on throughout the colonial period, and even later.[20]

Another clause of Ovando's instructions prohibited the bearing of arms by Indians. In another, Moors, Jews, heretics, *reconciliados* (i.e., persons who had been punished by the Inquisition and later "reconciled" to the Church), and New Christians were forbidden to go to the Indies; but Negro slaves and others born among Christians were allowed to do so.[21]

The repeated recommendations for interracial marriage are negative evidence that Spaniards were in no hurry to take native wives and settle down. Concubinage was the rule, much to the scandal of the religious. Native women were in great demand. A woman was worth a hundred *castellanos,* reported Columbus, as much as a farm, and even girls of nine and ten had their price. There was a market for women of every age, he added, and many merchants were doing a profitable business trafficking in them.[22]

Ovando brought a great company with him in 1502, some 2,500 men, but few who were in any way fitted to cope with life in the wilderness or willing to do so. They were soon in desperate straits. The Indians, seeing the increasing number of their guests, adopted a unique way of getting rid of them by refusing to plant any crops whatever, their own included. Ovando's representations at Court of the frightful conditions prevailing in the colony brought a series of royal edicts which definitely recognized the legality of forcing free Indians to work. These new instructions became the basis of the first code of Indian law, the Laws of Burgos, which will be treated in detail in another chapter.

The monarchs had heard, so read the instructions, that it was necessary for the salvation of the Indians that they be brought together in towns and not permitted to live separately from the whites. Each Indian was to be given a house for himself and his family and a farm for raising crops and cattle. Each town was to have a church with a chaplain to indoctrinate the Indians in the Holy Catholic Faith. Its government was to be the charge of some person of known virtue who in the King's name would administer justice, protect the Indians from abuse, "and make them serve in matters necessary to our service." This officer was to see that the Indians were paid for their work and not swindled; that is, explained the instructions, the goods given to the Indians must be worth at least *half* as much as the goods received from them.

The Indians were to be persuaded to wear clothing, like "reasonable men." The children of each town were to be brought together twice a week for religious instruction. They were also to be taught reading, writing, the sign of the Cross, the confession, the Pater Noster, the Credo, and the Salve Regina; and, of course, they were to be baptized and forced to attend religious services.

The caciques were not to be permitted to mistreat or oppress their followers "against their will," "in as much as it is our will that the said Indians be in everything well taught and well treated, as our vassals, provided that this be done in such a fashion as not to mistreat the caciques,"— a recognition of feudal privileges among the aborigines which must have been thought right and proper.

The Indians were to be persuaded to abandon their ancient evil ways, "and they are not to bathe as frequently as hitherto, for we are informed that it does them much harm." Spaniards were to be induced to marry Indian women, and Indians, Spanish women, so that the Indians might be taught in the Holy Catholic Faith and become civilized men and women. The indispensable labor supply was not overlooked. "And since we are informed that in order to get greater profit from the said gold it is necessary for the Christians of the island to make use of the Indians, we command the governor to discover what procedure should be observed in it . . . provided that the Indians be not mistreated . . . as they have been hitherto; and they are to be paid wages . . . and they are to be used with their consent and not otherwise." [23]

A secret instruction of the same date interpreted the labor clause more widely. The governor was to place the new Indian towns as near to the mines as possible, so that more gold might be extracted ("porque faya lugar de coger más"). And, although the Indians might resist this new mode of life because of its strangeness, they were to be persuaded to accept it, with the use of as little force as possible.[24]

Ovando interpreted the clause "to make the Indians serve in those things necessary to our service" as a mandate to force the Indians to produce food. Indeed, circumstances compelled him thus to interpret it, for he was confronted with the urgent problem of staving off famine. The natural solution which occurred to him was to transfer to Española the encomienda system with which he was familiar.[25] So he appealed to Isabella for permission to do so, and in reply received a royal cédula establishing a system which was to persist, with many modifications, until the eighteenth century, although its period of significant activity was limited to the sixteenth. The cédula is worth examining at some length.

Whereas, the King my Lord and I agreed, in the instruction which we commanded given to Don Frey Nicolás de Ovando . . .

that the Indian inhabitants of the island of Española are free and not servile . . . and whereas we are now informed that because of the excessive liberty enjoyed by the said Indians they avoid contact and community with the Spaniards to such an extent that they will not work even for wages, but wander about idle and cannot be had by the Christians to convert to our Holy Catholic Faith; and in order that the Christians may not lack people to work their holdings for their maintenance and extract the gold that there is on the island . . . and whereas we desire that the said Indians be converted to our Holy Catholic Faith and taught in its doctrines; and whereas this can better be done by having the Indians live in community with the Christians of the island and go among them and associate with them, by which means they will help each other to cultivate, settle, and reap the fruits of the island, and extract the gold which may be there, and bring profit to my kingdom and subjects,

[Therefore], I have commanded this my letter to be issued on the matter in which I command you, our said governor, that beginning with the day on which you receive my letter you will compel and force the said Indians to associate with the Christians of the island and to work on their buildings, and to gather and mine the gold and other metals, and to till the fields and produce food for the Christian inhabitants and dwellers of the said island; and you are to have each one paid on the day he works the wages and maintenance which you think he should have . . . and you are to order each cacique to take charge of a certain number of the said Indians, so that you may make them work wherever necessary, and so that on feast days and such other days as you think proper they may be gathered together to hear and be taught in the things of the Faith. . . . This the Indians shall perform as free people, which they are, and not as slaves. And see to it that they are well treated, those who become Christians better than the others, and do not consent or allow that any person do them any harm or oppress them.[26]

This amazing piece of sophistry clearly legalized forced labor, and it apparently authorized Ovando's proposed encomienda system, which seemed to be a reasonable way to implement it. In spite of its straining the meaning of freedom out of all recognition, it was the first bit of con-

structive legislation on the Indian labor question. It fixed
the status of the "free" native and hence tended to stabilize
Spanish-Indian relations, and it defined the bases upon
which the later and more humane code was erected, a code
which, in the more fortunate circumstances prevailing in
New Spain, at least, curbed the irresponsible exploitation
of the Indians by the Spaniards. The institution which
grew out of this act of Isabella, although shocking to
modern nerves, was in theory no more oppressive than the
European serfdom of her day. In practice, of course, it was
much more brutal, because there was no immediate bond
of sympathy between master and serf, who were of different
races, different languages, and different cultures. In view
of all these hazards it is remarkable that any good whatever came from the encomienda.

Isabella died on November 26, 1504. On her deathbed
she dictated a codicil to her will, appointing Ferdinand
regent of the Indies and leaving certain pious instructions
for their government. In the light of the documents which
we have examined it will be interesting to read its most
quoted clause.

Whereas, when the islands and mainland of the Ocean Sea were
conceded to us by the Holy Apostolic See, our principal intention
. . . was to procure, induce, bring, and convert their peoples to
our Holy Catholic Faith and to send to the said islands and mainland bishops, religious, clerics, and other learned and God-fearing
persons, to instruct the inhabitants and dwellers therein in the
Catholic Faith, and to instruct them in, and to bestow upon them,
good customs, exercising all proper diligence in this [therefore],
I beg the King my Lord very affectionately, and I charge and command my said daughter and the said prince her husband [Juana
"la loca" and Philip I] to carry this out, and that it be their principal purpose, and that they put into it much diligence; and they
are not to consent, or give permission, that the Indian inhabitants
and dwellers in the said islands and mainland . . . receive any
damage in their persons or goods, but are to order that they be

well and justly treated; and if they have received any damage it is to be remedied; and it is to be provided that everything enjoined and commanded us in the said concession be strictly observed.[27]

The sentiments expressed in Isabella's codicil have persuaded a good many historians that she was a farsighted humanitarian.[28] The contrary is not here argued. I merely wish to observe that Isabella was an accomplished and eminently practical administrator. Her instruction to Ovando is sufficient proof of it, if proof were needed. It is also difficult to avoid the conclusion that she licensed and encouraged Indian slavery, at least as a punitive measure, and profited by it. In short, she put the interest of the Crown, as she saw it, above all other considerations, a course to which she owed her prodigious success in unifying Castile.

2.

The Regency of Ferdinand

THE ELEVEN years of Ferdinand's rule of the Indies, including his brief joint regency with Philip I in 1506, were a period of almost unrelieved extortion. Without the piety of Isabella to modify the dictates of necessity, the Indian policy of the Crown was apparently reduced to a simple formula: get money, by fair means if possible, but get it! In the royal orders the conversion of the Indians continued usually to be mentioned as a matter of form, but with less emphasis. On the other hand, instructions were showered on the governors in the urgent business of increasing the revenue. The encomienda, which had become the recognized method of dealing with peaceful natives, may have acted as a brake on royal cupidity, for the colonists now had a stake in keeping them alive, at least; but that is only a surmise. The able and conscientious Ovando, who was to continue in office for five years longer, until 1509, may have been a controlling factor in preventing the total extinction of the natives. So far as can be judged from the royal correspondence, Ferdinand would have been in favor of enslaving the whole Indian population—which, indeed, is virtually what happened in any case.

In the colonization of Puerto Rico the precedents established in Española were followed. Vicente Yáñez Pinzón, one of the two famous brothers who had piloted Columbus's first voyage, was given a patent to "discover" that island in 1505. The land and the natives were to be apportioned among the settlers as in Española; the colonists were to contract to remain in Puerto Rico for five years; the title to the land was to remain in the Crown; a fifth of all profits was to be paid to the Crown; and so on. It may be significant that in the Pinzón contract the conversion of the Indians is not mentioned.[1]

In a later instruction to Ovando Ferdinand approved the granting of encomiendas in Española. He also urged the taking of slaves wherever the natives resisted, particularly among the Caribs of the Lesser Antilles and the Pearl Coast. The Crown concerned itself also with the delicate business of sex relationships between Indians and Spaniards: "As to what you say of the punishment of Indian women who wrong their husbands, it is my opinion that you should not proceed too rigorously against them, especially if the husbands do not accuse them, because much trouble would come of it . . . but you should warn the Christians not to have anything to do with them; or you might even punish them [the Christians], but in such wise that it come not to the notice of the husbands, as in that event it would cause a great scandal."[2]

The earlier suggested plan of promoting interracial marriages for the correction of these conditions and the increase of the population had very slender results.[3] The practical Ovando attempted to solve the problem by sending married men back to Spain for their wives. This must have been a prohibitively costly business, but it cost Ferdinand nothing, and he gave it his approval.[4]

Ovando served out his governorship until 1509 with little interference from the Crown. The few documents available for the period before the arrival of Diego Columbus as governor in that year do not indicate any amelioration in the general condition of the island. It had been thoroughly pacified by the stern Ovando, but continual starvation was still the lot of the settlers, while that of the Indians must have been much worse. Ovando protested against the sending of more colonists to the famine-ridden island, but drew a typical response from the King: "I should like to know why you request that no more people, even workmen, be allowed to go there until you ask for them. It is believed here that the more there are to work, the greater will be the profit." [5]

Affairs in Española had come to such a desperate pass by this time that Ovando sent two delegates to Spain to lay the situation of the colony before the King in person. These two men, Antón Serrano and Diego de Nicuesa (the latter soon to be famous in the disastrous colonization of Veragua), reported that the Indians of Española were rapidly disappearing and that Ovando recommended bringing those of the "useless" islands (the Bahamas) to replace them. ("Useless" meant that there was no gold in the Bahamas.) These new Indians, they argued, would thus have the privilege of living in contact with the Christians and would be converted, for the glory of God and the salvation of their souls.

This pious suggestion appealed strongly to Ferdinand, especially since gold mining was in danger of abandonment because of the labor shortage. So he readily granted permission to bring the Indians of the Bahamas to Española, but it was to be done with "as little scandal as possible," and these new Indians were not to be made slaves, or used

as such, but were to be paid wages and supplied with the
necessities of life, "just as is being done with the natives
of Española"—a witticism which apparently caused no
comment at the time.

The delegates reported further that the slave population
had developed the distressing habit of running away and
taking refuge among the peaceful tribes of the island, and
that it was impossible to recover them without doing some
violence to those tribes and running counter to the laws
that protected them. Ferdinand granted the colonists the
right to recover their slaves wherever they might be. It
seems not to have occurred to him that the colonists, to
whom all Indians looked alike, would seize some of the
peaceful Indians by way of compensating themselves, as
they did.

In the general distribution of land and Indians the
Crown had made grants to people in Spain—a practice,
complained the delegates, which worked great hardship on
the Spaniards of Española, because there were not enough
Indians to go round. For reasons of his own Ferdinand
made an evasive answer to this complaint, merely assuring
the delegates that in the future due regard would be had for
the interests of the island and its inhabitants.[6]

The delegates petitioned the King not to grant encomiendas of Indians to the priests and prelates sent to the island. Ferdinand's answer was a strong negative. Were, he
queried, priests less than other men? Obviously not! They
were not of less consequence than other men, but of more,
and they must have Indians to work their lands. He might
have added that if they did not have Indians to support
them they would have to be supported by the Crown.

A further complaint of the delegates, one which was
frequently heard, was that Spanish workmen, as soon as
they landed in Española, all became hidalgos and refused
to work at their trades. Rather, they wished to set them-

selves up as landed proprietors with encomiendas of Indians. Ferdinand decreed that they were not to receive Indians unless they worked at their trades.[7]

It will be seen with increasing clarity that Ferdinand looked upon the Indies only as a source of immediate revenue. Whatever vague rights the Indian population may have had were ignored on every occasion in which the fiscal interests of the Crown were involved. For example, in the patent which Diego de Nicuesa got for himself, with Alonso de Ojeda, to "discover" Urabá and Veragua, they were instructed to bring along forty Indians from Española experienced in gold mining so that they might teach the art to the natives of the mainland.[8]

Meanwhile, Ovando wrote the King that the people of Española, presumably the natives, were very happy, a rather astonishing statement in view of the lugubrious report brought to Spain by the two delegates. "I am pleased to learn," replied Ferdinand, "that the people are contented, and you are to provide that they be similarly treated always. . . . Our officials in Seville," he added, returning to his obsession, "have not as yet sent me the pearls. When I see them I shall let you know my opinion."[9]

Ferdinand's last communication to Ovando approved the plan to bring the Indians of the "useless" islands to Española, "for everyone tells me that there are very few Indians left in Española." He was disappointed in the quality of the pearls. Even so, he directed Ovando to send him all that had been found. He had heard that bad weather was interrupting the operations of the mines, but now, with God's help, they were going to have good weather, and he directed Ovando to put all available men to work in the mines and, somehow, to see that they were fed.[10]

For the preceding ten years Christopher Columbus and his son Diego had never ceased pressing their claims to all the land discovered by the Admiral. After the latter's death in 1506, Diego's fortunes brightened considerably with his marriage to Doña María de Toledo, niece of the Duke of Alva and grandniece of Ferdinand himself. Diego was named Admiral and Governor of the Indies on October 21, 1508, and assumed his duties the following year.[11]

The new Admiral's instructions began with the now meaningless injunction to convert the Indians to the Holy Catholic Faith; their conversion was to be the duty of the clergy, as well as that of the encomenderos; they were to be taught lovingly and in no wise by force, and so on, interminably. The question of the right of inheritance of the encomienda (which was to keep the encomenderos in a ferment for a century) had been brought to the King's attention. Although the encomenderos were insisting that their grants had been made in perpetuity and might be left to their wives and children, the Admiral was instructed to inform them that no such right existed.[12]

Ferdinand had shown some indignation, only a year before, when Ovando's delegates had suggested that the clergy should not be permitted to hold encomiendas. Now he discovered that they had been neglecting their divine duties because of their preoccupation with making money, and he instructed Diego Columbus not to grant Indians to the clergy.[13] The King's motive in this reversal, if I may venture a guess, was that he was less concerned over the clergy's neglect of their duties than with the fact that the Indians could be more profitably employed in the royal mines.[14]

Isabella had been content with a moderate profit from the Indian slave trade and had even protected that infant industry by reducing the tax from a third to a fifth. Even so, the price of slaves was too high, complained Ferdinand. A certain Gil González, it seems, had written him offering to bring Indians from the "useless" islands more cheaply. Ferdinand instructed Diego Columbus to come to terms with González, and he suggested that Diego might offer him and his associates a fourth of their take of Indians as their compensation, the remaining three-fourths being for the King! Moreover, added Ferdinand, since it might happen that the new slaves would not be so good at mining as the more experienced natives of Española, Diego was to give them to the encomenderos in exchange for their old Indians, and these latter could be sent to the mines.

The fixing of the civil status of the new Indians offered a problem. Although the original arrangement with Ovando was that the Indians of the "useless" islands were to be "free," and the rest, Ferdinand now hinted that it might simplify things if some pretext were found for making them out-and-out slaves. "And if by chance they do anything that may merit their being made slaves, I think it will be better to sell them, if anyone can be found to give a fair price for them, since in that case as many of the natives of the ['useless'] islands can be taken for our service as necessary." [15]

Diego Columbus was again warned not to grant encomiendas even for one life, but for two or three years at most, with the privilege of renewal for a like period. Indians given in encomienda were not slaves, but *naborias,* because Ferdinand felt that it would be a burden on his conscience to make them slaves.[16]

Another cédula of the same date regulated and equalized the distribution of Indians in encomienda. The first distribution, it seems, had not been made equitably, some Spaniards having received many Indians, some few, and others none at all. The Admiral was instructed to allot a hundred to royal officers and alcaldes, sixty to the married hidalgo who should bring his wife to the Indies, thirty to the simple farmer. Any surplus or deficit of Indians was to be apportioned among the colonists at the same rate. The encomenderos were to pay the Crown a gold peso a head per annum for all the Indians in their service, and they were to be held responsible for their religious instruction.[17]

The order for the redistribution of the Indians is one of the many instances in which the Crown, by abrupt and ill-considered measures, disarranged the rickety economy of the Indies in those chaotic days. The waste and confusion attendant upon such a revolution in a wilderness 30,000 square miles in extent was duly brought to Ferdinand's notice the following November. Thereupon he canceled the order for the redistribution, and everything was to remain as before. The reason given was what might be expected: the time lost in it would take the Indians away from gold mining. If any deserving citizens were without Indians they could be supplied from those brought in from the "useless" islands. A number of Spaniards were given kidnaping licenses. They might keep half their captives by paying the Crown half a peso a head. The remaining captives were reserved for the Crown. This expedient, explained Ferdinand, was necessary because of the labor shortage, "for, as you know, the greatest need of the island at present is more Indians, so that those who go there from these kingdoms to mine gold may have Indians to mine it with. You can imagine the profit that is being lost!" [18]

The colonists needed no encouragement in kidnaping. The Bahamas were rapidly exhausted and, when that source dried up, the kidnapers seized Indians wherever found and shipped them to Española. Exploring expeditions were organized with this end principally in view. The discovery of Yucatan was made by the slaving expedition of Juan de Grijalva in 1517, and within a few years Nuño de Guzmán was shipping boatloads of slaves to Española from his unlucky province of Pánuco.

The decree ordering mechanics to work at their trades was apparently impossible to enforce. Ferdinand had to repeat it—indeed, it was repeated many times during the colonial period, with noticeably little effect. What was more important, wrote Ferdinand, was that the colonists were not putting into gold mining all the diligence that they should. In the first twenty days and in the last twelve or fifteen of the semiannual periods between smeltings, he complained, they extracted as much gold as in all the rest of the time. Why, the very Indians were following the example of their Spanish foremen and idling after what they considered a just day's work! His remedy for this painful state of affairs was to shorten the periods between smeltings to four months.

Ferdinand did not approve of the lack of regard for social categories shown in the distribution of land, commoners having received in some cases as much as hidalgos. He instructed Diego Columbus to recognize the rank of claimants in the allotment of lands.

The destructive hurricane of 1508 had caused so much damage in Española that, as a relief measure, Ferdinand removed the peso head tax on encomienda Indians for one year, as well as the half-peso tax on kidnaped Indians, "because some of the Indians brought from the other islands die, while others become ill." The hidden premise seems to be that the need of labor was so great in Española that the kidnapers should be encouraged.[19]

That same day Ferdinand wrote to Miguel de Pasamonte, Treasurer General of the Indies, complaining that the mines belonging to private citizens were producing more gold than the King's own—a situation that called for remedy, because the royal mines were the richer.[20] All the efforts of Diego Columbus to appease his sovereign's insatiable appetite for treasure failed. In February, 1510, Ferdinand wrote him thanking him for his diligence in working the mines, but he ordered him at the same time to keep a thousand men continually at work, and later he was to send to the mines all the men who could be supported.[21]

The King's obsession with treasure interfered with the town-planning project which Ovando had been ordered to carry out (in the cédula of March 29, 1503, cited in chap. 1, n. 23). Ferdinand warned Diego Columbus to proceed in the matter with great caution, for the Indians were showing an unaccountable aversion to being removed; many might die as a result, "and a great deal of time for gold mining would be lost." If there were not enough Indians to keep the full quota of a thousand in the mines, he added, the shortage was to be made up by removing Indians from the less deserving encomenderos. Moreover, since the Lord had given such a generous sign of His approval of the deeds of the Spaniards by allowing them to discover gold, it might be a good idea to see that the Indians at the mines were well provided for.

The cancellation of the order for the redistribution of the Indians of the encomiendas was not, he ruled, to affect the holdings of the royal officers. On the contrary, they were to be given two hundred Indians, instead of the hundred originally assigned to them, because a hundred were too few for their proper support.

Diego Columbus had evidently suggested to Ferdinand that there were many Indians in the island of Trinidad who were doing nothing useful and whose souls were going to perdition for lack of instruction in the Faith. But Ferdinand refused, for the time being, to allow them to be kidnaped. His argument may be anticipated: he had heard that there was gold in Trinidad, and, moreover, if the Trinidad Indians were stirred up they might interfere with the pearl fishing.

The kidnapers of Española had complained that the royal tax of four-fifths on Indians brought from the Bahamas was excessive. Ferdinand reduced it to one-fifth, but he warned the kidnapers at the same time to confine their activities to the Bahamas and not to seize the Indians of

Cuba and Jamaica—evidence that by 1510 the Bahamas were already approaching exhaustion.[22]

The King's continual exhortations to Diego Columbus to dig more gold must have had some effect, for a year later he congratulated him on the excellent results of the last smelting. His appetite being thus whetted, he ordered Diego thenceforth to keep a third of *all* the Indians of the island at work in the mines. Inspectors were to be appointed to go about among the settlements to see that this provision was enforced.

Diego Columbus had suggested that those caciques whose followers had been reduced to fewer than forty should themselves be obliged to serve as naborias—a suggestion which met with Ferdinand's approval. First, however, he ordered a complete census of the island to be taken, including a list of all the caciques and their subjects; the numbers and social status of all the Spanish colonists, with or without encomiendas; and their rating according to their treatment of the Indians. Unfortunately, there is no record of such a census. The first one attempted was that of Rodrigo de Alburquerque, made in 1514.

Ferdinand changed his mind about opening Trinidad to the kidnapers. If it was learned that there was no gold there, he wrote, and that the Pearl Coast Indians would not rebel, Diego Columbus might bring the Trinidad Indians to Española, always provided that it could be done without hardship or danger to them. He had also been informed that the kidnaping expeditions to the Bahamas were not being conducted efficiently and that transportation and starvation had caused a heavy mortality among the Indians of those islands, so heavy that "it is somewhat burdensome to our conscience and not very profitable for business." [23] He punctuated this sentiment by a new appeal to Diego Columbus to put as many Indians as possible to work in the mines. He might even gather up the idle Spaniards and put them to work also, in the mines or plantations. This is the first mention of the plague of Spanish vagabonds which was to pester the administration of the New World for generations.

A minor internal squabble is suggested by a letter of Ferdinand to Treasurer Miguel de Pasamonte, who had been made responsible for seeing that a third of the Indians of the island were sent to the mines. Diego Columbus had evidently objected to having his included. Pasamonte was instructed to put a third of the royal Indians in the mines also, so that the Admiral would have no excuse for withholding his.[24]

The governor of Jamaica had reported that the natives of that island were submitting readily to Christianity. This was excellent, wrote Ferdinand to Diego Columbus, and he hoped that they would be better treated than the Indians of Española, "so that they may increase and multiply."[25] In the same letter he warned Diego to prevent Spaniards from bringing their Indian slaves to Spain, "because, as you know, all the good of those parts lies in there being a number of Indians to work in the mines and plantations."

At this time the royal correspondence first takes up the question of the use, and abuse, of Indian carriers, a controversy which was to rage for many years. Ferdinand had learned, he wrote, that excessive loading of carriers had been one cause of the diminution of the Indians and of their unwillingness to go to the mines, "which has been displeasing to our Lord and damaging to our rents, . . . and since it is a cruel thing and one which causes the Indians to leave the island . . . I command that no Indians may be used as carriers."[26] This prohibition had no discernible effect. The use of carriers, as we shall see, was abolished repeatedly, was reëstablished, regulated, reabolished, and persists today.

Ferdinand's conscience, which had been troubling him over the kidnaping of the Bahama Indians, was soon quieted.

Our Lord, he wrote, was well served in the bringing of the
Indians from the "useless" islands to those where gold was
to be had. The Lord was so well served indeed, and labor
was getting so scarce, that Ferdinand now excused the kidnapers from paying the tax of a fifth on their take of Indians.[27]

Despite the bringing of kidnaped Indians to Española, its
depopulation continued at an alarming rate. Ferdinand
wrote Diego Columbus that he was going to urge the Casa
de Contratación to send to Española Basques from Guipúz-
coa, "where there are many people and little to support
them." Meanwhile, he cautioned, the kidnapers should be
more careful, because the Indians received much harm in
the passage and some died of starvation.[28] The crisis in the
labor supply led him to issue a general permit for anyone to
take slaves among the Caribs of the Pearl Coast and certain
of the Lesser Antilles, because they had treacherously slain
several Christians of those parts. The only restriction was
that such slaves were not to be removed from the Indies.[29]

With the year 1511 we may allow that the Spanish experiment in colonization had completed its first stage. It is
surely one of the most dismal episodes in the history of exploitation and one which has excited the wrath of commentators from Las Casas' day to this. In twenty years the
native population of the Antilles had virtually disappeared,
and it was the shock of that fact which brought about the
beginning of a long series of corrective laws, the first codi-
fication of which was the Laws of Burgos of 1512. In those
dreadful years the future conquerors of New Spain served
out their macabre apprenticeship, and if that most fortunate of Spanish colonies was spared the disaster of the
Antilles it was owing to factors other than their ferocious
training in destruction. The period has only one faintly
bright spot: the germ of order and future adjustment was
present in the encomienda of Nicolás de Ovando.

3.

The Laws of Burgos

IT IS WELL to remind ourselves that the Spanish effort in the Antilles in the twenty years just reviewed was a very small affair, so small that Indian administration could be handled by two men, Bishop Juan de Fonseca and Lope de Conchillos, Secretary of the Council of Castile. Moreover, the adventure in colonization had been entered upon accidentally, with no adequate machinery of control and with no set rules applicable to its novel circumstances. It was particularly unfortunate that Ferdinand the Catholic looked upon his remote and unknown possessions merely as a source of revenue and upon their inhabitants as material to be exploited and hardly worth the keeping. It could not be expected that the Spanish colonists would be more humane and farsighted than their sovereign. Columbus's dream of a land of gold, milk, and honey, and of a profitable slave trade, had come to little, and in its stead the deluded conquerors found poverty, hunger, and death on every hand. So notorious had this condition become by the

period upon which we are entering that the Crown was repeatedly warned that the colony was on the verge of
abandonment.

Alburquerque's report of 1514, made before the dis-
coveries on the mainland had drawn off the greater part of
the colonists, gives the Spanish population of Española as
perhaps a thousand and the remnant of the natives as
29,000.[1] The destruction was on too vast a scale not to
excite some attention, and by 1511 plans were being made
to save the wretched remainder.

The passive attitude of the secular clergy of the island
in the face of this cataclysm is, perhaps, to be expected, given
their identity of interests with the colonists. That of the
dozen Franciscan missionaries who had arrived with Ovando
in 1502 is more difficult to account for. Records of those
early years are too scanty to justify Las Casas' wholesale
condemnation of them, but they did seem to consider the
woes of the natives as the visitation of the divine wrath
upon a wicked race, and they did little that we know of
to check their extinction.[2] Competition was soon to stir
them to more effective efforts.

A large part of the evil done in the islands is ascribed by
Las Casas and his followers to the interested indifference of
Bishop Fonseca.[3] Fonseca was clearly not particularly excited by the spiritual state of the aborigines, but his indifference may have been that of an administrator whose
first duty was to the Crown, and it may be doubted in
any case that Ferdinand would have looked amiably upon
any action that might have threatened his revenues.

Moved by the reports of the appalling condition to which
the island population had been reduced, Domingo de Mendoza, Cardinal-Archbishop of Seville and President of the
Council of Castile, was instrumental in having sent to
Española in 1510 a company of Dominican missionaries in
the charge of Fray Pedro de Córdoba. These pious and ex-

cellent men, although they arrived too late to stay the destruction, became, nevertheless, by their vigorous and unremitting protests, effective agents in mitigating the brutality of the laws by which the Indies were governed, and thus they determined to a considerable extent the later fate of the population of New Spain.[4]

The newly arrived Dominicans were shocked beyond measure by the callousness of the colonists toward the natives. Their horror may well have been given an edge by the unexplained silence of the Franciscans in the face of such wickedness, for the two great Mendicant orders were centuries-old rivals. However that may be, with courage and pertinacity they attacked the sickening abuses practiced upon the Indians, and within a short time they had stirred up such a deal of trouble that the colonists were forced to organize to protect their interests. A Franciscan friar, one Alonso de Espinal, was persuaded to present the colonists' case at Court. To oppose him the Dominicans sent their ablest preacher, Fray Antonio de Montesinos. A highly novelesque account of the meeting of the two men and of the defeat of Espinal is given in detail by Las Casas and need not be repeated here.[5] Montesinos eventually gained an audience with Ferdinand and pleaded his cause so convincingly that the King appeared greatly moved.[6] He pleaded ignorance of conditions in the islands and agreed to summon a council of theologians and learned men to suggest a remedy. The deliberations of this body resulted in the framing of a complete code of laws for the treatment of the Indians. It was promulgated in Burgos on December 27, 1512,[7] with an unimportant supplement added the following July.

To a reader of the twentieth century, the Laws of Burgos seem, in their practicable measures, a cold-blooded sanctioning of current methods of exploitation of the Indians. Since, however, they accurately reflect the attitudes of the Spanish lawmakers and state the premises upon which much of the subsequent Indian legislation was based, they must be examined at some length.

The preamble of the code states flatly that the Indians are by nature inclined to a life of idleness and vice, and not to the learning of the Christian virtues. It further states that the greatest impediment in the way of their redemption lies in their having their dwellings removed from those of the Christians, for which reason they cannot learn Christian habits and doctrines; whereas, if they should be gathered into villages where they might be kept from their vice of idleness and continually observe the practices of the Christians, they might be redeemed from their wickedness. From these premises the council drew up thirty-five articles which became the fundamental law governing Spanish-Indian relations for the following thirty years. They are summarized below.

Art. 1: provides that the Indians be settled in villages near the dwellings of their encomenderos, in huts (*bohíos*) fifteen by thirty feet in size, with garden plots for their maintenance. Upon the removal of the Indians to their new settlements their old houses are to be burned to discourage their return.[8]

Art. 2: provides that the removal shall be done gently, "with the least possible harm to the Indians."

Art. 3: provides that in each new village the encomendero build a church, with an image of Our Lady, and a bell to call the Indians to prayer, mornings and evenings; that the encomendero teach his Indians to make the sign of the Cross and to recite in chorus the Ave Maria, the Pater Noster, the Credo, and the Salve Regina.[9]

Art. 4: provides that every fortnight the encomendero conduct an examination of his Indians to ascertain what they have learned; that he further teach them the Ten Commandments, the Seven Deadly Sins, and the Articles of Faith—that is, those who have the capacity to learn them.

Art. 5: provides that, since it is impossible to maintain priests in all the native villages, churches be built to serve all the villages within the radius of a league; that the encomenderos bring their Indians on Sundays to hear Mass; that they feed them better on Sundays than on weekdays.

Art. 6: repeats the provision that no village be more than a league from a church.

Art. 7: charges bishops and clerics to supply priests for the Indian churches.

Art. 8: provides for churches at the mines.

Art. 9: provides that encomenderos having fifty or more Indians instruct a boy in reading, writing, and matters of the Faith, so that he in turn may instruct the others.

Art. 10: provides that priests attend the sick and the dying; that they oblige the Indians to confess once a year; that they assist bearing a cross at the burial of the dead; that they collect no fee for this service or for confession.[10]

Art. 11: forbids encomenderos and others to use Indians as carriers at the mines; permits Indians to carry their own household goods when they move.

Art. 12: provides for the baptism of all children within a week of birth; if no priest is at hand the encomendero is to perform the sacrament himself.

Art. 13: provides that Indians be obliged to mine gold five months of the year; that at the end of that period they rest for forty days; that none may be used for mining during the rest period except it be a slave.

Art. 14: permits the Indians to perform their ceremonial dances (*areytes*) on Sundays and feast days.

Art. 15: provides that encomenderos feed their Indians; that they give them cooked meats, at least on Sundays and feast days; that Indians working at the mines be given a pound of meat a day, or a pound of sardines and fish on meatless days.

Art. 16: provides that an Indian may have only one wife; that encomenderos be responsible for the lawful marriage of their Indians.

Art. 17: provides that the sons of caciques, thirteen years of age and under, be educated by the Franciscans for four years and then return to their encomenderos.[11]

Art. 18: provides that women more than four months gone in pregnancy be not sent to the mines; that they be used only in light household tasks.

Art. 19: provides that encomenderos supply their Indians with hammocks and not allow them to sleep on the ground.

Art. 20: provides that each Indian be paid a gold peso a year for the purchase of clothing.

Art. 21: provides that Indians may not change masters; that encomenderos may not take one another's Indians.

Art. 22: provides that caciques may use a limited number of their subjects in personal service.

Art. 23: provides that official inspectors keep records of all encomiendas; that they note their increase or decrease, and the amount of gold produced.[12]

Art. 24: forbids the beating or verbal abuse of Indians.

Art. 25: forbids the use of encomienda Indians in private trade and commerce.[13]

Art. 26: provides for the maintenance of Indians brought from villages remote from the mines.

Art. 27: provides for the indoctrination and maintenance of Indians brought from other islands, "unless they be slaves, because the latter may be treated by their masters as the masters please; but we order that it be not with that cruelty and harshness with which they are accustomed to treat their other slaves, but with much love and gentleness, so as better to incline them to the things of our Faith."

Art. 28: provides that upon the death or removal of an encomendero his successor compensate him or his heirs at a price fixed by appraisers; that his Indians may not leave his encomienda.

Art. 29: provides for the appointment of two inspectors for each village.

Art. 30: provides that these inspectors be chosen by the Admiral, royal officials, and judges; that they be compensated by being given Indians in encomienda, in addition to those they may already have.

Art. 31: provides that villages be inspected twice a year, once by one inspector and once by the other.

Art. 32: provides that inspectors may not retain runaway Indians, but must deposit them with "a person of good conscience" until they are restored to their masters.

Art. 33: provides that inspectors be given copies of these ordinances signed by the governor.

Art. 34: provides for the *residencia* of inspectors.[14]

Art. 35: limits the number of Indians who may be held by one person to not more than one hundred and fifty and not less than forty.[15]

News of the impending reform got back to Española, where the encomenderos were loud in their denunciation of the meddling Dominicans. Pedro de Córdoba, equally dissatisfied with what he heard of the Laws of Burgos, hastened back to Spain and arrived just after their passage. Properly shocked at the meager gains, he sought an audience with Ferdinand and persuaded him to reconsider the code. A few revisions were made in it and approved on July 28, 1513. None of them could have afforded much comfort to Pedro de Córdoba. Married women might not be compelled to work in the mines or anywhere else, save by their own or their husbands' consent. Children under fourteen might not be compelled to work, except at tasks fitting for children, such as weeding. Children might learn trades, if they wished, and nothing was to be tolerated which might interfere with their religious instruction. Unmarried girls were to be kept apart and taught apart from the others. Indians must give nine months of their time to the service of the Spaniards, and, in order to prevent their wasting their time in idleness and to assure their learning to live and govern themselves like Christians, they must spend the other three months working on their own farms, or working for wages. Indians, men and women, must wear clothing.[16]

That the agitation of the Dominicans thus far had been of no material benefit to the Indians needs no proof beyond a reading of the Laws of Burgos, which in naïveté and callousness can have few equals. It did, however, have the effect of making the Crown aware of the imminent danger of the abandonment of the Indies. This awareness is apparent in the increasing number of privileges granted to prospective colonists and in the renewed efforts of the Crown to promote interracial marriages. In 1514 Ferdinand prohibited any discrimination against Spaniards who took native wives, and the year following he repeated that whites and natives were free to marry whomever they pleased.[17]

The Laws of Burgos and their revisions did nothing to stay the destruction of Española. Conditions in the doomed island were so horrible that they supplied effective ammunition for the reformers for many years. The Dominican missionaries on the island wrote a powerful indictment of the regime to Cardinal Chièvres,[18] which repeats the details with which we are already familiar. We must allow a wide margin for the violent partisan feeling of the time and remember that there was little incentive to reveal anything good about one's adversaries. Even so, the Dominican indictment must be accepted as substantially just, if only on the basis that the entire native population of the Antilles, except a few wretched remnants, disappeared during those fearful years.

Although the Dominicans had failed in their effort to ameliorate the laws governing the Indies, they did succeed in arousing the conscience of one of the most extraordinary men in Spanish history. Bartolomé de las Casas had lived in Española and Cuba from 1502 to 1512. He had taken holy orders in 1510 and shortly thereafter had accompanied his friend, Diego Velázquez, in the conquest of Cuba. There he accepted an encomienda and exploited his Indians like his fellows. This period of iniquity, which he later bitterly repented, allowed him to witness the atrocities which he describes with such gusto in his *Brevíssima Relación*. Hearing of the preaching of the Dominican friars, with a sick conscience, and inspired by one of his own texts, he relates, he went to one of them to confess, but he was refused absolution on the ground that he was an encomendero. In his argument with the friar he was convinced of the wrong of seizing the property and bodies of the Indians, and he resolved to give the rest of his life to expiating that wrong.[19]

Las Casas forthwith gave up his encomienda and offered his services to the Dominican reformers. He brought to them the one element they needed: the fighting man, one who accepted their doctrine with all its inferences and consequences, one who never wearied of the struggle and who never varied by so much as a hair's breadth from his original stand. The philosophy of that doctrine (later to be elaborated by Francisco de Vitoria) may be stated in a few words: The New World was granted to Spain and Portugal by Pope Alexander VI solely for the purpose of converting the heathen. Hence the Spaniards had no right whatever to use the natives for secular purposes; nor had the Spanish Crown any right to use their bodies for profit, except so far as it furthered the purpose of the concession. The only just remedy for the evils suffered by the Indians was to remove the Spaniards from among them, that is, all except the necessary missionaries, who must bring them to a knowledge of Christ, but by peaceful and loving means only, using no force whatever.[20]

Las Casas' strength and his weakness lay in his inability to change. For fifty years after his conversion he kept up an uncompromising fight to impose his doctrinaire notions on the Council of the Indies. Long after most of the abuses which he attacked had been greatly modified by more humane laws and easier economic conditions, and after the encomienda had been reduced from a thin disguise for slavery into something like a social system, Las Casas was still attacking it as if nothing had changed since the dreadful days of Cuba and Española. His pertinacity and the constant agitation of the Dominicans were exceedingly useful to the designs of the Crown and culminated in the New Laws of 1542, which caused such a violent reaction that Spain all but lost her new empire.

But in 1515 Las Casas, with his single-minded zeal and long experience in the islands, was a mighty power at Court. Montesinos, who had returned to Española after the passage of the Laws of Burgos, was named by Pedro de Córdoba to accompany Las Casas to Castile. The two embarked in

September, 1515, and arrived at Seville in December. There Montesinos obtained a letter from Archbishop Mendoza presenting Las Casas to the King. Las Casas went directly to him, avoiding Fonseca and Conchillos who, he rightly suspected, would oppose him. Ferdinand listened to Las Casas and promptly referred him back to those same ministers, and, while Las Casas was being shunted back and forth between them, the aged Ferdinand died, on January 23, 1516.

Wasting no further time on the passing regime, Las Casas set out at once for Flanders to interview the young King Charles I (later to be the Emperor Charles V). On the way, however, he found a sympathetic listener in the Regent, Cardinal Ximénez de Cisneros, upon whom he made such a profound impression that the cardinal appointed another council to consider the situation of the Indies. The result of its deliberations was the most curious proposal in the history of government, namely, the administration of the Indies by three members of a monastic order.

4.

Theocracy

LAS CASAS' proposal, as presented by the council, was revolutionary. Among other things, it advocated the suppression of the encomiendas, the complete liberation of the Indians, and the administration of the native population by the religious. Cardinal Cisneros accepted the program; but the question then arose, whom to send on this new mission of redemption? Who was to bell the cat, the Franciscans or the Dominicans? Cisneros was himself a Franciscan and knew the long-standing rivalry between the two orders. The jealousy and confusion that would have resulted from placing one or the other in such a commanding position would have been damaging to them and fatal to the project. Cisneros, who was the greatest statesman in Spanish history, must have considered these implications when he ignored the Dominican candidate proposed by Las Casas and put the execution of the plan into the hands of the Order of St. Jerome. He left the selection of the personnel to Las Casas.

Las Casas' plan at the outset had several things in its

favor: a powerful and sympathetic regent, the disgrace of the two ministers who had opposed him, and the choice of the men who were to carry out his reform. His own position was to be that of adviser. He chose, after many consultations, three prominent Jeronymite monks: Luis de Figueroa, Bernardino de Manzanedo, and Alonso de Santo Domingo. He chose them for their rectitude and piety, and, it is reasonable to suppose, for their anticipated submissiveness to his will. If so, Las Casas made few greater mistakes than his misjudgment of these men. From the beginning they showed themselves restive under his dictation, and he soon convinced himself that he had erred in choosing them. According to his account, the Jeronymites were at once approached by those interested in defeating the new reform, and such was their lack of piety, so slight their faith in their leader, and so great the credence they gave to his enemies, that they frivolously decided to oppose him and throw in their lot with the oppressors of the Indians. Las Casas indignantly reported their defection to Cardinal Cisneros, who impatiently refused to substitute others for them. The most he would do was to give Las Casas a commission to accompany the Jeronymites under the somewhat ambiguous title of Protector of the Indians. The Jeronymites were by this time completely estranged from him and refused, in spite of his insistence, or, perhaps, because of it, to allow him to sail with them.

Their change of attitude, however, cannot be so easily accounted for. If these pious men could be so readily persuaded that Las Casas was an impractical visionary they must have had a more powerful reason than the interested propaganda of the encomenderos. Their experience with him was not unique. All his schemes met with the same fate. For some reason he rarely retained for long the confidence of his co-workers. He would tolerate no dissent or opposition. He was a prime example of what the Spaniards call an "exclusivista." His *Historia de las Indias* shows throughout that to disagree with him was to lay oneself open to charges of everything from folly to corruption. The Jeronymites were no exception.[1] But it seems improbable that these three men would voluntarily desert the calm and dignified life of the cloister to undertake a colossal and ungrateful task in a hostile community. There is evidence that they did so against their better judgment and against that of the general of their order, Pedro de Mora; but Cardinal Cisneros would not be denied and overrode their objections.[2]

Cardinal Cisneros was a justly celebrated statesman, but he must have been persuaded by his piety rather than by his intelligence in his hasty adoption of Las Casas' plan for the rehabilitation of the Indies. It is difficult to believe that he was convinced that three holy men from a cloister could prevail upon the lions and lambs of the Indies to lie down together. That he had some reservations about the plan is evident from his alternative instructions to the Jeronymites which will be discussed below. The amazing thing about the Jeronymite administration of the Indies is that it was not entirely unsuccessful; but whatever success it achieved must be ascribed to the good sense of the three friars and not to Las Casas' plan, which is a curious example of the workings of a mind trained to think a priori.

Upon their arrival at Santo Domingo, so read their instructions, the Jeronymite fathers were to call together the principal caciques and encomenderos and inform them that it was to be the policy of the Crown thenceforth to see that they lived together in peace and amity. They were ordered to solicit the opinions of both natives and Spaniards as to the best means of remedying the current situation. They were to assure the colonists that no hardship would be worked upon them and that nothing would be taken from them which was not rightly theirs, but that the Indians were free subjects of the King and were not to be mistreated, and more to the same effect. They were to persuade the caciques to move their people into towns and to pay the King a just tribute. The Spaniards who should be deprived of their encomiendas might be persuaded to accept a part of this tribute as a compensation for their loss, and the remainder of the Indians' earnings might be deposited with some reliable person who should see that it was not used wastefully.

The Jeronymites were instructed to select sites for Indian villages which would permit access to the mines with the least inconvenience. Each village was to be composed of three hundred Indians, more or less. It was to have a church, a hospital, and a common. It was to be governed by an Indian cacique, assisted by a priest and a Spanish administrator, "a man of good conscience." Spaniards were to be urged to marry the daughters of caciques, so that by their inheritance of the caciqueship they might save the Crown the expense of keeping an administrator in each village. This magistrate was to have as his especial care the instruction of the Indians in civilized ways of living; he was to persuade them to lead an orderly life; that is, he was to induce them to wear clothes, to sleep in beds, to content themselves with one wife, and the like.

A religious or priest was to be assigned to each village, to attend to the doctrinal education of the Indians and to the administration of the sacraments. The priest and administrator would receive a salary, half of which would be paid by the Crown and half by the Indians.

The number of men to be kept at the mines or on the farms, their hours of work and rest, what they were to do, and when, and how, were all prescribed to the uttermost detail.

The ousted encomenderos might be taken care of by having their estates bought by the Crown, or by being hired as miners, or by being given permission to mine on their own account, or by being made administrators of the new villages.[3] Some might prefer to emigrate to Tierra Firme, in which event they might be assisted to the amount of their transportation costs. Should these men be prevented from leaving because of their debts, some gratuity might be given them to keep them out of jail.[4]

This cool confiscation of the colonists' property—for, after all, their encomiendas had been legally granted them by the Crown—is the part of Las Casas' plan which, I suspect, made Cisneros anticipate some trouble in its enforcement. At any rate, he appended an alternative plan if the first should prove unworkable. The alternative provided that the Laws of Burgos were to be followed, save that certain changes in them were recommended, to wit: the Indians should not be forced to remove to the estates of the encomenderos; they should not be forced to carry burdens, or forced to work during their rest periods, save at light tasks on their own plots; they should be given meat every working day; they should be paid more than a gold peso a year; the women should not be forced to work, except at light tasks. The inspectors should not be given encomiendas but paid a salary by the Crown; the same should apply to other royal officers, as otherwise they would be tempted to neglect their duties. The importation of free Indians from other islands, except the Bahamas, should cease until further instructions.[5]

The Jeronymites were given very wide discretion in the interpretation of their instructions. The true nature of their office has given rise to some controversy. Las Casas, angry at what he considered their betrayal of his cause, denies that they came as governors, "but simply to oversee and execute what had been ordered concerning the Indians." [6] But the evidence is fairly conclusive that they were in fact royal governors. Alonso Zuazo, the *juez de residencia* who accompanied them, carried orders to consult them about everything. In the opinion of Serrano y Sanz,

the Jeronymites "were made true governors, especially of
the Antilles, since in Castilla del Oro they intervened considerably less." [7] It was under their authority that Diego
Velázquez organized the expedition of Hernán Cortés.[8]

Las Casas' instructions as "Protector of the Indians" are
fairly vague. He had two defined duties: (1) to advise the
Jeronymites concerning the best measures for the improve-
ment of the Indians, and (2) to keep the Crown informed
about everything that was done, or ought to be done, on
their behalf.[9] He was, of course, furious with the Jeronymites for failing to put his plan into instant execution.
Convinced that they were betraying their trust, he de-
nounced them before the juez de residencia, Alonso Zuazo.
Zuazo, however, refused to take action, and Las Casas
returned to Spain to complain to the Cardinal. He was
coolly received by Cisneros and, with this disappointment,
he seems to have abandoned all hope of saving the Indians
of the islands. For the next three years he busied himself
with a more ambitious scheme for colonizing the mainland,
in which we may leave him for a space and turn our attention to the interesting experiment in Española.

The Jeronymites arrived there on December 20, 1516.
Their first report to Cisneros is dated just a month later.
It is the letter of three puzzled men. Española, they wrote,
was a good land and a fruitful, but was woefully deserted.
Considerable distrust had been aroused by a rumor that
they were coming to free the Indians. To combat it they
had ordered the Indians to go to work, thus reassuring
the colonists and preventing their interference with measures which might later be put into effect. They had removed
the encomiendas of absentees, to the general rejoicing of
the colonists. They had ordered the miners (Spanish) put
on salary, because under the share system they had been
working their Indians excessively. The principal thing they
had learned thus far was that there was a vast difference

between the land they had heard about and the one they had before their eyes.[10]

Five months later they reported that the Indians were being well treated, a fact which they knew positively, because they had themselves visited the encomiendas and had had them visited by others. Anyone stating the contrary was not to be believed (this for Las Casas, who was on his way back to Castile with a walletful of complaints). They recommended the importation of Negro slaves, which would relieve the Indians and be a profitable business for the Crown. They also recommended the settlement of Española by colonists from Portugal and the Canary Islands, because there was a great need of farmers. Alonso Zuazo had begun the taking of residencias which, they found, was the cause of great disorder, for every man's hand was turned against his neighbor.[11]

The Treasurer-General of the Indies, Miguel de Pasamonte, paid tribute to their good judgment and moderation: "Regarding the Indians and the government of these parts which the Jeronymite Fathers have in charge . . . there is no necessity for me to say anything except that I approve of what they are doing, because they are looking after everything with great prudence, like wise and conscientious persons, and I hope that God and their Highnesses will be well served and that your Most Reverend Lordship will receive much contentment from having sent hither such persons as the said Fathers." [12]

In an interrogatory which the Jeronymites circulated, in order to learn whether or not the Indians were capable of self-government, they learned at least what the colonists thought of the Indians. The fifteen witnesses were unanimous about the personal habits of the natives who, according to them, were abandoned to drunkenness and gluttony, and preferred to live in the woods eating spiders and roots "and other filthy things" to living with the Spaniards. They had neither shame nor conscience, and took emetics to vomit what they had eaten. They did not wish to be subject to anyone but to be free and enjoy themselves in idleness. They smoked tobacco. They refused to recite the Pater Noster or the Ave Maria unless driven to it. They practiced sorcery and believed their witch-doctors, called *botates* in their language.

The witnesses were also agreed that the Indians were less capable of self-government and of leading a Christian life in complete liberty than the rudest Spaniard. They could do nothing without direction. They were, to be sure, capable of living as they were accustomed, but not one would dig gold without being driven to it. They had no business sense, for they exchanged things of great value for things of no value. Once two caciques had been set at liberty as an experiment to see whether they would retain their Christian habits, but they had immediately reverted to their old vices. If the Indians should be set at liberty they would never become Christians. Trade would cease, because they would have nothing to do with the Spaniards; and royal rents would cease, because the Spaniards would all abandon the island. The Indians loved to go about naked, and they held money and property as of no value, excepting only food and drink. They had no sense of shame and, when they were beaten by the Spanish authorities, or had their ears cut off, they had no feeling of guilt. They would not work for wages, they took no interest in commerce, and they had no conception of tithes or taxes.

On the expediency of removing the Indians to villages near to those of the Spaniards, opinion is for the first time divided. One witness thought that by all means the Indians should be brought within reach, so that they might be cared for and taught in the Holy Catholic Faith and saved from their vices. Another believed that some mortality might ensue among the young and the aged, and that others might kill themselves, "as they have done before for matters of no consequence," while others would escape to the woods. A third witness thought that there might be some present difficulties but that the ultimate result would be good, that is, the Indians would learn religion and the Spaniards would be spared the bother of going after them. A fourth thought that the Indians should not be molested; if removed they would kill themselves. A fifth, the Indians living in the wilderness were not visited by priests; they should be persuaded to come of their own volition.

They were all eloquent when asked whether the Indians should be removed from the encomienda system and put under the Crown. It should by no means be allowed. The Indians would be much worse off under salaried overseers than under their encomenderos, who treated them well. And above all, no more changes! The present laws, they thought, were sufficient for the protection of the natives, if they were enforced. It would be better if the two months' rest period were abolished, because during that time the Indians reverted to their old habits. The encomiendas should be made perpetual, because the encomendero, being dependent upon the labor of the Indians for his own support, would be more likely to protect them than a hired overseer. There was only one dissenting opinion. The tenth witness thought that if the Indians were set at liberty and allowed to pay tribute, "within twenty years, where there are now twenty-five souls in the islands, there will then be a hundred and five; whereas, if they are left in the encomiendas, as at present, the ratio will be only twenty-five to twenty-seven." The alcalde mayor of the island did not agree with the statistical witness, but urged that the Indians be given in perpetuity to the encomenderos, who would treat them well.[13]

The evidence of these citizens being in all likelihood a just index of the feeling of a great part of the colonists, it was good statesmanship on the part of the Jeronymites to aban-

don that part of Las Casas' plan which would have abolished
the encomienda. Any attempt to enforce it would certainly
have provoked strenuous resistance, and probably civil war,
as happened in similar circumstances in Peru and Panama
twenty-seven years later.

The immediate problem of saving the vanishing remnant
of the island population was a pressing one. Alonso Zuazo
advocated the introduction of Negro slaves who, he said,
would be vastly superior to the Indians as workmen. Gold
production was falling off and the colonists would soon
have to become agriculturists exclusively. The island offered
excellent opportunities for the cultivation of sugar cane,
and farmers should be encouraged to settle there.[14]

Zuazo reported to Cardinal Chièvres that the attempt to
build up the population of Española by importing the natives of the "useless" islands had been entirely inadequate.
Of the 15,000 brought from the Bahamas 13,000 had
perished, the rest having been sold as slaves at high prices.[15]

The Jeronymites supported Zuazo on the advisibility of
bringing Negro slaves from Guinea and the Cape Verde
Islands. The Indians, they said, would thus be relieved of
the heavy labor and would have leisure in which to learn
the Christian religion. There were very few of them left.
At the time of the coming of the Spaniards they had numbered several hundred thousand, and now they were "as
scarce as fruit left on the tree after the harvest." [16]

In their attempt to settle the Indians in villages the
Jeronymites encountered some opposition from the Spaniards—they do not mention how the Indians reacted. They
intended to settle the Indians in groups of four to five
hundred. Officers had been selected to administer the villages. The villages, however, would not be ready for occupancy for another year, for it would first be necessary to
find some means of supporting them. In all they estimated
that twenty-five or twenty-six villages would suffice to

house the remainder of the Indians. They had provided a married Spaniard and a priest for each village who would have to be paid a salary until the village could support them.[17]

During the Jeronymite regime in Española there was little interest at Court in that remote and unimportant colony. Charles I had his hands full adjusting himself and his unpopular group of Flemish advisers to a hostile country. The three friars were left in ignorance of their status. After a year of neglect they learned of the death of Cardinal Cisneros (November 8, 1517), and they resolved to send one of their number to Spain to petition the King to relieve them of their commission and allow them to retire to their cloister. Their emissary was Bernardino de Manzanedo, whose report on conditions in Española is at once the clearest and most objective document of the period. It establishes beyond any reasonable doubt the objectivity and moderation of the Jeronymite governors.

They had, reported Manzanedo, been at great pains to ascertain some remedy for the Indians which would, at the same time, satisfy the colonists. After exhausting all possible sources of information they had concluded that there was no plan which they could recommend in its entirety. Manzanedo, from his own observation, thought that the Indians were not capable of governing themselves after the Spanish fashion, and that they had no love for or desire to lead a Christian life. If left to themselves they would surely revert to their ancient ways, and their souls would be lost. On the other hand, if left in the power of the Spaniards, they would just as surely continue to diminish. The plan to set the Indians at complete liberty (that is, in the charge of the religious—Las Casas' plan) was, he thought, "the plain way for the soul," although the royal revenues would at first suffer from such a measure. An alternative was to continue the encomienda under the Laws of Burgos, with greater care in their enforcement. The religious, he said, Franciscans and Dominicans alike, were opposed to this, claiming that the Indians could not legally, and should not, be given in encomienda, "and they suggest other remedies, many of which offer no fewer difficulties than those which they reprehend."

Manzanedo suggested that a commission be appointed to study the problem dispassionately. Of all the plans thus far put forward he thought that the encomienda had fewer objections than the others. It might improve matters if the Indians could be relieved of the arduous work of mining gold, for they were a weak race, "drinking water and eating manioc, a bread of little substance." The Indians should be used exclusively in agriculture. Although the royal revenues might suffer at first, in time they would increase with the development of the country. Agriculture had thus far been neglected because the desire for gold was so great that no one would take his Indians from the mines.

"One of the principal causes of the depopulation of those parts has been the changes. Since no one has the assurance that he will be able to keep his encomienda Indians, he has used them like borrowed goods, and thus many have perished and are perishing." The fate of the slaves and *naborias perpetuos* was better than that of the encomienda Indians, because they were held in perpetuity. Any novel departure should be undertaken with caution, for it would in all likelihood do more harm than the evil it was designed to correct. Once, however, any disposition was made, it should be accorded all the stability possible, and no meddling should be tolerated, because otherwise "your Highness would be obliged to remedy the Indies every two months, as you are now doing." Another reason for proceeding with caution was that the Indians would be quick to take advantage of any slackness and would rise against the Spaniards, as they had recently done in San Juan (Puerto Rico).

If the encomienda should be continued, he suggested, it should not include more than eighty persons, counting children and the aged. It should be granted only to married men who intended to settle permanently in the country, and by no means to people in Castile, because much harm had come to the Indians in this fashion and the country had not been settled. Neither should encomiendas be granted to governors or judges, because they "will execute the laws very much better without them than with them." Mechanics and merchants should also be excluded from holding encomiendas, since they already had a means of living. A few naborias might be assigned to them as assistants and apprentices. Manzanedo advised against distributing the Crown Indians among the colonists, as they had requested, because the government would need them in many public works which the colonists were afraid to undertake. The colonists had also begged that ecclesiastics should be held ineligible for encomiendas, but Manzanedo thought that if the good of the Indians was the only thing to be considered, their fate under churchmen would be considerably better than under laymen.

He reported that priests were scarce and that both Indians and Spaniards were suffering from their absence. He advised that only men of good life acquainted with the problems of the Indies be chosen for this service. They should be given great authority in the administration of the Indians, with a minimum of interference from Castile. Up to that time he had seen little evidence of their effort to convert the Indians.

As long as personal service was demanded of the Indians, he feared, they would continue to diminish, and so it was very urgent that steps be taken to repopulate the islands. The new settlers should be married men, mostly farmers, because eventually the cultivation of the soil would be more profitable than mining. Colonization could be encouraged by allowing free emigration from Spain. All the ports should be opened to commerce with the Indies—which would make the Indies known to all the people of Spain, whereas at present only the people of Seville came into contact with them.

The colonists of Española were all clamoring for licenses to import Negro slaves. Manzanedo thought that this would be one remedy for the overworked Indians, and it would also increase the Crown's revenues. If sufficient colonists could be sent to the islands at the same time, there would be no danger from the Negroes in Española, although the same could not be said for Cuba and San Juan; in Cuba the Negroes would be dangerous because of the large number of Indians there, and in San Juan because of the frequent raids of the Caribs, with whom they would make common cause against the Spaniards.[18] The Negro slaves should include both sexes, with more women than men.

Because it was from the poorer classes that the Spanish colonists were recruited, Manzanedo thought that these people could be encouraged to emigrate if they were granted certain privileges; for example, their household goods might be shipped free of duty, as well as the goods they should bring over for the maintenance of their establishments, mines, Indians, and slaves. They might also be encouraged by gifts of cattle, oxen, seeds, and so on, and they should be permitted to buy slaves on deferred payments, so that they might begin to cultivate the land as soon as possible.

"I know nothing about colonizing," concluded Manzanedo, "and I beg your Highness to pardon me for what I have said least well and grant me permission to retire to my monastery, and the other fathers to theirs, because, as I have said, these are not things which we think are fitting to our cloth and our order."[19]

The Jeronymites seem to have made a sincere effort to execute one of the more important of their instructions.

By January, 1519, they reported, they had built thirty villages for the congregation of the Indians. Unluckily, just as they were about to transfer the Indians to them, a fearful epidemic of smallpox had broken out and a third of the population had perished. This disaster, they wrote, made it imperative to begin the shipment of Negro slaves at once, for if the pestilence should last another month no gold would be extracted that year.[20]

The mild reforms undertaken by the Jeronymite governors of the Indies satisfied no one. On the one hand they enraged Las Casas for failing to abolish the encomienda; on the other they invited the wrath of the colonists for the few things they had done to alleviate the condition of the Indians. Even Pasamonte joined their critics, and reports of graft and favoritism reached the Court. The anomaly of their government could hardly be allowed to continue in any case, and the judiciary was removed from their control in August, 1518. The following December they were relieved entirely and their powers were transferred to a new juez de residencia, Rodrigo de Figueroa.[21] Such was the leisurely movement of vessels in those days, however, that they continued in office until August, 1519, when, with the arrival of Figueroa, their administration definitely ended. They remained in Española a few months longer in an advisory capacity and finally returned to Spain some time in 1520. There they sought an audience with Charles V, but he refused to see them, much to the glee of Las Casas. "The cleric Las Casas," wrote Las Casas, "attributed it all to a judgment of God, who did not wish them to be heard by the King, or for him to pay any attention to them, because they had done so little to remedy the oppressed Indians." He recorded God's further displeasure with them displayed when Fray Luis de Figueroa was named Bishop of Santo Domingo several years later but died before setting out.[22]

The voluminous instructions of the new juez de residencia

included the entire code of Burgos as revised by Cisneros, most of the recommendations of Bernardino de Manzanedo, and a number of new notions which it would be idle to discuss, as they were never put into effect. Figueroa, of course, found himself faced with the same dilemma that had defeated the Jeronymites. If the Indians were removed from the encomiendas everyone agreed that the Spaniards would abandon the island; if they were left in the encomiendas they would perish. Figueroa tried the experiment of allowing two of the new villages to govern themselves, but discovered that they would do only enough work to keep from starving. He was convinced that the Indians were incapable of self-government, but, as he informed the King, if they increased at all the experiment would be justified.[23]

Charles V and his advisers on Indian affairs were convinced by this time that the encomienda could no longer be tolerated. This decision, made on the very eve of the conquest of Mexico, was to have important consequences. It was decided that "the Indians are free and should be given entire liberty, and we, in good conscience, cannot and should not give them in encomienda to anyone, as has heretofore been done." Figueroa was instructed that the Indians whom he had removed from the Crown and from absentees should be settled in villages, and that the same was to be done with the Indians held in encomiendas as soon as these should become vacant. The villages were to be administered as laid down in the instructions of the Jeronymites, with a priest, a layman of good conscience, and so on, although it had been suggested that they be administered after the manner of a Spanish feudal estate. Figueroa was to send his opinion on this matter to the King. Figueroa had reported that the Caribs were in the habit of eating human flesh which, it would seem, justified their being made slaves and brought to Española to relieve the Indians there.[24]

Before the scene shifts to the mainland it may be well

to reflect a moment upon the depressing record in the Antilles. The shocking calamity which overtook the native population was caused by the dislocation of their economy, the introduction of new diseases, and their exploitation in the mines and plantations. To return to the earlier thesis, a major factor in their extinction was the character and cultural background of the colonists. All ameliorative legislation (which, to be sure, was unrealistic and impracticable) met with the unyielding opposition of the Spaniards, an opposition which cannot be disposed of merely by calling it wicked. The men of the conquest were a military people. A large number of them had, and continued to have, no honorable occupation but war and no income but its spoils. They were proud, ignorant, credulous, unstable, callous to suffering, ambitious of rank, scornful of demeaning labor, and almost invariably hard up. The appeal made to such men by a country where gold was supposed to abound and where every white man might set himself up as a petty lord over a submissive population, was irresistible. But when they had come to the Indies these adventurers were caught in the net of their own incompetence and brought down with them the whole of the native population. The island people, in their turn, perished because their primitive economy could not support the burden of the harsh and wasteful parasite class which had been imposed upon them. It should be evident that the encomienda had little to do with their destruction. Properly administered, as it was to be in better conditions in New Spain, it might have developed into something no more vicious than the European feudal system. But Las Casas and the Dominican group now dominating the thinking of the Council of the Indies had convinced Charles V that the encomienda was responsible for the evil conditions in the Antilles, and when the news of the Mexican discovery reached Spain he resolved that it should not meet the same fate.

5.

The Partition of Mexico

THE SLAVE-HUNTING expeditions which had discovered the coast of Yucatan and Mexico spread through the islands the exciting news of the higher civilizations on the mainland. Nowhere else in the Indies had cities of stone and mortar, and well-clothed people been met. The discoverers also found, of course, that the new land was given over to the most hideous vices, the most abominable of which were cannibalism, idolatry, and human sacrifice. Its gods were stone and wooden devils. The disgusting habits of its people made it the manifest duty of the Christians to save them from themselves. And, if they resisted, well, it was a fair land and slaves were fetching a high price in the islands.

Cortés himself was struck by the superior civilization of Mexico. He had spent twenty years in the islands and had witnessed the disastrous effect of the Spanish occupation upon the natives there. He, like many enlightened men of his time, believed that the destruction was chargeable to the encomienda, and he resolved that the evil was not to be introduced into the new lands.[1]

In August, 1521, at the fall of Mexico City, Cortés had with him some 1,500 men who were under the most shadowy military obligation to their chief. These men had, in their great majority, been drawn from the Antilles. They had fought hard and suffered severely in the Mexican campaign. They had received no pay for two years except the small amount of booty left after Cortés had withheld his own not inconsiderable share and had sent a like amount to the Emperor to induce him to look kindly upon the conqueror's somewhat irregular conduct. The men were under no illusions about the motives of the conquest. They had learned in the islands how Indians could be put to profitable use. There was no reward for them but Indians, and Indians they must and would have. Cortés was too accomplished a statesman to allow principles to stand in the way of expediency and yielded to the threatening insistence of his men. There is also strong reason to believe that he was not without designs on the native population himself, but his letter to the Emperor argues that he was forced into this disagreeable surrender.

In a former letter [he wrote] I informed your Majesty that the natives of these parts are of much greater capacity than those of the other islands, and we thought that they were of such understanding and intelligence as would make them moderately capable, and for that reason I thought it a grave matter to compel them to serve the Spaniards as they did in the other islands. I also [thought] that if this [service] were abolished, the conquerors and settlers of these parts could not support themselves, and that in order not to force the Indians to serve them and to remedy the difficulty of the Spaniards, I thought that your Majesty should command that they be aided for their support from the revenues of your Majesty. . . . Since that time, in view of the many and continuous expenses of your Majesty, and [thinking] that we should increase your revenues in every way rather than cause ex-

pense, and in view also of the great length of time we have been
at war and the necessities and debts that we have all incurred
because of it, the delay in any disposition which your Majesty
might make, and especially in the face of the importunities of
your Majesty's officers and men which I could in no wise escape,
it was almost necessary for me to deposit the chiefs and natives
of these parts with the Spaniards—which I have done with proper
consideration for their rank and the services they have rendered
your Majesty. And so, until something further is ordered, or this
disposition is confirmed, the said chiefs and natives will serve the
Spaniards with whom they have been deposited and supply them
with what they need for their support.

This step was taken upon the advice of persons who are very
experienced in this country. Nothing could have been, and nothing can be, better or more necessary for the support of the Spaniards, as well as for the conservation and good treatment of the
Indians, as the delegates who are now on their way from New
Spain will explain to your Majesty. The best and most important
provinces and cities have been reserved for your Majesty. I beg
that your Majesty will command that this be approved. . . .[2]

In view of Cortés' speedy conversion to the encomienda
principle, his original glowing account of the natives, like
that of Columbus before him, was unfortunate. It reached
Court just at the time when the controversy over the
encomienda had been settled in favor of its abolition. It
must have made the most disagreeable impression on the
Emperor, who wrote back absolutely forbidding the continuance of the encomienda. He reviewed the whole case
against it: the Indians of the islands had been greatly
diminished by it; it had been an obstacle in the way of their
conversion; theologians and learned men at Court had decided that it was contrary to the bull of donation and that
the Emperor could not with a clear conscience give the Indians in encomienda, for the Lord had created the Indians
"free and not servile." "Therefore you will not make any
repartimiento or encomienda [3] in that land, or consent to
any assignment of the Indians, but you are to allow them

to live in liberty, as our vassals in Castile live, and if before the arrival of this letter you have given any Indians in encomienda to any Christians, you will remove them . . . and you will [also] take from them the vices and abominations in which they have been living . . . and you will inform them of the favor we are doing them in this . . . so that they may the more willingly come to a knowledge of our Holy Catholic Faith and serve us and have proper friendship and intercourse with the Spaniards. . . ."

The provisions of this instruction show a notable advance in humanity and statesmanship over anything done for the Antilles. In the matter of conversion the Mexican priests were to be given preference because of their great influence with the people, but they were not to be pressed too hard lest they should become offended. The Indians were to be encouraged in their high civilization and urged to lead an orderly life. They were to be persuaded to abolish human sacrifice, but if persuasion failed, they were to be forced to do so. They were to pay only the service and dues which they owed to the Crown in common with all other vassals. Free commerce between Indians and Spaniards was to be encouraged, since it would bring Indians into contact with Spaniards. The latter were to keep all promises made to the Indians.

The Christians were forbidden to make war upon the Indians or to take their property without payment. Anyone injuring an Indian was to be severely punished. "And thus the Indians will come into closer contact with the Christians, . . . and they will acquire a knowledge of our Holy Catholic Faith, which is our principal desire and purpose, and more will be gained converting a hundred by this means than a hundred thousand by any other."

However, it might so happen that the Indians would refuse to render obedience to the Emperor and that war would become necessary. In such a case no action was to be taken against them until they had been urged in their own tongue [4] to accept the authority of the Emperor, and even then the Indians must be the aggressors. But once war had been decided on, the Indians were to be made slaves. "But," continued the Emperor, "you are to bear in mind one thing, and that is that all the Christians will be greatly desirous of keeping the Indians warlike and not peaceful, so that they may be given in encomienda . . . and as they will always speak with this purpose . . . it will be well for you to take it into account before giving them credence."

Cortés was instructed to prevent the taking of the daughters and wives of the Indians by the Spaniards— which had been the cause of great friction in the islands.[5] He was to locate his townsites with a view toward minimizing the use of Indians as carriers. He was to distribute the land equitably among the colonists, who might receive title to it only after five years' occupancy.[6]

The distribution of the people and lands of New Spain was already an accomplished fact when the Emperor's peremptory order dropped upon Cortés. Nothing better illustrates the spirit of the great conquistador than his reception of his sovereign's letter. Presuming upon his new authority as Captain-General and Governor of New Spain,[7] and upon the magic of the ancient feudal formula of *obedezco pero no cumplo* ("I obey but I do not fulfill"), he indicated to the four royal officers who had brought the Emperor's order that he had no intention of executing it, and then wrote a long letter to the Emperor explaining the whole situation in detail and showing why the new provisions would not work.

In the first place, he wrote, free association of Indian and Spaniard would bring naught but disaster. If all the Spaniards were friars interested solely in the conversion of the Indians such a plan, perhaps, might succeed; but they were not. Indeed, "the majority of the Spaniards who come here are of low quality, violent and vicious . . . and if such were given permission to go freely among the Indian towns they would convert the Indians to their vices." Hence he had forbidden all Spaniards to go among the Indians, under severe penalties.

Cortés' argument justifying his establishment of the enco-mienda is carefully developed. Since his decision changed the course of the history of New Spain, reveals his quali-ties of statecraft, and gives some clue to the reason for the superior conduct of the conquerors of New Spain, his argu-ment is worth examining.

First, he wrote, the Spaniards had no means of support other than that offered by the service of the Indians and they would necessarily have to abandon the country if it were taken from them. Furthermore, his Majesty would lose his new empire and the natives their souls. (This, of course, was the ancient argument of the encomenderos of Espa-ñola.)

Second, it was not true that the natives would be free if the encomienda should be abolished. On the contrary, Cortés' method of distributing them in encomienda released them from the unbearable slavery in which they had been held by their former masters, who had been in the habit of seizing them for sacrifice to their idols. Their slavery had been so unendurable, in fact, that now it was only necessary to threaten to return them to their native masters in order to make them serve the Spaniards very willingly.

Third, Cortés wrote, he had lived in the islands for twenty-odd years and was familiar with the abuses com-mitted against the natives there, and he was going to take particular pains to see that the same situation did not occur in New Spain. He would not, for example, allow the Indians held in encomienda to be used in gold mining, or to be carried off to work in the plantations. Mining would be done by slaves, of whom there was a great abundance, both of those captured in war and those acquired by purchase from the natives themselves.

Fourth, it was illusory to suppose that the natives could be made to pay a money tribute to the Crown. In the first place, they had no money; in the second, if they paid in kind, his Majesty could not dispose of the goods. The towns already placed under the Crown had been almost ruined in the attempt to collect tribute, and Cortés had been forced to give these towns in encomienda to prevent their destruction. Since doing so, he had seen these towns rebuilt and the royal revenues from them increased to three times what they had been before. If any profit was to be made from such places it would only be when they were given into the hands of men who knew their business.

Fifth, if the encomienda were abolished, who then would hold the country for the Emperor? He would have to police it with several thousand royal troops paid by the Crown, and such a pestilence alone would suffice to destroy the country.

Finally, one reason for the destruction of the island population, he thought, had been the practice of granting encomiendas to the judiciary. He had forbidden it in New Spain.[8]

There is nothing in Cortés' instructions or in his commission as Captain-General which gave him such extraordinary discretion. The chronic suspicion of its servants which was to become typical of the Spanish Crown seems to have been justifiable in the case of the conqueror of Mexico, whose talent for intrigue was combined with a magnificent audacity, imagination, and intelligence. First, he had met and captured Francisco de Garay, who was "discovering" the province of Pánuco with a far better title to do so than Cortés' own. Then he had bribed, cajoled, and otherwise cozened the large force of Pánfilo de Narváez to join him in the conquest of Mexico, and had imprisoned Narváez himself. Cristóbal de Tapia, who had been sent by the Audiencia of Santo Domingo to keep an eye on him, had been persuaded, by bribery, it was charged, to go back to the islands. And now Cortés had gone to the length of shelving the Emperor's direct command.[9]

In its attempt to abolish the encomienda in New Spain the Crown, acting, to be sure, on the recommendation of Cortés himself, had failed to take into account the momentum it had acquired in the long years of its practice in the Antilles. Like preceding governments, that of Charles V showed itself ready to upset the established economic system of the Indies—if, indeed, we are justified in so qualifying the near-chaos which we have been describing—for short-term considerations of policy. In the resulting instability the encomenderos, in Manzanedo's picturesque phrase, used the Indians like "borrowed goods" and had no thought for anything but immediate profit. Cortés' decision to retain the encomienda can be defended from a more realistic conception. Not only was he faced with the ticklish business of finding some means of rewarding his men, but he was evidently convinced that he could make the encomienda over into something like an orderly society with a feudal basis. He had also assigned to himself an immense share of the human spoils and was of no mind to give them up. He showed himself a master of the *fait accompli*, and the Crown had to make the best of it. "As this evil practice," wrote Solórzano, "had already struck root, it was not easy to pull it up. Indeed, the governors and colonists made such complaints and pointed out so many difficulties in the way of the execution of these new provisions . . . that they were suspended." [10]

Charles V's admiration for Cortés, which was great, was not great enough to make him overlook insubordination, and he resolved to send that dreaded officer, a juez de residencia, to find out what Cortés was up to.[11] The Crown was obviously opposed to an extension of New World feudalism on such a scale, and from this point onward pursued a consistent policy of reducing the power of Cortés.

At the moment, however, Cortés was flying very high and there was no apparent limit to his impudence. Satisfied that his letter had settled the acceptance of the encomienda in New Spain, he followed it with another in which he urged that it would be of great benefit to Indians and Spaniards alike if it were made perpetual. With stability and prosperity thus assured, he wrote, his Majesty's revenues would increase proportionately. It would also help to stabilize the country if a number of religious of good and holy lives should be sent over to convert the natives to Christianity.[12] But the principal need of New Spain, he repeated, was the perpetuity of the encomienda. The Crown might receive a steady income from it by imposing a sales tax on all its products, or by requiring the encomendero to pay a fixed perpetual tribute. Above all, the encomienda must be given stability in order to protect the Indians.[13] The disinterestedness of Cortés is doubtful in view of the vast estate which he persuaded the Crown to grant him. Although it was contrary to Hapsburg principles to permit such an anachronism as the Marquesado de Valle to be set up, the Crown had no choice. The conquest was privately financed and the conquistadores had to be lavishly rewarded, or the whole business would come to a stop. Meanwhile, the swelling stream of officers sent over to keep an eye on Cortés may have convinced him that he had gone too far. Possibly to restore his credit with the Emperor by another such dazzling exploit as the conquest of Mexico, possibly to avoid the royal officers, he set out on his famous and disastrous march to Honduras.

His immediate excuse for absenting himself from Mexico was the reported defection of Cristóbal de Olid, whom he had sent to Honduras to forestall the expedition of Gil González de Avila, who had a patent to "discover" the land to the northwest of Tierra Firme. Olid, perhaps in imitation of Cortés, perhaps in connivance with Diego Velázquez, Cortés' ancient enemy, soon gave unmistakable signs of wishing to operate on his own. Cortés had already sent his kinsman, Francisco de las Casas, to Honduras, but, having heard nothing from him, he resolved to go there in person, leaving the government in the hands of the four treasury officers, Alonso de Estrada, Rodrigo de Albornoz, Peralmíndez Chirinos, and Gonzalo de Salazar.[14]

It was an odd arrangement and one which shows that Cortés must have been in a most pressing hurry to get away. He could hardly have expected it to work. Estrada, the treasurer, and Albornoz, the accountant—so read his instructions—were to have first try at running the government, and if it should prove too much for them they were to be superseded by the other two, Chirinos and Salazar. Nothing could have been better calculated to set the colony by the ears. Without the prestige of Cortés to restrain them, the Velázquez and Cortés factions were immediately at each other's throats. Cortés was no more than out of town before Chirinos and Salazar overtook him with scandalous tales of the misbehavior of Estrada and Albornoz. He sent them back to the capital with orders to assist Estrada and Albornoz in the government, but, by changing their orders, they were able to expel their rivals and set themselves up as dictators of New Spain. The prolonged absence of Cortés gave them an excellent opportunity to enrich themselves. They easily got together a following from among the numerous malcontents of the Velázquez faction and distributed among them the encomiendas of the men who were with Cortés. They even disposed of Cortés himself by publishing a report of his death. Their usurpation bore most heavily on the Indians, whose new masters, suspecting that their tenure was to be short, amassed wealth in the speediest way possible, which was to squeeze the Indians of their encomiendas for all they were worth.[15]

Cortés was very much alive, however, and turned up again in May, 1526, to the confusion of the usurpers, who were clapped into jail at the first news of his arrival at Vera Cruz. He at once set about repairing the damage caused by his absence, but had hardly begun when the royal juez de residencia, Luis Ponce de León, arrived and made him a private citizen again. But the conqueror's star had not yet set. Ponce de León had been in Mexico City but a short time when he was stricken with a fever and died.[16] Before his death he assigned his commission to his companion, the aged inquisitor, Marcos de Aguilar; but Aguilar's health was too feeble for him to take an active part in the government, although Cortés made a show of turning it over to him. Aguilar had no alternative but to restore Cortés in his duties as Captain-General, an action in which he was supported by Cortés' friend, the treasurer Estrada.[17]

The arguments of Cortés against the abolition of the encomienda bore fruit at Court. At least there is no evidence that any attempt was made to enforce the act, and he was left for the time being in charge of the administration of the Indians and the distribution of encomiendas. If Ponce de León had lived, things might have been different, for the feeling against Cortés at Court is well illustrated by Ponce's instructions.

Cortés, they stated, had been ordered not to make any distribution of the Indians in New Spain, because the encomienda had been responsible for the diminution of the island population and a consequent loss of Crown revenue. He had not only failed to execute that order, but he had even suppressed it and had distributed all the peaceful Indians provisionally among his men, and they were being used for building houses, supplying the Spaniards with food, and bringing gold from the mines. And, although Cortés had maintained that it was impossible to collect tribute from the natives and that it would be preferable for the Crown to take its fifth from the encomenderos, others had said that it could be collected without difficulty. Ponce was instructed to confer with Cortés and the religious on this question and on the best way to convert the Indians to the Holy Catholic Faith, "for their good treatment, the maintenance of justice, and our own service and profit." They were to decide whether it would be better for the Indians to remain in encomienda and serve the Spaniards, or whether it would be better for them to be given as vassals, like those held by the nobles of Castile, paying the Crown such tribute "as you think can be imposed upon them." All these opinions were to be submitted to the Crown for decision.[18]

As might be expected, Cortés gave a good account of his stewardship. "The country," he wrote, "is somewhat fatigued by the recent disturbances, but with the friendship and good treatment of the Indians, which I always strive to maintain, it will be restored, God willing, for the Indians, although they have necessarily received some vexations from our people because of the change of masters, are multiplying and increasing so rapidly that it seems that there are more natives now than when I first came to these parts. The religious . . . are doing much good, especially among the children of the caciques. The Christian religion is being so well planted that your Majesty owes many thanks to God for it." [19]

The ordinances which Cortés issued for the government of the Indians are hardly more than a repetition of the Laws of Burgos. The Indians were told that they were to be taught in the Holy Catholic Faith, that they were to provide food for the Spaniards to whom they had been assigned, that they were to work on the Spaniards' farms, and serve them. The encomendero was not to be allowed to remove any woman, or any child under twelve, from the native towns for any reason whatever. The Indians assigned to work parties (*repartimientos*) must be counted both coming and going before a lieutenant of the governor, and were to have thirty days' rest between assignments. They might not be taken out before sunrise or brought back after sunset, and they were to have an hour's rest at noon. Their encomenderos were charged to do away with idolatry in their villages and to build churches in their encomiendas within six months. Indians could not be ordered to serve on work parties by anyone except a deputy of the governor, and they were to be assured a wage from their encomenderos of half a gold peso a year.

His ordinances for the government of the Spaniards, on the other hand, go considerably beyond the Laws of Burgos in their protection of the Indians. Every encomendero was obliged to destroy idols and forbid their use. He was to forbid the practice of human sacrifice. A house of prayer or a church was to be built in every encomienda. The encomenderos were obliged to bring all male children to the monasteries for religious instruction. Where there were no monasteries the alcalde or regidor of each town was to hire a priest at his own expense to teach the Indians, except where the encomiendas were too small, in which case two or three adjoining encomiendas could support one in common. The encomendero was forbidden to demand gold of his Indians. Title to an encomienda could be proved only by eight years' residence in it. Cortés promised to petition his Majesty to grant the encomiendas for life and for the life of one heir, and for tenure during good behavior. Married encomenderos must send to Spain for their wives; otherwise they must marry within six months or lose their encomiendas. They were also required to build houses in their encomiendas, and to live in them, within eighteen months.[20]

Supplementary instructions which he issued for the government of newly conquered territory went even farther in providing for the protection of the Indians. His kinsman, Francisco Cortés, for example, who was sent to "pacify" the province of Colima, was to see that any Spaniard harming a native was to give redress to the latter's satisfaction.[21] This unusual step may have been taken because of the warlike character of the tribes of the west, but it obeyed at the same time a wise policy adopted by Cortés since the beginning of the conquest, and it was a long advance over the practice in the Antilles, which was to exterminate or enslave all natives who showed resistance. This innovation is not to be taken as meaning that Indian slavery was a thing of the past. Prisoners of war were regularly and legally made slaves, and a constant supply of them was needed for the working of the mines. So long as the wars of conquest lasted, there had been no lack of slaves, but now that the country was in a fair way toward complete pacification the supply threatened to run short—hence the abuse of acquiring Indians by purchase, which is described in detail by the accountant Rodrigo de Albornoz.

The Indians, he wrote, seemed to hold slavery as a thing of no consequence among themselves. A man might gamble away his freedom, or sell himself to pay a debt, with little regret for his lost liberty. But then they did not use one another in the killing work of gold mining. Nothing was easier for a Spaniard to do than to descend upon a village with a demand for tribute. The Indians would protest that they had no gold to give him, but would he accept a few slaves instead? He would. So the slaves were brought forth and duly branded and sent off to the mines chained together. Sometime, indeed, the cacique of a village might be running low in slaves, but then he had only to bring out some of his own tribesmen, or his own kin, for that matter, and force these unfortunates to swear that they were legitimate slaves, in order to satisfy the demand for tribute.[22]

The buying of these *indios de rescate* was difficult to regulate. Cortés made an attempt to prevent the enslavement of free Indians, with, it seems, only moderate success. His instructions for the government of Trujillo (Honduras) prescribe the manner of acquiring slaves from the Indians. "Since his Majesty has given permission to all the citizens of New Spain to buy slaves from the native lords of the country, you will issue licenses to those who have Indian towns and their lords in encomienda to buy slaves from these lords . . . in any quantity you may see fit. . . . You will issue such licenses with the proviso that all slaves thus acquired are to be brought before you and your notary, and in the presence of the lord who is selling them you will have them asked what method they formerly pursued among themselves in making slaves. Then you will take the said slaves to one side, their lord not being present, and you will learn from them how and why they were made slaves. And if it appears that they are slaves according to their own custom, they are to be given to the person buying them . . . and you will brand them with the iron of his Majesty, which is to be kept in the strongbox of the cabildo." [23]

The control of Indian slavery continued to occupy the thoughts of the Council of the Indies, which was now under the presidency of Fray García de Loaisa, general of the Dominican Order and the Emperor's confessor. In November, 1526, it instructed Ponce de León, the news of whose death had not yet reached Spain, not to tolerate the taking or branding of slaves without due process of law; nor was he to allow Indians to be brought to Spain, save only certain children who might be sent there for education.[24]

Even under the leadership of Loaisa, the Council of the Indies continued its policy of trying to appease reformers and colonists alike. In a general cédula prescribing the conduct of exploring expeditions it provided that each expedition was to include two religious who were to have authority in all matters pertaining to the Indians. The latter, if it was thought necessary for their conversion, might be given in encomienda, with the consent of the two religious. Acts of violence perpetrated by Spaniards against Indians everywhere were to be investigated by royal officers and the guilty parties were to be punished. These officers were to set at liberty all slaves who had been unjustly taken. Liberated slaves were to be treated as free men; they were not to be given an excessive amount of work; nor were they to be sent to the mines against their will. The Indians of newly discovered territories were to be persuaded, by peaceful means if possible, to accept Spanish rule. They were to be taught good habits and dissuaded from eating human flesh and from indulging in other unpleasant vices. They might be enslaved only if they resisted Spanish rule. They might not be forced against their will to go to the pearl fisheries, mines, or plantations. All these things were ordered "to prevent the former harm and difficulties, and to provide what is best for the service of God and the King." [25]

The reader will suspect that this attempted regulation of slaving, like the Laws of Burgos, hardly did more than recognize the standard practice. Giving authority over the Indians to the religious was a favorite measure of the Dominicans. The title "Protector of the Indians," which was first held by Las Casas, was continued, although no one ever knew precisely what the prerogatives of a "protector" were. The new bishop-elect of Mexico, Juan de Zumárraga, was given that title. Among his duties he was to see that the Indians were well treated, and taught in the Holy Catholic Faith. With the help of the new Audiencia of Mexico he was to enforce all orders for the protection of the Indians, and the president and oidores were commanded to give him all the aid and favor he should need in the performance of his duties.[26] As the Council of the Indies should have foreseen, this anomalous office did little but stir up antagonism between the civil government and the "protector." It did, however, in the turbulent government of the first Audiencia, give Zumárraga a kind of authority to oppose the lawless exploitation of the Indians of which Nuño de Guzmán and his accomplices were guilty.

Meanwhile, Cortés was steadily losing favor. The death of Ponce de León and a long complaint from the accountant, Rodrigo de Albornoz, brought about the temporary appointment of the treasurer, Alonso de Estrada, as governor, a position which Cortés looked upon as his by right. He could not bring himself to accept his diminished status and quarreled bitterly with Estrada, who exiled him from Mexico City. It was probably this humiliation which determined Cortés to return to Spain to look after his interests in person.

Estrada's appointment was merely a stopgap. The time had come to set up a regular government for the Kingdom of New Spain, and in 1528 an audiencia was sent out under the presidency of Beltrán Nuño de Guzmán, a notorious enemy of Cortés. The turbulent spirit of this extraordinary man was the single element needed to throw the country back into the chaos of 1524–1526. The history of the encomienda under him was almost a repetition of its history in the Antilles and deserves a chapter to itself.

6.

The First Audiencia

IT MAY BE well at this point to summarize the situation in New Spain which the Council of the Indies was trying to correct. Cortés, acting in accordance with the Laws of Burgos, and yielding to the pressure of his troops, had distributed among them a large number of encomiendas. In that distribution, however, he had given preference to the men of his original army and had slighted the men whom he had persuaded to join him in his famous encounter with Pánfilo de Narváez. These men we may properly call the Velázquez faction because Narváez had been sent by Diego Velázquez to take over the conquest of Mexico. The Velázquez men were understandably resentful of their treatment, particularly since they were in the majority, and they had joined Chirinos and Salazar in the 1524–1526 interlude in an attempt to get their share of the spoils, with the disastrous results that we have observed. Cortés, in the short period of his restoration, could do little to rehabilitate his party. The appointment of the treasurer, Alonso de Estrada, as temporary governor, merely increased the bitterness between the factions. New Spain, in a word, was the victim of two competing gangs.

It is likely that the Council of the Indies had a distorted view of the situation. Certainly the Velázquez party had, ever since 1519, done everything in its power to discredit Cortés and play up his apparent ambition to make New Spain a feudal empire, with himself as *primus inter pares*. Nothing else explains the desperate measure which the Council of the Indies now thought it necessary to adopt, which was, in effect, to put the government of New Spain into the hands of the Velázquez faction headed by Beltrán Nuño de Guzmán. At the same time the Council of the Indies must have been aware of the danger of civil war if it came down too heavily on the encomenderos of Cortés. Anyway, their credit had gone up lately with the arrival in 1527 of the picturesque and swashbuckling Pedro de Alvarado, whose reputation was second only to that of Cortés himself. The upshot of all these factors was that the instructions issued to the first Audiencia were milder than might have been expected; they seemed to promise, indeed, a pleasanter era all round for the conquerors of New Spain. The Council underestimated the bitterness of the feud and probably had no clear notion of the character of the man to whom the new government was entrusted.

The Audiencia, stated the instructions, was immediately to assemble a council in Mexico City which was to include the bishops of Tlaxcala and Mexico, the prior of the Dominican Order and the guardian of the Franciscan, three religious from each of them, and the president and oidores (justices) of the Audiencia. These men were to consider ways and means of reducing the native population to Christianity as soon as possible and of distributing land and Indians among the conquerors in an equitable fashion. The King had been convinced by the arguments of Hernán

Cortés and others that the conquerors should be rewarded
by grants of encomiendas in perpetuity, with preference
given to those who intended to establish themselves permanently in New Spain. The capital towns (*cabeceras*) of
provinces, however, and those necessary to the royal service,
with their inhabitants, were to be reserved for the Crown,
and a reasonable number of Indians and lands should be set
aside for the use of future settlers. The rest of the towns were
to be distributed among the conquerors and settlers according to their quality and services. The president and oidores
of the Audiencia were forbidden to share directly or indirectly in the distribution, since they had been assigned
competent salaries; but each of them might have ten Indians for his personal household service only.[1]

A second instruction of the same date provided that all
encomiendas becoming vacant during the investigation of
the council were to be given preferably to married men, as
it was thought that they would remain longer and treat the
Indians better,[2] and a long special instruction to Nuño de
Guzmán contains a paragraph forbidding the Indians to
have arms or horses.[3]

The Audiencia arrived at Mexico City in December,
1528. It had originally consisted of five members: President
Nuño de Guzmán, and four oidores. Two of the latter had
died, however, on the voyage, leaving New Spain in the
hands of Nuño de Guzmán and the two survivors, Diego
Delgadillo and Juan Ortiz de Matienzo. It soon developed
that these three interpreted their instructions as a mandate
to despoil the Cortés men and enrich themselves and those
of the Velázquez faction.[4] The only impediment in the way
of the new dictators was Bishop-elect of Mexico Fray Juan
de Zumárraga, who took seriously his responsibility as Protector of the Indians. He made a vigorous attempt to secure
the enforcement of the laws restricting the exploitation of
the Indians, but, unfortunately, his commission was so

vaguely worded and it so evidently overlapped the civil authority that his efforts brought about frequent and violent clashes with the Audiencia. Their disagreements led to explosions from the Franciscans (Zumárraga was a Franciscan) and to repressive measures on the part of the Audiencia. Guzmán refused to recognize Zumárraga's authority as Protector, and the bishop thundered anathemas from the pulpit and granted sanctuary to Guzmán's enemies. Guzmán relieved his feelings in a ninety-two-page letter to Charles V.

His work in New Spain, he complained, was like to be barren, and all because of the excessive zeal of Zumárraga, who had rushed off to the Indies without waiting to be consecrated and hence had no more authority than a common friar. Guzmán had circulated an interrogatory among the principal men of Mexico City concerning the unparalleled conduct of Zumárraga and his Franciscans, and these witnesses were unanimous in their condemnation of it. In the first place, they charged, Zumárraga was working for Cortés and his faction.[5] Furthermore, Zumárraga had published that he alone had the power to adjust the tributes paid by the Indians and that the Indians owed him obedience as Protector. The result had been that the Indians no longer obeyed their masters or the civil authorities, but ran to the bishop with their complaints. Zumárraga was himself using the Indians in his personal service, and the Franciscan friars were holding most of the sons of caciques in their monastery on the pretext of teaching them the Christian doctrine, though their real purpose was to teach these boys to obey and reverence the friars.

The friars, he continued, were in the habit of punishing the Indians with great cruelty for slight cause. For example, they punished drunkenness and absence from Mass by putting the Indians in irons, hanging them up by their arms, flogging, and the stocks. The friars were loose in their

relations with women. One friar of Cuernavaca was reported
to have got as many as eight Indian girls with child. The
friars were sending boys out to preach before they had been
properly taught. They were building a sumptuous monastery at Huejotzingo and were using the Indians in its
construction. They had sent Indians for materials as far as
Vera Cruz and some of the carriers had died of it. They
were also using a great many Indians in the building of an
aqueduct at the same place, without having asked permission of the Audiencia. Fray Toribio de Benavente (the
famous Motolinía) was reported to have sent to Castile
700 *castellanos de oro,* and, since he had no estate, he must
have extorted the money from the Indians.

Thus the first half of the letter. The rest of it is a
thorough whitewashing of the Audiencia.[6] If that is all
Guzmán could dredge up against Zumárraga in his in-
flated and sanctimonious letter, it can hardly be argued
that the bishop was greatly abusing his powers. Guzmán's
case was further weakened by the rigid censorship he
thought necessary to establish at Vera Cruz in order to
prevent adverse criticism from reaching Spain. Zumárraga
tried twice to get a letter through to the Council of the
Indies, and succeeded the second time by making the painful
journey to the coast in person and smuggling the letter into
the hands of a Basque sailor (Zumárraga was also a Basque),
who hid it in a barrel of oil and delivered it to the Council.
Zumárraga's letter is possibly the most important ever
written from the Indies. It is a thoroughgoing indictment
of Guzmán and his regime and, in spite of its heat, gives
a circumstantial and convincing picture of those troublous
times in New Spain.[7]

Such was the prestige of Cortés that, with his arrival in
Spain in May, 1528, the Crown began to veer sharply
toward his party. The first evidence of its changed attitude
was a cédula ordering the Audiencia of Mexico to withhold

two-thirds of the salary of the four treasury officials, if it should be found that they had received Indians in encomienda.[8]

In that year the Indian question engaged the attention of the Council of the Indies to a remarkable extent. It cannot be charged that the Spanish Crown, once awakened to its responsibility in the matter, failed through lack of laws. If anything, the balance dipped the other way and the mass of legislation threatened to smother its execution. An effort was made to license and control Indian slaving, the abuses of which had been reported by the accountant, Albornoz. All Spaniards, stated one decree, claiming ownership of Indian slaves, were required to bring them before a royal officer for registry and examination. Those discovered to have been unjustly taken were to be set at liberty forthwith.[9] At the same time Spaniards proposing to go on slave raids were required to obtain a royal license, on pain of death. A third cédula directed that such licenses must specify the particular rebellious natives who were to be taken, because the Spaniards had been in the habit of enslaving peaceful Indians along with the others.[10] The most minute instructions regarding the treatment of the Indians were showered on the Audiencia and, as was now the custom, on the bishops and on the priors of the two Mendicant orders, as "protectors" of the Indians. There is a certain monotony in the pathetic repetition: no Indians were to be forced to carry burdens against their will, nor otherwise used, except for pay; but they might be required to bring their tribute to their encomenderos as far as twenty leagues—not, however, to the mines, unless they were paid for it; neither might they be used for carrying goods for sale to the mines. The Council had been informed that many persons having Indians in encomienda carried off women to the mines to make bread for the slaves and to work as household servants. This practice was forbidden, even though the women should say that they went of their own accord. It was further ordered that encomienda Indians might not be used to help the slaves at the mines; nor in building houses to sell; nor in transporting supplies from the seaports. They might, however, be hired of their own volition to unload ships, provided they were not required to carry the cargo to a point more than half a league distant. It had also been reported [11] that the Spaniards had been demanding a gold tribute of the Indians, and had been seizing them and torturing them and frightening them into giving slaves to satisfy the demand, such slaves being in some cases the Indians' own children. Thenceforth, it was ordered, no person might take gold from the Indians except such as they might give of their own accord. During the planting and cultivating seasons Indians might not be removed from their farms. Certain Spaniards, it had been reported, had gone to New Spain, not to settle, but to live at their ease by robbing the Indians, taking whatever they fancied and committing many other outrages. Such vagabonds were to be expelled from the country and thenceforth no Spaniard might demand of the Indians anything which they would not give freely. The Indians who had been sent from New Spain to the islands had suffered great hardship and even death, and they had thus conceived a hatred for the Spaniards and kept their women and children from contact with them. Thenceforth no one might remove Indians from New Spain, even though it should be claimed they were slaves. [12]

Although the Crown had surrendered to Cortés on the encomienda question (temporarily, as it turned out), the clamor of theologians in Spain and the continued reports of abuses of Indians in the colonies were used as a pretext for reopening the matter. The Council of the Indies called a conference of theologians and other "learned men" in Barcelona in 1529 to render an opinion on the legality of using free Indians in forced labor. Their opinion, as might be anticipated, reflected the prevailing attitude of the Council of the Indies. Nonresisting Indians, it was decided, were entirely free and were not obligated to perform personal services beyond those demanded of other subjects of the Crown, and they might be assessed for tithes and tributes only according to the quality and value of their lands. It was illegal to give them in encomienda, not only because of the ill treatment they received, but also because they were free men. Until the Indians should be instructed in the Holy Catholic Faith and should adopt Spanish customs and learn to live in an orderly manner (*en policía*), the King might not legally give them to anyone, either temporarily or permanently, "for experience has shown that the laws made in their favor have been observed by no one; nor is the pretext of looking out for their good a sufficient reason for the evil treatment to which they have been subjected by others than the King." [13]

The findings of the Barcelona conference gave the Crown the needed authority for adopting a tougher policy toward the encomenderos. The implied promise of perpetuity, made both in the instructions of Ponce de León and in those of the first Audiencia, may not have been made in bad faith; but clearly by the time of the Barcelona conference the Council of the Indies was determined to destroy the encomienda system, as is evident in the instruction issued to the second Audiencia in 1530. In 1529, however, the encomenderos had enough friends at Court to prevent the Barcelona resolutions from becoming law. Cortés was there and surely had a say in the matter. Their arguments are already familiar to the reader. If such laws should be passed, they said on this occasion (and on every occasion the question came up), New Spain would inevitably be destroyed. It was hardly just to bring everyone to ruin merely because in some cases the Indians had been mistreated. The great majority of the colonists took pains to teach the Indians and protect them, and, indeed, treated them like their own children. Clearly the Indians would lose their chance of salvation if they should be removed from the encomiendas, because there would be no one to instruct them in the Holy Catholic Faith and Christian ways. Anyway, the Indians of the encomiendas were no worse off than the vassals of the lords of Castile.[14]

During the next four years, while Charles V was absent from Spain, the Council of the Indies kept a confusing stream of ordinances flowing to New Spain over the signature of the Queen. It is difficult to find a guiding principle in them.

It had been learned, said one, that the interpreters had a good opportunity for graft in a country where much of the business had to pass through their hands and that they were using their borrowed authority to extort gifts from the Indians. Accordingly, they were forbidden to demand or receive presents, such as jewels, clothing, women, food, or anything whatever.[15]

In answer to Nuño de Guzmán's charge that the Franciscans were using the Indians in personal services, he was instructed that Indian women might come to the monasteries and bake bread for their children (who were in school there), provided they did so of their own accord.[16]

It had been reported that the encomenderos were renting out the services of their Indians, a practice which resulted in harm to the Indians. They were forbidden to do so.[17]

The Council was evidently irritated by the various officials' habit of shelving inconvenient laws by invoking the old formula of *obedezco pero no cumplo*. Thenceforth laws relating to the treatment of the Indians were to be obeyed *and* fulfilled.[18]

A law had already been issued prescribing the registration and examination of Indian slaves. It was now further ordered that all slaves not brought before royal officers for

such registration and examination should forthwith be declared free. The branding iron was to be kept in a double-
locked strongbox, one key to which should be held by
Bishop Zumárraga.[19]

Some inkling of the state of affairs in New Spain had
evidently got past Guzmán's censorship even before Bishop
Zumárraga's sensational letter. The correspondence of the
Council of the Indies took on a sharper tone. The Queen
had learned, for example, that Guzmán, Matienzo, and
Delgaldillo had been using free Indians in the mines and
plantations. The treasury officers were ordered to withhold
their salaries if this charge should be proved.[20]

The encomenderos' ancient dream of perpetuity seemed
about to be realized, in spite of the Barcelona resolutions.
Some efficient lobbying was probably back of a new cédula
which stated: "In view of the information and opinions of
the religious and our governor, Hernán Cortés, and many
others, and with the approval of our Council [of the In-
dies], it being our will to favor the conquerors and settlers of
New Spain, especially those intending to remain there, we
have agreed that a permanent distribution be made . . ."
Guzmán and the Audiencia were instructed to make the
distribution, but they were to have no part in it beyond the
ten Indians allowed for household service; moreover, they
were to give up Indians they had already taken.[21]

It is tempting to speculate about what lay behind this
decision which, if it had been allowed to stand, would have
had the most important consequences. It was plainly against
the policy implied in the Barcelona resolutions, and it was
plainly against the interests of the Crown. It would seem
that there was a profound split in the Council of the Indies.
In any event the split was soon repaired, for the only
encomienda to be granted in perpetuity was that of Cortés.
Zumárraga's letter may well have had something to do with
the matter.

The Council of the Indies laid such business aside while it considered the problem of putting New Spain under a permanent and responsible government. Using the Kingdom of Naples as a precedent, it set up the Kingdom of New Spain as a viceroyalty, which was to be headed by an officer who should represent the King's person. The man eventually selected was Antonio de Mendoza, a member of one of the most powerful families in Spain, knight of the military order of Santiago, royal chamberlain, and ambassador to Hungary. Accepting the recommendation of Zumárraga, the Council had evidently decided that only a man of Mendoza's stature could control the turbulent elements of New Spain. Mendoza, however held out for five years while he dickered with the Crown over his salary.[22] Meanwhile, a second Audiencia was appointed to rule New Spain *ad interim*. Its president was to be Sebastián Ramírez de Fuenleal, Bishop of Santo Domingo and president of the Audiencia of Santo Domingo, a man whose proved virtues and long experience in the Antilles were rightly considered as adequate preparation for his new and difficult post.

The first Audiencia of Mexico had been a calamitous failure. Too hastily chosen, its members were mistaken in their concept of their duties, and their open pillaging of the country and their tyrannical behavior showed them to be the kind of irresponsible adventurers who had been the curse of the Indies since the beginning. The fate of the Indians under such a regime is now familiar to the reader. The documents of the time all repeat the same distressing story of extortion, oppression, and slavery. As Bishop Zumárraga had made clear, there was nothing to be done for either colonist or Indian until stability should be achieved, and such was to be the task of the remarkable body of men who made up the famous second Audiencia of Mexico.

7.

The Second Audiencia: First Phase

THE IMPORTANCE of the second Audiencia is manifest in the stature of the men who composed it. Four oidores were appointed to serve with President Fuenleal: Vasco de Quiroga (who later became famous as the humanitarian bishop of Michoacán), Alonso Maldonado (who earned the nickname of "el bueno"), Francisco de Ceynos, and Juan de Salmerón, all *licenciados* and jurists of standing. Their appointments were made on April 5, 1530, but their instructions were not written until July 12. The Audiencia sailed on September 16 and arrived in Mexico City December 23.[1] They had planned to stop at Santo Domingo to pick up Bishop Fuenleal, but bad weather prevented their landing. In any case the bishop was apparently not enthusiastic about taking the post in New Spain and did not join them until a year later, and then only after repeated urgings.[2]

The Council of the Indies was determined to risk no such fiasco as the first Audiencia had turned out to be and

typically sought to prevent it by issuing instructions to the
new Audiencia which fill eighty-five pages in Puga's *Cedulario*. One of its most delicate assignments was the suppression of all the encomiendas granted by Nuño de Guzmán
which were to be placed under the Crown in a centralized, Crown-controlled system of Indian government, the
corregimiento. This explosive was prudently concealed in a
secret instruction which has considerable importance here,
because it reveals the new thinking of the Council of the
Indies on the encomienda question and its stiffening attitude
toward the incipient feudalism of New Spain. It should be
read in its entirety.

> I command that as soon as you arrive you inform yourselves
> regarding the Indians that have been seized since the said presi-
> dent and oidores [of the first Audiencia] were appointed, and to
> whom they have been assigned, and, above all else, to declare null
> and void, as we declare them to be, all the encomiendas which the
> said president and oidores have made of the Indians that have
> been seized. And we order you immediately to remove them from
> the persons to whom they have been given in encomienda and set
> them at liberty, assessing them such tributes as you think they
> can and should properly pay, and [the Indians] shall deliver them
> to our officers, whom you will make responsible for all this. And
> you will appoint competent persons reputed to be of good con-
> science to administer justice to the said Indians and have them
> instructed in matters of our Holy Faith. And you will do the
> same with all those [Indians] who have been, or shall be, seized
> in any way, until such time as we, having seen your report, shall
> order whatever may be necessary for our service and for the good
> and peopling of that land. The persons who are thus put in charge
> of such towns shall be called *corregidores,* so that even by their
> titles the Indians shall know that they are not their lords.[3]

The ousted encomenderos might be compensated, if found
worthy, by being made corregidores; otherwise, they might
be made constables (*alguaciles*).

It is noteworthy that this plan for establishing a centralized system of Indian government under royal officers is reminiscent of, if not actually derived from, Las Casas' plan for the government of Española which the Jeronymites failed to realize. The corregidor, like Las Casas' administrator, was to have as his principal duty the education of the Indians in his charge, a duty in which he was to have the assistance of a priest. His salary, like that of the priest and the alguacil, was to be paid from the tributes of the Indians, and the balance was to be remitted to the Crown. Any provisions which these officers might need—and only absolute necessities were to be demanded of the Indians—were to be charged against them and deducted from the tribute.

The corregidor was to ascertain from his Indians how much tribute their former encomendero had been getting from them, and he was to reduce the amount if he thought it excessive. He was to keep an eye on his neighboring encomenderos and report any transgressions of the law on their part; that is to say, whether they were living apart from their encomiendas and working their Indians through overseers (*calpisques*); whether they were exacting an immoderate amount of tribute from them; whether they were maintaining priests in their encomiendas, etc.[4]

Further duties of the corregidores were to warn their Indians against committing bigamy and idolatry and to punish them only if they persisted. The Indians were not to be punished for fighting, unless they used weapons. Spaniards mistreating Indians were to be punished as for a public crime. The Indians, to be sure, might not be allowed to remain idle, but should be persuaded to work on farms, or at trades, in order to accustom them to proper Spanish ways of life. Attendance at Mass was obligatory, as was the observance of feast days, and the corregidor must teach them proper deportment in church, among other things. In order to convince the Indians that their sovereign held them in the same esteem as he did his Spanish vassals, the corregidor

was instructed to appoint one Indian alguacil in every town
—which would also serve to train the natives in Spanish
ways of government. The Indians were to be informed,
moreover, that it was the King's will that they should enjoy
the use of their goods without hindrance or abuse by the
Spaniards.[5]

It is apparent by this time, to judge from the similarity
between the ideal functions of corregidores and encomenderos, that it was the purpose of the Crown to make the
King the only encomendero, with the corregidores as his
agents. The salaries assigned to the new posts were modest.
The corregidor was to receive from 320 to 380 *pesos de oro
común* a year; the alguacil from 120 to 140; the priest from
150 to 170.[6]

The instructions to the new Audiencia were, in effect, an
answer to Zumárraga's letter. The oidores were forbidden to
hold encomiendas directly or indirectly, and this disability
was extended to their servants and relatives. The Indians
were to be paid for the work they had done for the first
Audiencia. The census was to be completed. The Audiencia
was to coöperate with the Protector of the Indians (Zumárraga), and it was to make an effort to suppress the Indian
slave trade, although the slave traffic among the Indians
themselves was to be dealt with according to "reason and justice."

The new program included the education of the Indians
in self-government. With this in mind the Audiencia was
to appoint Indian councilmen (*regidores*) to serve equally
with the Spaniards in the native town governments. The
Indian members were to have votes and were to be treated
with respect by their Spanish colleagues. Every Indian town
was to have at least one Indian alguacil. This coöperation
was intended to bring about greater cordiality between the
two races and to teach the Indians the practices of the Holy
Catholic Faith. The Audiencia was enjoined to discourage

the Spaniards from having Indian mistresses, but in this it was instructed to proceed as quietly as possible. The ever-present fear of a native uprising is reflected in a new prohibition of the use of arms, horses, and mules by the Indians; but they might still carry such native arms as they should need for hunting. In its census report the Audiencia was instructed to include such unconquered provinces as could be easily pacified, so that they might be made available for encomiendas for new settlers; but in granting encomiendas the Audiencia was to give preference to the original conquerors and first settlers.[7]

There is an apparent contradiction here between the Crown's plan to establish corregimientos on a large scale (as is evident in the secret instructions cited above) and this promise of further extension of the encomienda system. This inconsistency may have been owing to a prudent realism. The Crown had evidently determined to replace the encomienda eventually by the corregimiento, but at the moment it would have been dangerous to stir up organized opposition among the powerful class of encomenderos. It should also be borne in mind that the conquest had not yet been consolidated and that the only effective military force in New Spain was the encomenderos.

Meanwhile, the encomenderos did little to encourage the Crown to treat them with greater leniency. For example, they were continually trafficking in Indian slaves. The monotonous decrees repeat the familiar story of the enslavement and intolerable abuse of free Indians. Moved by such reports, the Council of the Indies issued a general cédula definitely prohibiting further traffic in Indian slaves and ordering the registration of all slaves then held.[8] Indian slavery, however, was to persist in New Spain for twenty years longer, because the shortage of labor at the mines made it profitable to take Indians "in rebellion" whenever they could be badgered into resistance.

Bishop Zumárraga had requested more definite powers for his protectorship, and in reply was given a special cédula which shows how weak that office really was. The Protector, it said, might, with the approval of the Audiencia, send persons to visit any part of his territory. Such persons, or the Protector himself, might make investigations of reported abuse of the Indians, submitting their findings to the Audiencia for action if the abuse should merit punishment. In the less serious cases, involving fines of not more than fifty pesos, or ten days in jail, the Protector might have jurisdiction. He might also visit the corregimientos, but he had no jurisdiction over the corregidores and was obliged to submit his reports about them to the Audiencia, "because it is not our intention that the Protector should have superiority over the said magistrates." [9]

The protectorship was thus reduced to a device for keeping the Council of the Indies informed on Indian affairs, and its power to interfere in the administration was removed. In effect it turned the missionary into a spy on the encomenderos and corregidores and tended to destroy the cordiality which must exist between them if any progress was to be made in the evangelization of the Indians. The able Fuenleal saw the anomaly when he came to Mexico and recommended the suppression of the office.[10]

The second Audiencia had a difficult assignment in the revocation of the encomiendas granted by the first.[11] The oidor Salmerón, in one of his numerous reports to the Council of the Indies, enumerates some of their difficulties:

The organization of the country is being undertaken, as her Majesty has been informed, but, since circumstances at present are such as to prevent its completion, it has been thought necessary to halt proceedings in the revocation and reallocation of the encomiendas of Indians which her Majesty ordered in the secret instruction. This is going to cause a great deal of bitterness, but we shall not neglect it because of the difficulty of its execution and shall begin it soon again, endeavoring to go as gently as possible, that it may be felt less. And if this should not suffice, let those who will become angry, for what has been commanded by her Majesty shall be done. Although it may harm the Spaniards here it cannot be denied that it is in the interest and for the conservation of the Indians, and therefore just and right.

Salmerón goes on to lament the disorder in the government of New Spain. It had, indeed, been without a master, for those in charge had been too interested in their own affairs to give it any attention. He thought that in the dispute between Franciscans and oidores over the treatment of the Indians there had been some reason on the side of the former. They, however, had allowed themselves more licence in their preaching than was proper. Lately they had also insisted on having a finger in the administration of the royal lands, claiming that it was all for the sake of religion, but they had been induced to submit to the Audiencia.[12]

Two months later the oidores lamented that they were making little progress in supplanting the encomiendas with corregimientos, a failure which they attributed to the absence of their President, Bishop Fuenleal. "We are impatiently awaiting our President," they wrote, "who is still in Santo Domingo. We have encountered a thousand difficulties in the way of executing the new ordinances, particularly the one which suppresses the encomiendas and orders them converted into corregimientos. We have removed the Indians of more than a hundred persons and we are not giving them to anyone whatever, and this is exciting a universal clamor. The same holds for our having reduced the tributes imposed on the Indians by the governors who preceded us."

The oidores regretted that they might not give Indians to certain individuals who had rendered great service to the King, and it was still more painful for them to remove the Indians of widows and children of deceased conquerors.

But they would not yield to sentiment! Those who complained of these actions were being told that their cases would be referred to the King. "These promises, mixed with reprimands and punishments, have produced a good effect."

In their obvious effort to get the Council of the Indies to modify the secret instruction on the encomiendas, the oidores dug up the venerable argument used by the encomenderos since the days of the Laws of Burgos. The encomenderos, they reported, were refusing to cultivate the farms they had established because they no longer had Indians to do the work. Those who still had their encomiendas, suspecting that the Crown purposed to remove them, were no longer interested in cultivating the soil or in raising cattle, but were making every effort to extract the greatest profit out of their Indians in the shortest possible time, fleecing them and sending them to the mines in droves. "And this is the reason why the land is not being cultivated; nor will it be cultivated so long as nothing is stable."

In order to rid New Spain of its pest of Spanish vagabonds the oidores had founded a new town near Cholula which they had named Puebla de Los Angeles.[13] They had induced them to settle there by assigning them fifteen to twenty Indians apiece. These Indians were to work for them for a limited time in agriculture and trades, and would thus learn European methods. The caciques of certain villages had been ordered to send boys to be apprenticed to trades at Puebla, and the boys had been promised that as soon as they attained the grade of master they would be respected and would earn as much as the Spanish mechanics. The latter, however, had refused to accept them as apprentices and wished to use them as perpetual slaves. There was an unbelievable amount of muttering among the colonists over this matter, grumbled the oidores, but it would do them no good.

Nuño de Guzmán had been informed of the new ordinance which prohibited slaving, but he had replied that it would be the ruin of his people in Pánuco, "because they have no business other than taking slaves and sending them to the islands."

The oidores recommended modification of the ordinance on the use of Indian carriers. The Indians, they said, were accustomed to bearing burdens from childhood—indeed, they have never had any other means of transport and many of them had no other way of earning a living. Two or three hundred of these *tamemes* came to the marketplace of Mexico City daily for hire. If carrying should be abolished it would result in a great loss for the colony. On the other hand, there was no denying that terrific abuses had been practiced upon Indian carriers. When, for example, Nuño de Guzmán had gone off on his conquest of New Galicia he had taken along 15,000 tamemes, most of whom had died.

On the slavery question the oidores also discovered that there was something to be said on both sides. The mines were already suffering from a shortage of labor since the prohibition of slaving, and commerce had declined generally. Moreover, the Indians were getting bolder in their new freedom. They had lost their fear of horses, which they had once regarded with such dread, and now they mingled among them in the *juegos de cañas* quite fearlessly and with the greatest agility.[14]

It should be fairly apparent, to judge by the general tenor of the oidores' letter, that they had yielded ground all along the line, if, indeed, they had not gone over entirely to the colonists' point of view. Like their predecessors, the Jeronymites, they found the pressure of reality too great to be resisted inflexibly. It is a fair guess that in both cases the ties of a common speech and common culture that united them to the colonists tended to make them modify their harsh instructions. It was perhaps inevitable that every government sent to New Spain should go through a similar change of attitude and come to be regarded by certain members of the Council of the Indies as traitors to the cause. It was this conflict between the doctrinaire legalism of the Dominican element and the necessary practical adjustments in local administration that convinced zealots of the type of Las Casas that colonial officers were infected with an insidious diabolism.

The oidor Salmerón, who seems to have had a special commission to report directly to the Council of the Indies, added his argument in favor of continuing Indian slavery. Its abolition, he wrote, had doubtless been very just in the light of past experience, but how were those Indians to be punished who attacked the peaceful Indians of the encomiendas? If it were permitted to make them slaves they would be deservedly chastised and his Majesty would profit, because they could then be put to work in the mines. Anyway, this procedure would be less cruel than killing them outright.

The Franciscans, he reported, although they had been sharply reprimanded for interfering in the government of the Indians, were still doing so, although they were, to be sure, supporting the measures of her Majesty, to the disgust of the colonists. The prior of the Dominicans, on the other hand, had been answering their arguments in very good style, "speaking more to the taste of the Spaniards, pointing out their merits and the demerits of the Indians." [15]

Five months later the oidores were not finding the going any smoother. They had to work, they lamented, ten to twelve hours a day and, for their pains, they were made the targets of many charges by the colonists, who complained that they were taking the side of the Indians against their own countrymen. For example, in the late uprising of the Opilcingos Cortés had sent his lieutenant, Vasco de Porcallo, against them, and Porcallo had taken some 2,000 prisoners, whom Cortés had distributed as slaves among his men without the consent of the Audiencia. The oidores had immediately released all the old men, women, and children, but had sent the rest to the mines by way of punishment, without, however, making them slaves. Cortés was very bitter about what he considered an unjustifiable interference with the prerogatives of the Captain-General. He had, moreover, been using the Indians in the building of a sumptuous palace in Mexico City (the other fellow's palace was always *suntuoso*). The Audiencia had ordered him to pay them wages, which he had agreed to do, but thus far he had not complied.

The oidores were using the Indians in the vicinity of the capital in the erection of public buildings, a service which they performed "very willingly" in lieu of the tribute which they owed his Majesty. They were also being used in constructing a convent for women and a "suntuoso" Dominican monastery. For work on the public buildings they were being paid half a *celemín* (about two quarts) of maize a day, which was causing surprise, "because it is a very novel thing in this country to pay the Indians for working for the government."

The Spaniards were still complaining about having their encomiendas turned into corregimientos. They were no longer willing to spend their money, and business was suffering as a consequence. Some of the colonists were returning to Spain in despair, and others were leaving to join Pedro de Alvarado in Guatemala, or to serve in New Galicia under Nuño de Guzmán, because they had nothing to live on. This exodus of colonists had determined the Audiencia to found another Spanish town in Jalisco (Guadalajara) so that the country might have some protection in the event of an Indian uprising. The Indians were, to be sure, very gentle, but they were so blindly obedient to the caciques that the Audiencia felt that it was always necessary to be on one's guard.

The abolition of Indian slavery was the cause of great discontent. Pedro de Alvarado in Guatemala and the people of Pánuco were raising an outcry against it, because, they argued, it would keep new colonists away from those parts and thus retard the subjection of the country. The oidores admitted that the Spaniards treated their Indian slaves like dogs—which was not true among the Indians themselves, who treated their slaves like relations and vassals. It was true that the Indians had occasionally sacrificed their slaves to idols, but in the main they used them kindly.

The oidores were convinced that so long as the Indians lived scattered about the country little progress could be made in their conversion. They recommended that the Indians be congregated in villages in the proximity of the Spanish towns.[16]

Salmerón was much more severe with the colonists. "You cannot imagine," he wrote, "the avarice, disorder, and laziness of the Spaniards in this country. Those who have encomiendas think only of making the greatest possible profit out of them, without bothering the least bit in the world about the welfare or religious instruction of the Indians. Those who have none complain impudently to us and demand something to live on. If told that they are young and well able to work, they answer saucily that they took part in such-and-such a conquest." Some fifty Spaniards had settled in Puebla and were building houses. He suggested that the Indians assigned to help these men should not be obliged to serve them more than about thirty-five days a year. After ten or twelve years of this service the Indians would be accustomed to the habits of civilized people and it could be abolished. Some opposed even this moderate use of the Indians, "but they do not choose to understand that this keeps the Indians from indulging in vice. Is it acting the part of a good father not to chastise one's son and to allow him to give himself up to laziness?" [17]

A certain Jerónimo López voiced the grievances of the old conquerors. He wrote the Emperor that when the first Audiencia had suspended the encomienda three years before, it had created great distress among the colonists and many of them had gone to Guatemala and Peru. Now during the past week more than a hundred had left for Peru, and all those without Indians were thinking of doing the same. Many of the conquerors had remained in the hope of a new distribution of Indians, but most of them were living in poverty, whereas many of those who had taken no part in the conquest were enjoying great estates. López himself had married, as his Majesty had commanded the encomenderos to do, and he now had a daughter and no means of supporting her.[18]

Jerónimo López turned out to be an inveterate letter writer. In a second communication to the Emperor he repeated his standard arguments, but ended on a more hopeful note. The Audiencia had told the colonists that his Majesty intended to make a new distribution of Indians among the colonists, who were now easier in their minds. He added the plea that the encomiendas should be made perpetual, which would eliminate all the practices which had made them objectionable; that is, the encomenderos would in that event treat the Indians as their own property, and so on. If the new distribution was not made, he warned, there would be a general exodus of Spaniards from New Spain and the Indians would revolt.[19]

The new distribution promised by the Audiencia (evidently based on the cédula of July 12, 1530, cited above), as reported by López, is a further indication that the Audiencia was swinging over to the colonists' side. Certainly the danger of removing the only military force from a land where the Indians had no reason to love their conquerors was a valid argument for keeping the encomenderos. Letters to the Council of the Indies repeated it frequently.

Meanwhile, someone in the Council thought up an original device for holding the encomenderos in check. It consisted in having the Audiencia keep a kind of ledger in which the good or bad conduct of every encomendero in New Spain was to be posted. Every two years the Audiencia was to make up a balance sheet and send it to the Queen. "It may be well," concluded this humorous cédula, "that both natives and colonists should know of our purpose and the watchfulness we are exercising." [20]

The specter of the natives' idleness, which had haunted all governments from the time of Columbus, was the subject of another cédula, in which the Queen approved the use of Indians in the rebuilding of Mexico City, with their consent, of course, and for wages, because it would never do to allow them to live in idleness.[21]

The suggestions made by the Audiencia the preceding August were incorporated in a long cédula. The Indians should be congregated in villages, since this was clearly the best means of converting them, but they were to be persuaded to come of their own accord, and gently. "Everything," admitted the Council of the Indies, for once, "is experimental." The Indians' tributes were to be gauged by those they had paid to Montezuma. The carrier question might be decided by the Audiencia and the Protector. It was wrong for priests to have encomiendas, which were incompatible with their duties as protectors of the Indians, although an exception might be made for tonsured laymen. The Audiencia was instructed to incorporate the encomiendas of absentees in the Crown and make them over into corregimientos.[22]

The principle that the encomienda was valid only during use and that it escheated to the Crown otherwise, was invoked in the cancellation of an undetermined number of encomiendas. It is further evidence of the Crown's determination to absorb them. The principle was strengthened by another cédula which established that the encomendero had no absolute dominion over his encomienda, or his Indians, or their tributes.[23]

The first phase of the rule of the second Audiencia ended with no significant change in the situation of the encomenderos. If anything, they were in a stronger position because of their growing influence with the oidores. They had successfully resisted the determined assault on them made by the Council of the Indies and had got the oidores to admit that they had a case—all this, to be sure, in the absence of Fuenleal. There is reason to believe that the Audiencia would have been less flexible if he had been at its head. The stern old bishop was to be, in effect, acting viceroy for the next three years, a period of great significance in the history of New Spain.

8.

The Second Audiencia: Second Phase

PRESIDENT FUENLEAL arrived at Mexico City early in 1532, while the Audiencia was wrestling with the carrier question. It had established the rule that the tamemes might be used to a moderate extent and had fixed a schedule of rates for their pay: married persons while traveling might use four to eight tamemes, depending on the size of their party; single persons, two. Tamemes might be used only voluntarily. They were to be paid a hundred cacao beans a day,[1] and in no case were they to be removed more than one day's journey from their villages. The Audiencia reported that it was having some trouble enforcing this ordinance. Cortés, for example, was building two brigantines for a new exploring expedition and was having the materials for them transported by tamemes from Oaxaca to Acapulco. The Audiencia had sent two alguaciles to stop them, but Cortés had ignored the order.[2]

Fuenleal, whose actions must be read against the tragic background of Española, immediately took issue with the oidores. He saw no justification, he wrote Charles V, for permitting the use of carriers at all, for they were treated with great cruelty. Moreover, there were pack animals in abundance to do that kind of work. He recommended that merchants be obliged to import she-asses to sell to the Indians for breeding. The Indians would then, he argued, no longer make trouble, and anyway, "burdens should be carried by beasts and not by men."

He also disagreed with the oidores on the slavery question. They regarded slavery as a necessary punishment for rebels and as a means of replenishing the supply of labor for the mines. He, however, appealed strongly for the total abolition of Indian slavery, "because in the license and disorder customary in taking and buying them Our Lord has been disserved and this land has lost much."

He had been obliged to ignore the royal cédula which limited the jurisdiction of the oidores for inspection trips to a radius of five leagues from the capital. With such a restriction they had no control over disputes between Indians of remote villages or over the conduct of overseers (*calpisques*) in charge of encomiendas, many of which were at a great distance from the city. These native overseers were in the habit of killing the Indians left in their charge, using them as carriers, ravishing their women, and mistreating them generally. The Audiencia had to have wider jurisdiction so that corregidores might be sent to check such abuses.[3]

Given Bishop Fuenleal's experience in Española, it might be expected that he would see little good in the encomienda or in the encomenderos, and he tended to be less lenient with them than did his four colleagues who had come directly from Spain. He decried the holding of encomiendas by unmarried men who were not even conquerors, a conqueror being, in his definition, a man who had been in New Spain before the fall of Mexico City (1521). He deplored the habit of encomenderos of leaving their encomiendas in the charge of calpisques, who treated the Indians more abominably than did their masters. He recommended that the encomiendas of unmarried men be incorporated in the Crown. For all his apparent sympathy with the thesis of the reforming element of the Council of the Indies, he begged Charles V to pay no attention to irresponsible persons at Court who gave him gratuitous advice about the government of the Indies, "for this Audiencia is responsible for what is to be done, and not they." [4]

In spite of Fuenleal's feeling about the encomienda, there is no evidence that he pushed the execution of the Audiencia's instructions beyond the limit of strict prudence. He was convinced, however, that the corregimiento was far superior to it as an instrument for governing the Indians. He wrote that the Indians were now beginning to understand what a great privilege it was to be vassals of his Majesty, and they were even threatening to bring their grievances to Court. The Tlaxcalans were very loyal to the Spaniards, and he was using them as police in various parts of the country, a charge which they considered a great honor.[5]

Fuenleal's enthusiasm for the corregimiento, in the light of its later history, seems excessive. In his opinion its establishment was a measure "directed by God," and the more Indians who could be brought into the system the better, for it would conserve them and, at the same time, would provide an inducement for Spaniards to settle in New Spain as corregidores. The Indians would become more peaceful as they learned the difference between being held in encomienda and being vassals of his Majesty and were no longer "subject to the tyrannies and deaths" which they had suffered under native rule. His Majesty, therefore, should not take too seriously the complaints of Spaniards who, because they were not being given slaves or encomiendas, cried that the country was being ruined. Fuenleal also advised against the Crown's acting hastily about granting the perpetuity of the encomiendas.

He reported that the Spaniards were trying in every way to acquire slaves, because the discovery of new and rich mines had sent the price of an Indian slave up to forty pesos. He warned the Crown, however, that it would do immense harm to the country if slaving should be allowed. It was the Crown's duty to protect the Indians, for it was they who supported the country. So long as the Indians were numerous the country would yield a profit and there would be an abundance of new settlers, although he thought that the presence of many settlers would interfere with the conversion of the Indians. At the moment there were enough Spaniards in the country to defend it, because many of those who had gone away were returning. He advised that new settlers should not be promised encomiendas (as in the cédula of July 12, 1530, cited above), but married men might be attracted by the prospect of being made corregidores over two or three hundred Indians. After five years in that service they would become attached to the land and would settle permanently. Bachelors, however, should be discouraged from coming to New Spain, for they were a disorderly and restless lot, and few of them ever settled down for long or devoted themselves to honest labor. The whole country, he concluded, was now pacified from New Galicia to Guatemala.[6]

Fuenleal's colleagues of the Audiencia did not share his high opinion of the corregimiento. "Our government," they wrote, "is still complained of by the Spaniards, but the Indians are tranquil and contented, and are beginning to be civilized. The corregidores no longer dare to abuse their powers, because we have frightened them by removing several. The Indians have learned to complain for themselves; they come from a distance for this purpose and face and accuse their corregidores. We are keeping almost all the corregidores in Mexico City and only rarely allow them to visit their jurisdictions. Thus the city is kept full of people and they do not dare molest the Indians." Cortés had built up a large following among those who were discontented with the government because of the suppression of the encomiendas. The oidores recommended that he and five or six others be expelled from the colony. They reported that the young Indians who had been educated by the religious were being settled in separate villages in order to protect them from contamination by their old religion. The tributes had been somewhat reduced and the Indians, understanding the benefit they were receiving, were now coming from long distances to solicit further reductions.[7]

Juan de Salmerón added his customary postscript. The new town of Puebla, he wrote, was not prospering, for several reasons. One, it could not be given all the aid it needed for its maintenance until the proper orders should be received from Spain; two, the encomenderos were very much opposed to it, saying that the new settlers were ruining everything by proving that the country could get along without encomiendas.[8]

The Franciscans saw in the new regime the salvation of their work. They were particularly delighted at being made protectors of the Indians. The change, they hoped, "would stop the discords among the Spaniards, as well as the ill treatment of which the Indians have complained." They were very busy teaching and converting the natives. Some of the Indian boys whom they had trained were out preaching among their people and destroying idols, and frequently risking their lives.[9]

The praise of the corregimiento voiced by the Franciscans and President Fuenleal was more to the liking of the Council of the Indies than were the strictures of the oidores. The Queen, stated a cédula, was gratified to learn that the

Indians in the corregimientos were getting to understand Spaniards better and to love Christian doctrine. The corregidores were ordered to remain in their corregimientos where they were to busy themselves in the instruction of the natives, the maintenance of justice, and the destruction of the heathen religion. The same cédula (evidently as a result of the recommendation of the Audiencia) abolished the office of Protector. Thenceforth official visits were to be made by two of the oidores, accompanied by the heads of the two religious orders.[10] That is, four men in a body were expected to patrol a territory larger than Spain, holding court, punishing abuses of the Indians, adjusting disputes, and so on, while at the same time, we presume, they might not neglect their duties in the Audiencia! The ignorance which continued to prevail in the Council of the Indies with respect to the physical barriers in the way of effective administration is difficult to explain. Or perhaps such an instruction merely reflects the faith of the legal minds of the Council in the efficacy of the written word to overcome all obstacles. Or perhaps, as President Fuenleal had complained, the fault lay in the willingness of the Council to accept recommendations from persons who had had little experience in the administration of the colonies. An illustration of the type of impracticable proposals which irritated Fuenleal is afforded by a long "brief" opinion on Indian government prepared by the Council for Charles V when he returned to Spain in the summer of 1533.

It recommended that monasteries be erected in all Indian towns capable of supporting them, for the education of Indian children, and that schoolmasters be sent from Castile to teach Latin grammar.[11] It was the opinion of the Council that the Indians were entirely free and not obligated to perform any personal service whatever, any more than free persons in Spain, and that they might be required to pay tribute only to the extent of their ability. They should not be given in encomienda to anyone, or in any way be put under the power of the Spaniards, not only because of the great cruelties practiced upon them, but because they were free men. The Council advised his Majesty not to place any reliance upon the efficacy of ordinances for the protection of the encomienda Indians, because experience had proved that they were not effective. The branding of slaves had been done by trickery, and his Majesty was advised to have the slaves examined in order to determine whether or not they had been taken legitimately. Indians should be forbidden to sell their children, servants, and relatives into slavery. The use of tamemes should also be forbidden altogether.

Another recommendation made by the Council was that the Indians be governed by their own caciques to some extent; that is, they could force the Indians to work and they could escort parties of men to the mines. The mines should be worked for the profit of the Indians, allowing, of course, for the deduction of the King's fifth. With this source of revenue assured, argued the Council, the Indians would be able to pay tributes and tithes. They should also be allowed to keep their lands if they showed any disposition to cultivate them. New settlers could be attracted to New Spain by promises of corregimientos, benefices, free land and houses, and they might be allowed also to bring with them a limited number of Negro slaves.[12]

These proposals, which were obviously dictated by the Dominican group of the Council, had the great weakness of refusing to recognize the well-established claims of the conquerors, who had been repeatedly encouraged by the Crown to regard their encomiendas as vested rights. As Fuenleal had pointed out, it was easy for persons in Spain to propose laws based upon ideal justice, so long as the responsibility for their execution fell to others. All the experience of administrators in the Indies, from the Jeronymite government to that of the second Audiencia, supported his argument.

The return of Charles V did not interrupt the flow of instructions to the Audiencia. A church was ordered built in every corregimiento and town of importance. The Indians, naturally, would have to pay for them, but, lest they should resent it and get a mistaken notion of the purpose of the churches, they were not to be assessed directly for them. Instead, their tribute was to be increased to cover the additional outlay, and the extra tribute was to be removed after they had learned to pay tithes.[13]

The Audiencia's visitation of the encomiendas provides the first concrete information about a part of the new Marquesado del Valle. One Pedro García, an interpreter, was commissioned to visit the province of Cuernavaca. His report is the translation of an Indian *pintura*, which lists the tributes and services provided by that rich district. Cortés, complained the Indians, was treating them like slaves, seizing their lands and exacting excessive tributes from them, so much so that the province was being abandoned.[14] For Cuernavaca (province) they were obliged every eighty days to deliver 4,800 *mantas* (a *manta* was a piece of cotton cloth about a yard wide and four yards long), 20 rich shirts, 20 rich skirts, 10 fine bedcovers, 10 coarse bedcovers, 4 cotton pillows. They had also to supply field and house servants, and food. Every year they had to cultivate for the Marqués 20 fields of cotton, 8 of maize, and they had to harvest and store the crops. Every thirty days they had to carry to the mines of Taxco 140 *cargas* (of 50 pounds each) of maize, 6 of chili peppers (*ají*), and 4 of beans, and they had to send men to work in the mines. The town of Cuernavaca had to give, every second week, 15 cargas of maize for the household of the Marqués, 10 "chickens of the country" (turkeys), 10 chickens of Castile, 3 doves, 2 rabbits, 10 partridges, 80 baskets of tor-

tillas (each containing 20), fruit, salt, peppers, wood, and
hay as needed. On fast days they supplied 200 eggs, and
fish as needed. They were also expected to supply crockery,
food, and service for the overseers, and wet nurses for the
Marqués's servants—all this without pay. Every day they
had to bring 80 cacao beans. In the year 1532 the Marqués
had demanded forty slaves to work in his fields, and now
he was building a house in Cuernavaca with the labor,
and at the cost, of the Indians. Moreover, he had told them
to deceive the Audiencia about their numbers, promising
them a reduction in their tribute if they did so, but he had
not kept his promise.[15]

In defense of Cortés it should be said that no other
Spaniard among the conquerors ever commanded the love
and respect of the Indians to an equal degree. When he returned to New Spain in 1526 and 1530 his way was strewn
with flowers and the Indians came from great distances to
do him homage. Salmerón reported that his word was law
among the Indians, and this made him a powerful and dangerous man. "The affection which they bear the Marqués,"
wrote the Audiencia, "arises from his having conquered
them and, to tell the truth, because he has treated them
better than any other."[16]

The increasing demand for slaves to work the mines,
their rising value, and the report to the effect that since the
abolition of Indian slavery the unconquered natives had
become very bold and dangerous, influenced the Council
of the Indies to modify its stand in the matter. It argued
that, since the slaves kept by unconverted Indians had no
chance of salvation and since they would be slaves in any
event, it was manifestly better that they should be slaves
of the Christians. The Council decreed, therefore, that hostile Indians might be punished by enslavement, but that
their women and children might only be made naborías.[17]

With the growth of the secular Church of New Spain the

question of the tithing of the Indians began to assume considerable importance. "A special series of rulings arose out of the existence of the encomienda. Under the rules governing the royal decisions, tributes ordinarily would not have been subject to tithe, but the needs of the new dioceses led the King to extend the levy to all tributes which encomenderos, including himself as the greatest encomendero of all, received from the Indians. The obligation covered payments in specie, agricultural products, fowls, and livestock, but did not extend to services. When the tribute paid was a mixture of tithable commodity and services, the courts drew a fine distinction to separate the two categories. Cotton cloth, for example, was declared tithable for the value of the cotton in it, but exempt from payment on the increase in value due to spinning and weaving." [18] A further important point here is that the government was forced to keep account of the tithes assessed against Indian tributes, both in the encomiendas and the corregimientos. The earliest tithing list is that of 1560, which is an invaluable document bearing on the population of New Spain and its economy.[19]

The question of whether or not the Indians should be tithed directly was argued for the better part of a century, with the regular orders opposing (partly, it would seem, because they could not share in the benefits), and the secular Church arguing for them. The settlement varied somewhat from diocese to diocese, but in general the Indian was eventually held liable for tithing only on crops introduced from Spain, which in the sixteenth century were limited to wheat, silk, and livestock, as Borah points out (article cited in n. 18).

In its lengthening list of recommendations for the government of the Indies the Council had included the prohibition of forced labor. One result which was not envisaged at the time was that Indians might not be used in the erection of priests' houses, so the Council issued a cédula permitting parish priests to do so.[20] That they were not slow to take advantage of the privilege is apparent from the numerous complaints of its abuse in the records of the Juzgado General de Indios.[21]

The encomenderos' propensity to pack up and leave at the rumor of any new discovery brought two curious ordinances designed to correct the evil. The Council of the Indies ordered that colonists who had been in possession of their encomiendas for ten years or more might not remove to another province, on pain of losing their titles. Those who had held their encomiendas for a shorter period were apparently free, by implication, at least, to remove without penalty. Another device which aimed at fixing men to their encomiendas was that they must erect stone houses in them within two years.[22]

The last year of Fuenleal's administration was little disturbed by communications from the Council of the Indies, which was probably saving its ammunition for the benefit of Viceroy Don Antonio de Mendoza. Mendoza's debt to Bishop Fuenleal was great. Thanks to Fuenleal's tact in persuading both the Council of the Indies and the encomenderos to trust him to do the right thing, Mendoza found New Spain generally at peace, the rival factions relatively quiet, and the more flagrant abuses in the encomiendas and corregimientos on their way toward correction. It seems likely that the great viceroy could hardly have achieved the success with which he is credited without the pioneering of the second Audiencia. Fuenleal even accomplished the miracle of winning the enthusiastic approval of the Council of the Indies. Upon his return to Spain he was appointed to the bishoprics of Tuy, León, and Cuenca; he served as president of the Audiencias of Valladolid and Granada; and he finally achieved the highest honor of all, a seat in the Council of the Indies. He died in 1547, fittingly in the same year as his erstwhile rival, Hernán Cortés.[23] The regard which Bishop Fuenleal enjoyed in New Spain, even among his former adversaries, is best expressed in the words of that most typical of conquistadores, Bernal Díaz del Castillo: "And because he was a good judge he was raised to the state that I have said; and at that time death came to call him; and it seems to me that, in accordance with [the teachings of] our Holy Faith, he is in Glory with the blessed, for . . . in everything he was righteous and good." [24]

9.

The First Years of the Viceroyalty

THE ARRIVAL of Antonio de Mendoza was hailed with joy by all the elements of New Spain, with the probable exception of Hernán Cortés, who saw himself cheated of the high place which he might justifiably have looked upon as his by right and who must have seen in the establishment of the viceroyalty the end of his feudal autonomy. But the rest of the citizenry were well pleased to see a definite end of the instability and factionalism which had kept the country unsettled since the conquest. Mendoza reached Mexico City in the middle of November, 1535, and was received with a rousing celebration. "Trumpeters with gaily colored cloaks and the roll of kettle drums greeted his arrival as the city dignitaries, knights, and commoners, went out to meet him arrayed in fiesta attire. Games in the plaza and a repast for the viceroy, his gentlemen, and the contestants, following the solemn reading of his commission by the public crier in the presence of the Audiencia, cabildo, and citizens, completed the official ceremonies provided

at the cost of the city."¹ Nor were the citizens defrauded
in their expectations. Mendoza continued the moderate
administration of the second Audiencia, as a result of which
the first nine years of his reign offer few developments in
the history of the encomienda.

No pains had been spared to invest Mendoza with all
the apparatus calculated to impress the populace with the
dignity of his high office, for he represented the King's person. "Mendoza's qualifications are immediately apparent.
He came from an ancient and influential family and would
command respect as a member of the older nobility. His
family had been distinguished for generations on the Spanish
frontiers and he had grown up exposed to frontier conditions in the conquered province of Granada where his father
and brother had ruled. He was drawn from the immediate
circle of the Empress and his personality, ability, and loyalty were well known at Court. Above all, he had no interest in the factional disputes which were raging in New
Spain and could be trusted to place imperial concerns before his own." It was thought, moreover, to put him above
temptation by assigning him the substantial income of 6,000
ducats a year, plus 2,000 more for household expenses. His
official titles were Viceroy, Governor-General, and President of the Audiencia of New Spain.²

The manifest purpose of the Crown in creating the viceroyalty was the reconquest of New Spain for the Crown, but
few hints of that purpose are apparent in Mendoza's instructions, which, with respect to the government of the
Indians, contain no novelties whatever. He was immediately to complete the census and to ascertain how much
tribute the Indians were paying, and to learn whether they
were able to pay more. He was to suppress their custom of
paying tribute in kind, because in the disposal of the produce
the royal revenues suffered a loss. If he should discover that
some Indians were unable to pay a cash tribute, it was sug-

gested that they be allowed to work out the amount of their assessment in the mines, voluntarily, of course. He was informed that the Indians were lazy by nature and was instructed to encourage them to work for themselves in the mines (as recommended by the Council of the Indies in their opinion already mentioned). Such an arrangement would be of great profit to them, because it would save them from their besetting sin of idleness, and the Crown would gain by the tax on their earnings. Mendoza was instructed also to investigate the report of the exorbitant tributes being exacted by native caciques, which were so heavy that the Indians had not enough left to pay the Crown.

The royal mines were to be worked with Indian and Negro slaves—which leads us to believe that the Council's agitation about Indian slavery was not meant to imply that it approved of abolition. Unfortunately, we have no record of the extent of the Crown's interest in Indian slaves. Monasteries and fortifications were to be erected with Indian labor, but without harm to the Indians. The viceroy was to see that Spaniards and Indian caciques committed no fraud in slave-trading. He was to inform himself concerning the manner of using carriers and to see whether the present laws were sufficient for their protection. The Council also wished to know whether it would be better for the Indians to have Spaniards settled in their towns or separately —this with a view toward the conversion of the Indians.[3]

The paragraph of the instructions to Mendoza forbidding payment of tribute in kind discloses a great weakness in the corregimiento system, as he soon came to recognize. The Crown Indians had no money and therefore had to pay in kind or work out their tributes. Since the corregidor had to squeeze the tribute out of his charges in one way or another, it is difficult to see how the Indian benefited from being a "vassal of the Crown." The Crown also suffered, because the corregidor, who had to convert the tribute into cash, had to dump produce on the market at harvest time, and the resultant glut brought prices down.[4]

Thus the Crown was forced into precisely the same situation for which the encomienda was so bitterly blamed by Las Casas. The wealth of the Indies was needed to support Charles V's European adventures. Whether it came from slaves, or forced or free labor, it had to come, and no administrator was allowed to forget that essential fact.

In these first years of Mendoza's reign the encomenderos were little interfered with—which may have been owing to a wise policy of allowing the viceroy to get established before attempting any radical innovation. It had been reported to the Council of the Indies that the encomenderos were exacting an excessive tribute from the natives, and Mendoza was instructed to see that the excess was restored. Whatever lands the encomenderos had taken from the Indians were likewise to be restored.[5]

About this time the encomenderos were granted an important concession. As early as 1509 the Crown had established that the encomienda might not be inherited, but was to escheat to the Crown upon the death of its holder. The governors of the Indies had never consistently enforced this rule, and the Crown itself, in the instructions issued to the *visitador* Ponce de León, had recognized the injustice and hardship of leaving the widows and children of deceased encomenderos destitute, and gave him permission to make such disposition of titles as seemed prudent.[6] The practice of allowing widows and children to inherit was further legalized (in Cuba, at least) by cédulas of 1528, 1529, and 1532. The first Audiencia, on the other hand, had been instructed to incorporate in the Crown all encomiendas which should become vacant upon the death of their holders. The second Audiencia reversed this procedure and consented to the "deposit" of encomiendas with the widows and children of deceased encomenderos. The

Council of the Indies now legalized the matter generally. It was the royal will, stated the famous Ley de Sucesión of 1536, that encomenderos should settle permanently in their encomiendas—which they would do the more readily if they knew that upon their death their widows and children would be provided for. "Upon the death of any inhabitant of that province who has Indians in encomienda and who has a legitimate child, the child is to be given the Indians that his father had in encomienda. If the encomendero has no legitimate children the encomienda is to go to his widow. If she should marry again, the encomienda shall go to her second husband, but if he should have an encomienda already he is to have his choice of one of the two." [7]

The law of 1536 was clearly encouragement to the encomenderos to look upon their titles as proved, at least for two "lives." There is certainly no hint that the Council was contemplating the drastic Article 35 of the New Laws of 1542 (see below, chap. 10) which incorporated all encomiendas in the Crown at the death of their holders. It is easy to see why the vacillation of the Crown in this and other matters was one of the most trying aspects of all government of the Indies. A possible explanation of this temporary favor which the encomenderos enjoyed was the fear of a native uprising. They were, it must be repeated, the only military force in New Spain. Mendoza was instructed to see that the encomenderos had arms in readiness at all times to defend the colony; that they resided in their encomiendas; that they should leave only with the viceroy's permission, on pain of loss of their Indians. If they should overstay their leaves they were to suffer the same penalty. [8]

The corregidores were also obliged to live on the job, and they were reminded that it was their duty to instruct the Indians in civilized habits, in husbandry, and the like. They were warned also that they might not accept anything from the Indians beyond their salaries [9]—which is evidence that they were already looking upon their places as opportunities for self-enrichment—an abuse which was soon to become notorious.

The low morality of the Indians was a source of grief to the Council of the Indies, and a number of cédulas were issued through the years in an effort to induce them to have one wife at a time. The absurdity, however, of trying to suppress concubinage among the Indians in view of the growing multitude of half-breed children running about must have impressed the Council, and it instructed Bishop Zumárraga, who had charge of the moral policing of the colony, to refrain from fining the Indians a mark (eight ounces) of silver for keeping mistresses. He must, of course, continue in his efforts to reform them, but *poco a poco*.[10] Another possible reason for relaxing the law against concubinage is suggested by a letter of Bishop Zumárraga written four years later in which he said that certain grafting secular priests were making a handsome income by going about fining the Indians for concubinage and pocketing the proceeds. He gives a dismal picture of the morals of the seculars.[11]

The moral obligations of the encomenderos and corregidores were again outlined in a long cédula addressed to the viceroy. The only way, stated this document, to bring the Indians to a true notion of obedience to, and reverence for, their natural lords (i.e., the Spanish monarchs) was to indoctrinate them in the Holy Catholic Faith, and so Mendoza was to see that religious were sent wherever there was the least knowledge of God and the greatest need of doctrine. The encomenderos and corregidores were directed to assume as their special concern the teaching of their charges, the building of churches, and the support of priests, wherever the tribute was sufficient to permit it. They were to set aside each day certain hours for the teaching of the Christian doctrine. Even the slaves were to be taught along with the others. To facilitate the work the religious and the secular clergy were to be encouraged to learn the native languages. The danger of allowing the Indians to read profane literature was to be avoided by giving them only Christian books to read; otherwise they might conclude that all printed books had the same authority as the Scriptures. The viceroy was to induce the religious to cease from squabbling with one another, lest the Indians get a false notion of their piety. For the same reason the laity was to refrain from sinning in public. The colonists were admonished to treat the Indians kindly, and they might take and brand slaves only according to law. Idle Indians were to be induced to work, as free persons, that is, and for wages. Indians might not possess horses. One oidor was to be kept continually in the provinces as an itinerant judge, to report on conditions among the Indians, to try cases, and to settle local disputes.[12]

The viceroy had the power to use his discretion in the execution of such instructions, but it was typical of the Council of the Indies that it could not refrain from meddling in local administration, and it kept up a running fire of comment, criticism, and ordinances which would have strained the patience of any responsible officer. It even intervened in favor of a poor blind conqueror who had three marriageable daughters and not enough Indians to afford them a suitable dowry.[13]

From this point on to the passage of the New Laws in 1542 there is little in the royal cédulas that hints at the violent reforms which were to shake the Indies. It would almost seem, to judge by the generally favorable tone of the legislation, that the Council of the Indies was deliberately lulling the encomenderos into a feeling of security. What it actually did was to make their opposition so desperately bitter, when the test came, that the whole framework of government was endangered. Meanwhile, a few scattered instructions kept the viceroy and the colonists reminded that the Crown had the good of the natives nearest its heart. The encomenderos were ordered to maintain priests for the indoctrination of the Indians. If there were not enough priests to go round they must spend the money on the erection of churches.[14] After a silence for the better part of a year the Council attempted to put a stop to the cheating of Indians by interpreters by allowing the Indians to bring a friend with them.[15] The piety of the Council did not prevent its approval of the use of forced Indian labor in public works. Bishop Vasco de Quiroga of Michoacán was given permission to use the Indians of the vicinity in the erection of the cathedral, those of the corregimientos as well as those of the encomiendas, with, of course, "as little vexation to them as possible." A "reasonable house" for the bishop was included. There is no mention of wages. The work was one in which "Our Lord is served." [16]

There was nothing new in such use of forced labor. Public institutions, such as hospitals, monasteries, and the mint, were all at first supported by grants of encomiendas and temporary repartimientos of labor, although on a limited basis. The Indians assigned to the mint, for example, served two years.[17] All such encomiendas were abolished by Article 31 of the New Laws.

Of far greater interest than the monotonous ordinances of the Council of the Indies is Mendoza's first report on the state of New Spain after nearly three years of his government. He wrote that the city of Puebla de los Angeles was being erected by drafts of laborers from neighboring villages. The Tlaxcalans had apparently objected to this service as a violation of their charter. Mendoza advised their exemption from it in view of their good work in the conquest of the country; and then they might be needed again should an uprising occur. The Indians of the provinces were suffering from lack of supervision, because he had been unable to keep an oidor on the road as an itinerant judge. He had only two oidores and, if he sent one away, the remaining one could not possibly carry on the work of the Audiencia. He urged the appointment of permanent provincial governors, alcaldes mayores, who should be given power to control the conduct of Spaniards toward the Indians.[18]

Mendoza had found that the government of Indian towns by corregidores was utterly ineffectual. "If your Majesty thinks that it is enough to put corregidores in the towns, I assure you that nothing is more necessary for the relief of your royal conscience than to remove them. The persons appointed are incompetent and, moreover, they have no interest in the Indians except to take their tributes and steal from them everything they have left . . . I think that in order to remedy this situation the corregidores should be removed and put on a pension so that they may have a livelihood, and that alcaldes mayores should be given charge of the collection of the tributes in their provinces."

The royal mines were suffering from a shortage of labor, and Mendoza asked for money to buy slaves for their operation. The mint was in danger of having to cease functioning, because the grant of the town of Xiquipilco was for only two years, and the term would be completed in another four months. The Indians had developed a talent for counterfeiting coins, which were as good as the originals. Even cacao beans were counterfeited with such perfection that they passed for genuine among the Indians.

In Mendoza's opinion certain of the remote territories (probably those being conquered by Nuño de Guzmán in Sinaloa) should not be distributed as encomiendas, because their great distance made proper supervision impossible.[19]

The importance of Indian slavery may be gauged by the fact that Mendoza takes it up no fewer than three times in the course of his letter. Since the prohibition of slaving

(1530), he reported, the Spaniards of New Galicia had not been able to support themselves. He had refused to allow them to take slaves and had had to subsidize them with a thousand pesos' worth of tools to keep them from abandoning the province. He suggested that the Crown put them on a salary.[20] He made it fairly clear that he considered the resumption of slaving necessary, although he would exempt the Tlaxcalans. The Indian governor and cabildo of Tlaxcala had ordered the emancipation of all the slaves in that province, and Mendoza thought that their act should be approved.

Mendoza made the very practical suggestion of securing the loyalty of the Indians who showed the greatest progress in Christianity and service to the Crown by establishing an order of nobility for them, complete with appropriate titles and insignia—an inexpensive device which was not adopted, although the legal recognition of Indian hierarchies and privileges (such as the exemption of caciques from tribute, personal service, and corporal punishment) had much the same effect.

He reported that the silk industry was showing great promise, and he suggested that the King send over a couple of spinners to teach the natives to spin. Nothing more would be needed, he explained, because the Indians were so clever that they would soon master the art.[21]

Zumárraga's school for Indian boys was proving a great success. Mendoza had personally examined them in Latin and found them very proficient in it, given the time they had been at it. In his opinion these boys would do more for the propagation of the Faith than all the friars in the country. Zumárraga had requested that another town be allotted to him for the support of this school, as well as for the support of a convent for the education of Indian girls. Mendoza thought that his Majesty would do well to support such worthy enterprises, even though it might necessitate using some of the Crown Indians. "But, since I have seen the difference between the Indians held by the Crown and those held in encomienda, I say to your Majesty that I am very doubtful that I am right in advising your Majesty to remove them from the Crown. Some Indians of Coatepec made me the most confused man in the world, because when I told them that they were to serve the treasurer by order of your Majesty there was as much weeping as if I had ordered them to be hanged. But they cleared it up later by telling the treasurer that their tears had been tears of joy because they were going to belong to him." [22]

The reader can hardly be less confused than the viceroy at this point, after the gloomy picture just painted of the failure of the corregimientos. The contradiction is unexplained. Mendoza was certainly beginning to regard the encomienda more benevolently, as is borne out by his backing the encomenderos during the New Laws crisis a few years later. His reign had by this time settled down into a fairly comfortable routine, and during the next five or six years he was little interfered with by the Council of the Indies.[23]

Thus far Mendoza's reign had been singularly free from the disturbances that might have been expected. The habitual grumbling of the encomenderos had been almost silenced by the Ley de Sucesión of 1536 and by the viceroy's judicious interpretation of his instructions. It may be that Mendoza, like his predecessors, had begun to look upon the encomienda with less distrust as he fell into the colonists' way of thinking. The encomenderos had shown that they were indispensable by undertaking the defense of the kingdom in the short and terrible Mixtón War of 1540–1541. It seemed, indeed, that Mendoza had achieved a stability based upon mutual respect and tolerance between Crown and colonist. If, however, anyone had any such illusion it was soon to be dispelled by the most violent departure in the history of colonial legislation, when the revitalized Council of the Indies issued the radical code known as "The New Laws of the Indies for the good treatment and preservation of the Indians."

10.

The New Laws

ALTHOUGH the mild rule of Mendoza may have quieted the fears of the encomenderos for the time being, yet it should have been evident to them that the sending of a viceroy, equipped with the power and dignity of a sovereign, was meant to end once and for all the anachronistic feudalism which was taking root in New Spain. It was during the latter part of Mendoza's reign and the one following that the two systems met head on, and the events of the civil wars of fifteenth-century Spain were repeated on a smaller scale in the Indies. The great difference between the two situations was that by the middle of the sixteenth century the centralized despotism of the Hapsburgs was immensely stronger than the struggling monarchy of Isabella the Catholic, and that in New Spain the feudal party of the conquistadores, weakened by age, death, and internal faction, was not able to resist the power of the Crown. Even so, protected by the distance from Spain, and unnecessarily irritated by the rigidity of certain royal officers, the encomenderos fought the absorption of their encomiendas bitterly for the next half century and managed finally to salvage the remnants of the institution in the form of a pension system.

To understand properly the crisis which was about to explode like a bombshell in all parts of the Indies, it is necessary to review briefly the activities of Bartolomé de las Casas, for, beyond all others, he has been given the credit and the blame [1] for the extraordinary measures now thought necessary to conserve the Indian population.

We left Las Casas in Spain in 1517 when, disgusted with the Jeronymite governors of Española for their failure to dispossess the encomenderos, he had stormed back to denounce them. Unsuccessful in persuading the Crown to intervene, he used his astonishing energy during the next three years to promote a model colony on the Pearl Coast of South America. His central idea was to recruit among the peasants of Castile a group of pious men who would form a kind of crusading order, complete with a distinguishing habit, a white robe with a red cross on the breast. Their purpose would be to convert the savages by giving them an object lesson in the practice of the Christian virtues. They were to be known as the Knights of the Golden Spur. The colony would be governed as a theocracy, with Las Casas as high priest. So great were his powers of persuasion and so recent the age of chivalry and the crusades (and, it might be added, so great was the Crown's need to pacify the fierce tribes of the Pearl Coast who were interfering with the pearl fishing), that he was granted an enormous strip of unknown territory for his experiment. He even succeeded in recruiting a small company of peasants. He prepared the way by sending on ahead a Dominican mission, which established itself at Chiribichi. Las Casas followed in 1520 with his band of crusaders, but, upon landing at Puerto Rico, he learned that the Indians of Chiribichi had risen and slain a missionary and

a lay brother. He got this discouraging bit of news from
Gonzalo de Ocampo, who was heading a punitive (read
"slaving") expedition against them.

Las Casas failed to persuade Ocampo to abandon his raid;
so he left his Knights of the Golden Spur in Puerto Rico
while he hastened to Española, where he vainly tried to prevail upon the Audiencia of Santo Domingo to recall Ocampo.
Even so, such was his fixity of purpose that, when Ocampo
returned to Española with a cargo of slaves, he still thought
his colony a possibility. The Audiencia, with a sense of
humor not common among Spanish administrators, got rid
of Las Casas by commissioning him to lead a new military
expedition to the Pearl Coast. It sailed in the summer of
1521, stopping at Puerto Rico to pick up the crusaders, but
they had somehow lost their enthusiasm for a godly life in
the tropics and Las Casas had to go on without them. At
Cumaná his troops became disobedient and mutinous, some
deserted, and Las Casas quarreled violently with the com-
mandant of the neighboring island of Cubagua. He remained
at Cumaná only long enough to build a storehouse for his
supplies and then hurried back to Santo Domingo to report
the misdeeds of his troops to the Audiencia. His voyage
was delayed by bad weather and, when he finally reached
Santo Domingo, he learned that the savages had fallen upon
his settlement and wiped out every vestige of the hated white
civilization, along with a priest and five laymen. It was the
single time that Las Casas admitted defeat. He found a
grateful refuge in the Dominican monastery of Santo Domingo, the prior of which, Fray Domingo de Betanzos,
persuaded him to join the order.

Thus ended one of the most illuminating episodes in the
annals of Spanish colonization. It is retold here because it
illustrates, better than all the dialectics of the time, the kind
of medieval mentality which would attempt to build on

earth an Augustinian City of God. The Laws of Burgos and the New Laws cannot be understood apart from that background.[2]

Little is known of Las Casas' activities during the seven years following his admission to the Dominican order in 1522. According to our one authority, Antonio de Remesal, he returned to Castile in 1529 and was instrumental in securing the passage of a stringent antislavery law, presumably that of August 2, 1530.[3] In 1531 he seems to have got a commission to go to Peru with two other Dominicans, Bernardino de Minaya and Pedro de Angulo. It is doubtful that the three men ever reached Peru, because in 1532 they were in Nicaragua, where Bishop Osorio urged them to remain and found a mission. From Nicaragua Las Casas was called to Santo Domingo by the president of the Audiencia, Alonso López de Cerrato, to aid in the pacification of the rebel chieftain Enrique. He persuaded Enrique to capitulate and thus avoided another of the butcheries which had drenched that tragic island.[4]

From Nicaragua, Las Casas, Minaya, and Angulo went to Guatemala, where they were allowed to put into practice Las Casas' doctrine of conquest by persuasion. After three years' work among the *indios de guerra* of the province of Tuzulatlán, Las Casas negotiated a treaty between them and the Governor of Guatemala, Pedro de Alvarado. The province was renamed Vera Paz to commemorate the manner of its conquest.[5] This signal accomplishment enhanced Las Casas' reputation beyond the reach of detractors. At a general council of the Dominican order held in Mexico City in 1539 it was decided to send him to Spain to solicit protective legislation from the Council of the Indies and to recruit missionaries for Guatemala. The value of Las Casas as an adviser in the writing of the contemplated reform of the Indian code was recognized by the Council, which kept him in Spain for several years, although what his actual contribution was to the New Laws is not known.[6]

The encomenderos of the time, however, as well as Motolinía, saw in Las Casas the cause of all their woes. Whatever his countribution to the New Laws was, the thesis upon which they were based was the ancient one of the Dominicans which was used in the Laws of Burgos. Its best expression was voiced by Francisco de Vitoria in his two lectures, *De Indis recenter inventis* and *De jure belli Hispanorum in barbaros,* delivered at the University of Salamanca in 1532. Vitoria's conclusions struck at the very foundation of Spanish temporal power in the New World. They are, in brief:

1. Since unbelief does not preclude ownership of property, the Indians are not precluded from owning property, and they are therefore the true owners of the New World, as they were before the advent of the Spaniards.

2. The Emperor is not the lord of the whole world, and, even if he were, he would not therefore be entitled to seize the provinces of the Indians, to put down their lords, to raise up new ones, and to levy taxes.

3. Neither is the Pope the civil or temporal lord of the whole world. He has no secular power except in so far as it subserves things spiritual. He can have no power over the dominions of unbelievers and therefore cannot give such dominions to secular princes. A refusal on the part of the aborigines to recognize the power of the Pope cannot therefore be regarded as a reason for making war upon them and seizing their goods. If the Christian religion had been expounded to the Indians with never so much sufficiency of proof, and they still refused to accept it, this would not render it lawful to make war upon them and despoil them of their possessions.

4. The Spaniards, on the other hand, have the right to go to the lands of the Indians, dwell there and carry on trade, so long as they do no harm, and they may not be prevented by the Indians from so doing. If the Spaniards have diligently informed the Indians that they have not come to interfere in any way with the

peace and welfare of the Indians, and if the Indians still show hostility toward them and attempt to destroy them, then, and only then, will it be lawful to make war upon the Indians. In the event of war the Indians may be despoiled of their goods and reduced to slavery, because in the law of nations whatever we take from the enemy becomes ours at once, and so true is this that men may be brought into slavery to us.

5. The Christians have the right to preach the Gospel among the barbarians. The Pope has the right to entrust the conversion of the Indians to the Spaniards alone and to forbid all other nations to preach or trade among them, if the propagation of the Faith would thus be furthered. If the Indians do not hinder the preaching of the Gospel they may not be subjected by war, whether they accept it or not.[7]

In spite of the uncomfortable implications of Vitoria's thesis, the Crown found it very useful in its attack upon the encomienda. Las Casas elaborated it in his "Eighth Remedy for the Ills of the Indies" which he presented at Valladolid before a special council summoned by Charles V to draw up a new Indian code. It is unnecessary to repeat Las Casas' argument, which had not changed essentially since the time of the Laws of Burgos. His conclusion will explain two things: (1) his usefulness to the Crown, and (2) why he aroused such bitter resentment in the Indies. "Let your Majesty," he said, "order and command . . . that all the Indians in all the Indies, those who have been subjected as well as those who may be subjected, be placed and reduced and incorporated in the Royal Crown of Castile and León . . . as the subjects and vassals which they are, and let none be given in encomienda to any Christian Spaniard. Rather, let it be an inviolable royal constitution, determination, and law perpetually that neither now nor at any time may they ever be taken or alienated from the said Royal Crown, or given to anyone as vassals, or in encomienda, or in deposit, or by any other title, mode or manner of alienation, or taken from the Royal Crown because of services rendered by anyone, or because of any merit he may have or need he may suffer, for any cause or pretext whatever." [8] In short, let there be one encomendero, the King. It is probable that Charles V was moved to take this grave decision by the current anarchy in Peru, where the squabble between Pizarro and Almagro had begun the long series of civil wars which all but destroyed that rich kingdom. However it was, it is here submitted that only such a consideration could have induced the sagacious Charles to approve the dangerous innovations of the New Laws. It may be allowed that he was not unaffected by the pious arguments of Las Casas; but he was first of all a Hapsburg despot engaged in consolidating his vast empire, and he could not consistently have tolerated feudalism in the Indies. He was also perennially in need of funds, and the seizure of the wealth of the encomenderos must be reckoned among his motives.

The gravity of the issues and the lengthy debates of the council of Valladolid prevented an early decision; in consequence it was reconstituted and reconvened at Barcelona. The influence of Dominican thought on its conclusions is at once apparent. Of the fifty-four articles of the New Laws, twenty-three concerned the status and treatment of the Indians, and all but a few of the most radical were eventually incorporated into the *Recopilación*. The twenty-three are summarized below.

Art. 10. The Indians are free persons and vassals of the Crown, and it has always been the royal purpose to have them treated as such. The Council of the Indies is therefore commanded to see to the execution of the laws for their benefit and protection.

Art. 24. It is one of the principal duties of the audiencias to enquire into and punish excesses committed against the Indians.

Art. 25. Lawsuits among the Indians are to be decided summarily and according to their usage and custom.

Art. 26. We order and command that henceforth, for no reason of war or any other, even though it be by reason of rebellion or purchase, may any Indian be made a slave, and we wish them to be treated as our vassals of the Crown of Castile, which they are. No person may make use of any Indian, either as naboria or tapia, or in any other way, against his will.

Art. 27. Since we have ordered that henceforth in no wise shall Indians be made slaves . . . we order and command that the audiencias, having summoned both parties, shall summarily and briefly, without quibbling, the truth only having been ascertained, set them at liberty, if the persons who hold them as slaves do not show title of legitimate possession; and in order that, because of failure to petition . . . the Indians do not remain slaves, we order the audiencias to place persons to plead these suits for the Indians, and let them be paid out of the court fines, and let them be men of confidence and diligence.

Art. 28. The use of Indian carriers is to be permitted only in those places where it cannot be avoided, and then only with their consent, moderately, and for pay.

Art. 30. No free Indian is to be brought to the pearl fisheries against his will; if the loss of life in pearl-diving cannot be avoided, pearl-fishing is to be abandoned.

Art. 31. All Indians held in encomienda by the viceroys, by their lieutenants, royal officers, prelates, monasteries, hospitals, religious houses, mints, the treasury, etc., are to be transferred forthwith to the Crown.

Art. 32. Excessively large encomiendas are to be reduced in size and the surplus of Indians is to be distributed among those first conquerors who have none.

Art. 33. Those encomenderos who have mistreated their Indians are to lose their encomiendas, which will be placed in the Crown.

Art. 35. Also we order and command that henceforth no viceroy, governor, audiencia, discoverer, or other person, may give Indians in encomienda by our provision, or by renunciation, donation, sale, or in any other form or means . . . but upon the death of the person holding the said Indians, let them be placed in our royal Crown; and the audiencias have the duty of informing [us] immediately of the person who died, his quality, merits, and services, and how he treated his Indians, and whether he left a widow, children, or other heirs; and let them send us an account of the quality of the Indians and the land, so that we may provide what is best for our service and make a grant, according to our pleasure, to the widow and children of the deceased; and if meanwhile it is

the opinion of the audiencia that the widow and children should
be given some support, let them do so with the tributes paid by
the Indians [of the deceased's encomienda], giving them a moderate sum, but leaving the Indians in our Crown, as has been said.

Art. 36. The Indians removed from the encomiendas are to be
well treated and taught in the Holy Catholic Faith as free vassals of
the Crown, and that is to be the principal concern of the presidents and oidores of the audiencias. These Indians are to be governed in the manner now prevailing in New Spain for the Crown
Indians [i.e., in corregimientos].

Art. 37. In the distribution of corregimientos the first conquerors are to be preferred.

Art. 38. Lawsuits involving Indians are no longer to be tried
in the Indies, or by the Council of the Indies, but must be pleaded
before the King himself.

Art. 39. In expeditions of discovery no Indians are to be used,
save only perhaps three or four as interpreters. One or two religious are to accompany each expedition. Nothing may be taken
from the Indians except in fair trade.

Art. 42. The tributes of newly discovered Indians are to be
fairly assessed and delivered to the royal treasurer.

Art. 43. The Spaniards have no authority whatever over newly
discovered Indians and may not use them in any way whatever.
They may have the use of only such tributes as the governor shall
approve.

Art. 45. The Indians left alive in the islands of Puerto Rico,
Cuba, and Española are relieved of all tributes and services, so
that they may multiply and be taught in the Holy Catholic Faith.

Art. 46. Those first conquerors and their heirs who have no
Indians in encomienda are to be provided for out of the tributes
of the Indians removed from encomiendas.

Art. 47. Corregimientos are to be assigned preferably to those
conquerors who were not provided for [in the distribution of
encomiendas], and to their sons.

Art. 48. Encomenderos must reside in the provinces in which
their encomiendas are located.

Art. 49. The tributes paid to encomenderos and to the Crown
are to be fixed at a lower rate than that which obtained under the
native rulers.

Art. 50. The Indians are to be well treated as free vassals of the
Crown, which they are. Anyone mistreating them is to be punished according to the laws of Castile.

Art. 51. No encomendero may exact a greater tribute from his Indians than that fixed by the viceroy and the Audiencia.[9]

Although there was very little in the New Laws that had not been projected or enacted already, it was evident to the colonists that this time the Crown meant them to stick. Many of the "first conquerors" had already died, and their encomiendas were held by their widows and heirs. Many others were aging and faced the prospect of leaving their dependents with nothing but a vaguely promised pension. The encomenderos also, with some justice, it must be admitted, looked upon themselves as a vested aristocracy, but for whom there would have been no New World for the Spanish Crown to enjoy. The progress of the councils of Valladolid and Barcelona was anxiously watched from every corner of the Indies, and the publication of the New Laws was awaited with sullen resentment. Cortés, who had his ear to the ground along with the rest of the worried encomenderos, wrote to the Council of the Indies what was to become a standard form letter in support of the encomienda. After reminding the Council that the encomenderos were the only military force in New Spain, he hinted darkly at "the indignation it would cause to remove them [the Indians], not only among those who have them, but among those who are supported by them [i.e., the clergy]." The removal of the encomienda would destroy commerce and, with it, his Majesty's revenue. Anyway, whatever harm the Indians suffered from the encomienda could be avoided by giving them "to the proper people," who would conserve them, "and his Majesty's rents would increase and become permanent." [10]

The Crown did not entrust the execution of these unpopular laws to the existing authorities in New Spain and Peru, where opposition was the strongest. Four men were commissioned to enforce them: Blasco Núñez Vela, for

Peru; Francisco Tello de Sandoval, for New Spain; Miguel Díaz de Armendáriz, for Tierra Firme; and Alonso López de Cerrato, for the Antilles and the Pearl Coast. Blasco Núñez Vela was unlucky enough to arrive in Peru during the rebellion of Gonzalo Pizarro, and was promptly captured and beheaded. It is not unreasonable to assume that New Spain would also have suffered the horrors of a civil war if Antonio de Mendoza and Juan de Zumárraga had not been able to persuade Tello de Sandoval to suspend the laws affecting the encomienda until an appeal could be presented to the Council of the Indies.[11]

The articles of the New Laws which most profoundly affected the administration and economic life of the colony were numbers 26 and 27, abolishing Indian slavery; 31, prohibiting the holding of encomiendas by public servants and institutions, by the secular clergy and religious establishments; and 35, forbidding new encomiendas and providing that encomiendas escheat to the Crown upon the death of their present holders. This last was the one which aroused the fiercest opposition and which the Crown was soon forced to abrogate.

In New Spain there was an unexpected unanimity of opinion opposed to the abolition of the encomienda. Tello de Sandoval circulated the inevitable interrogatory, in order, we may safely conjecture, to cover himself at Court. It contained three questions: (1) Is it necessary for the service of God and his Majesty to have the Indians held in encomienda? (2) Should the new law concerning this matter be set aside? (3) If many Indians should be left idle because they were not held in encomienda, what difficulties would arise?

Of all the replies received that of the Dominican chapter at Mexico City is easily the most significant, because it was that order which had most violently opposed the encomienda from the beginning. One of its signers was Domingo de

Betanzos, old friend and supporter of Las Casas, and the one who had induced him to join the order in 1522. To the first question they replied that it was necessary for the Indians to be held in encomienda, because it was apparent to all men that the Indians were so fickle by nature that they would never of themselves retain the religion they had received. There could be no permanence in the land without rich men, and there could be no rich men without encomiendas, because all industry was carried on with Indian labor, and only those with Indians could engage in commerce. Moreover, it was necessary to have rich men for defense against enemies and for protection of the poor, as was true in Spain and in every other well-regulated republic. Also, if there were rich men in the country with a permanent title to their estates trade would increase, and with it his Majesty's revenues.

The Indians [they wrote], receive great benefits from having the Spaniards hold their towns, for the Spaniards treat them as if they were their own children and the inheritance which their children are to receive. For this reason they try to conserve them and govern them, and to foment Christianity and bring religious to their towns. It may be allowed that there has been some negligence in the matter, but no one now desires anything but the good treatment of the Indians because of the justice and order which the viceroy has established, and because of the affection which the Spaniards now have for their Indians, as well as their own interest, for they know that their wealth depends upon the prosperity of their towns. And if the Indians cannot pay their tributes on time we know that their encomenderos will not press them, and that they frequently forgive them [the payment]. Such is not the case with the towns held in corregimiento, for the Indians there are commonly thrown into jail on this account. Allowing that there are some good corregidores, yet it commonly happens that all they do is to collect their salaries and the tributes, and no good comes to the towns, but rather vexations and violence, as everyone knows. And, since the corregidores are poor and are so frequently changed, the saying is true that they do nothing but skin the Indians.

The encomenderos were necessary for the defense of the country, because they maintained and supported men in their encomiendas and fitted them out every year. Without the encomenderos to protect them, what would become of the poorer Spaniards? In that event the poor could not live in the country, unless they should become servants of the Indians, "which would be a great insult to the Christians and to the Spanish nation."

If the law should not be repealed it was certain that most of the people and the best people would leave the country rather than abandon their wives and children to the Indians. The estates of the encomenderos had become worthless and without price since the publication of the new law, and many of the married men were leaving the country, despairing of being confirmed in their encomiendas. If confirmation should not be received soon all would leave who could find buyers for their property, "and it is a most true fact that if they leave, your Majesty will not in a long time be able to reëstablish this country with people as noble and as attached to the soil as they are."

To the second question the Dominicans replied that the new law revoking the encomiendas might have been fitting and even necessary in certain other parts of the Indies, but not in New Spain, where the abuses of the Indians had ceased and the Indians were generally well treated. They also thought that since his Majesty had made the grants of the encomiendas after such abuses had ceased and the encomenderos had married and had many children, it was not just that these grants should be revoked without any present blame on their part. Rather, since they had won the country for his Majesty at their own expense and with great hardship and peril, it was just that his Majesty should renew the grants and make them perpetual, because otherwise the discontent and troubles of the present time would be repeated.

To the third question they made the hallowed *pro forma* reply: "As everyone knows, the Indians are weak by nature and are satisfied with having enough to get along on from day to day. And if there is any way to bring them out of their laziness and carelessness, it is to make them help the Spaniards in their commerce. In it the Indians are benefited through their wages, and thus they will become fond of commerce and profits, as, indeed, some of them have already done, in imitation of the Spaniards. . . . And, besides this, great good comes to the state and to his Majesty from having the Indians help the Spaniards in their commerce and on their estates, because without Indians all trade and profit cease. . . ." [12]

It would not be difficult to pick flaws in the logic of the Dominican friars, or, at least, to challenge their assumptions; but we must consider them in their time. They accepted an Aristotelian world of masters and servants; they belonged to the master class and recognized their responsibilities. We cannot believe that they would have composed such a document from motives of worldly interest alone. The saintly life of Domingo de Betanzos and his companions is proof to the contrary. It must be concluded that they had come to accept the encomienda, as the Franciscans had long since done, as the best means of Christianizing the Indians and of bringing them to a proper (European) way of life. In a word, they had accepted the colonial attitude toward the Indians. [13]

The Bishop of Oaxaca, Juan de Zárate, wrote a gossipy letter to Prince Philip which reveals not only his attitude toward the encomenderos and the New Laws, but also sheds some light on conditions in that stronghold of Cortés.

Temporal affairs in this city of Antequera are completely ruined
. . . because, since the estate of the Marqués del Valle has not
been defined and since Oaxaca (which is the same thing as Antequera) [14] is his, the viceroy has not come to see it or visit it, and
the citizens of the said Antequera suffer great necessities, hardships, and difficulties, because there are few who are rich, and if
there ever were any [rich] they are dead. . . . The city [of Ante-
quera] is abandoned and without people and in great danger, because there is not a fort or any defense whatever, and the natives
have not given up their thought of rebellion, as there [in Spain]
it is alleged. . . . In short, one cannot help regretting that . . .
the city of Antequera of your Highness and the Oaxaca of the
Marqués are held by two different lords—which is good neither
for the Spaniards nor the natives, because the Spaniards have no
place to sow or reap except in the lands of the natives; nor does
the city have a common, or approaches, or pastures of its own. For
this reason the natives cannot be as well treated as they should,
because [the Spaniards] cannot avoid doing them harm with their
cattle. . . . For the same reason there is no wheat in the city
except that of the Marqués; nor are there any provisions except
those brought in by his Indians, and all at such excessive prices
that no one can support himself there. . . . The city is almost
abandoned by the Spaniards, so much so that there are not above
thirty citizens left, and they are looking for some way to leave,
as they will, and it will be a desert (I mean without Spaniards)
unless the matter is soon remedied by [your] ordering all those
who have Indians to remain in the city and [by ordering] corregimientos given to those who live there . . . so that as a city, and
one of the most important in this country, it may have a common
and a pasture, and its citizens lands on which to sow and to plant
trees, because for our sins vines do not yield there, although they
have been planted, with no little expense and hardship, and with
too many conflicts with the natives and with the servants of the
Marqués. . . . The natives have increased and have intruded into
the outlying parts of the said city, not leaving the Spaniards any
egress for their cattle, or any common or pasture land for their
cattle, or lands to work and cultivate.

The corregimientos, according to Bishop Zárate, were in
very bad shape. The corregidores had to travel as far as a
hundred leagues to Mexico City to collect their salaries and

deliver their tributes. Not a few of them had to spend their
entire salaries in the collection of tributes and in the government of their corregimientos. If they did not bring their
tributes to Mexico City they destroyed them and, in order
not to have to account for them, they jailed the Indians (to
prevent the news from getting out), so that they might receive their appointments for the coming year.

Not so with the encomenderos, "who, by giving [the In-
dians] terms [in the payment of their tributes] and by
teaching them the commerce of Castile and helping them
over hard times, collect their tributes and make a living.
Thus one small town [in encomienda] supports a Spaniard
very well, while four towns [in corregimiento] do not
produce enough to pay the salary of a corregidor." The execution of the new law would soon make this fact patent,
when his Majesty's revenues would diminish and the country would be abandoned, a process which had already begun.

In the treatment of the natives the conscience of his Majesty
is well acquitted, and that of your Highness may rest easy, because
everything is being done [for them]. It is not allowed to collect
excessive tribute from them, or to treat them ill, or to use them
as carriers against their will; and so much attention is being given
to the matter that no Spaniard now dares to harm an Indian. On
the contrary, the natives are so favored that they dare to mistreat
the Spaniards, not giving them anything to eat except for money
and at high prices, and only when they wish and not when the
Spaniards request and need it. There are alguaciles among them
who dare to arrest a Spaniard and tie him up and bring him before
this Audiencia. . . . They know how to file complaints about
anything at all, and, when they see that they are given more
credence than the Spaniards, at times wrongly, and when they
learn that for any small matter of mistreating an Indian they
can destroy the one who does it, things are no longer what they
used to be, but everything is in such good order that it could not
be more so. For this reason the natives are masters of their estates
and many of them are rich, and all of them have what their fore-
fathers never had, so much so that all the money in the country

belongs to them, because they own all the provisions and sell them at such high prices that no one can live in this country. A hundred-weight (*fanega*) of wheat sells for a peso, and it cannot be had; maize for half a peso. . . . They raise, sell, and traffic in cattle and silk, in such quantities that there is a town in the Mixteca where the natives produce [yearly] for themselves 2,000 pounds of silk, and they pay in tributes only 900 pesos in gold dust.[15]

The replies of the Franciscan friars of Mexico City, of Francisco Terrazas, a prominent encomendero, and of Presbyter Gómez Maraver of New Galicia all repeated substantially the same arguments against the abolition of the encomienda and need not be summarized.[16]

Once Tello de Sandoval had consented to a temporary suspension of the New Laws affecting the encomiendas, a delegation was immediately chosen by the encomenderos to plead their case before the Council of the Indies. The delegates were Jerónimo López and Alonso de Villanueva. The three religious orders were represented by Francisco de Soto, for the Franciscans; Domingo de la Cruz, for the Dominicans; Juan de San Román, for the Augustinians. They left for Spain on June 17, 1544.

A year later the delegates of the encomenderos presented a lengthy and well-reasoned petition, the arguments of which repeated the testimony given in reply to Tello de Sandoval's interrogatory. They urged two measures: (1) the immediate suspension of the New Laws; (2) the perpetual encomienda. They rang again the familiar changes of the argument for the encomienda, but their conclusion had weight. The encomenderos, they said, were the ones who, in the expectation of perpetuity and succession, had thus far supported the country, but now that they saw the New Laws driving them from their homes, they were saving what they could in order to return to Spain, preferring to return poor to waiting until they and their wives should be killed, because if they should abandon the land the Indians would seize it.[17]

The Council of the Indies faced the undeniable fact that the New Laws would have to be amended if serious trouble in the colonies was to be avoided. One member handed down an opinion generally supporting the defenders of the encomienda. In short, he approved of the encomienda, but he suggested that its evils might be mitigated by a more careful selection of the men to whom it was granted and by certain additional restrictions: (1) The tribute should be fixed at a moderate sum and adjusted from time to time. (2) No personal services should be required of the Indians, save moderate work on farms at a small wage. (3) In assessing the tribute a small amount, say one-twentieth, should be set aside for the King. (4) The oidores should visit the encomiendas, with or without complaints from the Indians. If the encomenderos should be found to be mistreating them their encomiendas should be incorporated in the Crown.[18]

Two strong voices were raised in favor of retaining the New Laws unchanged, Sebastián Ramírez de Fuenleal and, of course, Bartolomé de las Casas. The rest of the Council of the Indies may have encouraged the delegates from New Spain to go directly to the Emperor at Malines in Belgium, where they persuaded him to repeal Article 35, which abolished the encomienda upon the death of its present holder.[19] It was, however, only a qualified victory for the encomenderos. The law restricting the succession of the encomienda to one heir remained in force, although it was never rigidly applied; the encomenderos were deprived of the privileges of using the labor of the Indians (i.e., of considering the personal services of the Indians as tributes), of taking slaves, and of using the Indians as carriers. These measures were, to be sure, modified from time to time as necessity dictated, but it was evident from this point on that the encomenderos enjoyed their privileges only on a permissive basis. As the second generation grew old, the question of the succession of the encomienda and its escheating to the Crown came up again, and eventually led to the unlucky conspiracy of the Avila brothers in 1566.

Meanwhile, Mendoza had his hands full trying to enforce the New Laws affecting personal service and Indian slavery. Petitioners against the abolition of slavery argued that it was unjust to penalize the men who had acquired their slaves by purchase, and that mining could not be carried on without them. One petition was read to the Council of the Indies by Bernal Díaz del Castillo, who was acting as a delegate of the encomenderos of Guatemala.[20] The enslavement of rebellious Indians was left to the discretion of the Audiencia by a cédula of 1549.[21] It seems likely that the Council of the Indies was persuaded to keep slaving as a punitive measure by the dangerous rebellion of the Maya in Yucatan, in 1546–1547.[22] At the same time, the encomenderos were forbidden to use their Indians in the mines, and the Audiencia was directed to prevent the commutation of tributes into services in the mines. The New Law concerning Indian carriers was soon modified to permit their use where there was a shortage of pack animals, but their loads were to be moderate and their journeys short. The Council also decided that the present wage of carriers amounted to their working for nothing, for they received 8½ maravedís (equivalent to ¼ real, or 1/32 peso) a day. It reminded the Audiencia that it was the ultimate purpose of the Crown to abolish personal services entirely.[23]

The viceroy analyzed the carrier and personal service question with his usual realism. He suspected, he wrote the Council of the Indies, that the law forbidding the use of carriers had been adopted on the advice of people who did not know the facts. The stories of the abuse of carriers had been exaggerated. Carriers were needed to take supplies to the new mines of Zacatecas, for there were not enough pack animals by one-twentieth to handle the traffic. In fact, there was no way to travel in New Spain without carriers for one's personal effects. The missionaries were obliged to use them, and even Tello de Sandoval had been forced to transgress the law in this respect. Indian merchants were allowed to use carriers without restriction, and thus they were gaining an unfair advantage over their Spanish competitors. Military expeditions were impossible without carriers, and if government officials were obliged to rent pack animals every time they went from one place to another their entire salaries would not suffice to cover the cost of a single trip. After all, a fifty-pound load was no heavier for an Indian than it was for a Spaniard. Now, wherever a Spaniard went he was held up by some corregidor, scale in hand, to discover whether his Indians were carrying two or three pounds above the prescribed load. Indian merchants had to suffer no such annoyance.

Mendoza thought that the laws against the use of carriers and against personal services might work some benefit in New Spain if he were allowed to use his discretion in their application. The Spaniards, he reminded the Council, had not invented personal services, which had been customary among the Indians since time immemorial. Their whole system of government depended upon personal services, and even the Spanish system could not dispense with them. It was absurd to make services voluntary, even for wages, because the Indians would not work for the Spaniards unless forced to do so. And now that the slaves had been freed, the mines could not be worked because Negro slaves were too expensive. Also, the new industries, which were manned by natives, would all be ruined if made dependent upon voluntary labor.[24]

Now that the first enthusiasm for reform had cooled off a bit, the Council of the Indies, impressed by the reasoning of Mendoza and the rest, adopted a less magisterial attitude. Mendoza was undoubtedly in the right, for the government of New Spain could not function without forced services of one kind or another. The Council decreed that carriers might be used, but they were to be hired in the presence of royal officers, who were to fix the weight to be carried, the wages, the length of journeys, and to issue licenses. No mestizo who was not the legitimate son of a Spaniard might use carriers.[25] It also decided that, although government officials had been forbidden to use carriers, the government itself could not be so restricted. The new cathedral of Michoacán was to be completed by subscription: the Crown would bear a third of the cost (out of the tributes of the Indians), the encomenderos a third (*idem*), and the Indians a third.[26]

There was considerable literary activity in the Council of the Indies during the closing years of Mendoza's reign. One long cédula reviewed the whole question of the encomienda and forced services and showed the Council to be still impaled upon its ancient dilemma. It seems that certain encomenderos had objected to having religious in their encomiendas, so the Audiencia was directed to see that the religious were free to go where they pleased and erect monasteries. Carriers might be relieved by the building of roads and bridges. Indians held at the mines against their will were to be released, but the Audiencia might not allow them to remain idle. Cattle were to be kept away from the Indians' *milpas*. Sites were to be chosen for Spanish towns where no harm would come to the Indians from them. The New Laws, except those which had been repealed, were to be enforced. The Audiencia might mitigate the vagabond nuisance by putting the offenders to work or by exiling a few of them by way of example. Crown officers were again reminded that they were forbidden to use Indians in personal service.[27]

Bishop Zárate's complaint about the corregidores, or

others like it, brought a cédula forbidding these officials to collect the tribute, which thereafter was to be handled by an officer appointed for the purpose—another dead letter. Native overseers (calpisques) hired by encomenderos and corregidores were to be examined in the future for good character before being licensed.[28]

The illicit traffic in Indian slaves proved difficult to control because of the shortage of labor in the mines and the high prices commanded by the slaves (up to forty pesos). A typical remedy suggested by the Council of the Indies was that the Audiencia should appoint the Franciscans as the special guardians of Indian slaves. The Audiencia would then appoint a prosecutor to handle the cases of abuse reported by the guardians.[29]

That Mendoza no longer considered the encomienda to be a problem may be gathered from his failure to mention it in his instructions to his successor, Luis de Velasco. The New Laws had, indeed, purged it of its most notorious fault, the power to coerce labor, and had taken from the encomendero his quasi-feudal independence, reducing him to the status of a pensioner of the Crown. He received the tributes of the Indians entrusted to him, he looked (presumably) after their welfare, and in return for his privileges he acted as militiaman when necessary. In reality the Crown was now the only encomendero in the old sense, because it alone had the power to assess tributes and to coerce labor "for the good of the state." [30]

11.

The Tamed Encomienda

ALTHOUGH the amended New Laws had, for all practical purposes, fixed the status of the encomienda for the rest of its existence, the restriction of the succession to "two lives" remained a source of uneasiness and irritation among the encomenderos.[1] They never ceased in their effort to have the encomienda made perpetual, and their failure kept them in a rebellious mood which led some of the younger bloods to dream of cutting loose from the old country and setting up a feudal empire under Martín Cortés, the second Marqués del Valle.[2] The widening rift between the descendants of the conquerors and Spanish officialdom was one of the most active ingredients in the nascent nationalism which split New Spain permanently into two factions, *criollos* and *gachupines*. The feeling became so deeply rooted, irrational, and bitter that it is tempting to accept the thesis of González Obregón and ascribe the independence movement of the nineteenth century to the lasting rancor stirred up in the sixteenth by the suppression of the encomenderos.[3]

Articles 24, 26, 27, 32, 33, 49, and 51 of the New Laws, all those, in short, which restricted the use of the Indians in personal services, regulated the tribute, and emancipated the slaves, were a body blow at the economic power of the encomenderos, who resisted their execution to the utmost. The classic Spanish method of enforcing unpopular laws was invoked, and visitadores with ample jurisdiction were sent into the provinces. These magistrates were true courts, empowered to examine all encomiendas and corregimientos, to take depositions of witnesses (including Indians), to punish transgressors by removing their encomiendas, to reassess the tribute, and to free the Indian slaves. They had, however, no jurisdiction over corregidores, charges against whom had to be submitted to the Audiencia for action. The most famous of these provincial visitas was that of Diego Ramírez, a friend of Las Casas, who seems to have been an honest but inflexible bureaucrat and who evidently looked upon himself as a prosecuting attorney. He was given the uncomfortable assignment of investigating the large territory north and east of the capital, as far as Pánuco,[4] which had been notorious for abuse of the Indians since the slave-catching days of Nuño de Guzmán. In the territory lay the rich textile region of Metztitlán (in modern Hidalgo) which was controlled by two wealthy and vigorous encomenderos, Diego de Guevara and Alonso de Mérida.[5]

Ramírez appeared in Metztitlán late in 1551 and found himself stalled by an appeal to the Audiencia in which Guevara and Mérida claimed exemption from the visita, because Metztitlán was not specifically mentioned in Ramírez' instructions. Ramírez countered by appealing directly to the Council of the Indies, which authorized him to visit Metztitlán and at the same time told the Audiencia that it might not receive appeals from Ramírez' decisions. The encomenderos, who seem to have been firmly en-

trenched in the Audiencia, got that body to send out a special
judge to investigate the actions of Ramírez. As must have
been anticipated, the judge found that Ramírez had been
exceeding his instructions and put him under arrest. Ramírez even had to suffer the ignominy of being paraded on
horseback through the Indian towns, to let them know,
we may safely guess, who was master. He was soon released
by Viceroy Velasco and returned to Metztitlán in a proper
fury. The upshot of his visita was that he sentenced Mérida
and Guevara to the forfeiture of their encomiendas and to
exile from Metztitlán for two years.

It soon became apparent, however, that it would take
more than an isolated visitador armed with a piece of ambiguous paper to bring the encomenderos to heel. Backed
by a friendly Audiencia and not opposed, apparently, by
the viceroy, they had little difficulty in getting the Council
of the Indies to annul their sentences. It was fairly obvious
that visitadores of the type of Ramírez could not hope to
prevail against the universal hostility of all classes, and after
several experiments the Council of the Indies settled down
to a policy of gradual attrition and local visitas performed
by corregidores with limited commissions.[6]

The execution of the New Laws was Viceroy Velasco's
most trying task, and his vexation is manifest in a number
of letters he wrote to the Council of the Indies. He urged
in one the immediate distribution of vacant encomiendas
to the needy. "I have written like a loyal servant what I
think of this distribution, that is, that your Majesty should
not defer it, because in [the case of] most Spaniards who
have Indians in encomienda the two lives will end in the
one generation for which they have been granted. There
are so many penniless men in this land 2,000 leagues from
Spain that I fear their necessity will cause them not to observe the loyalty which they owe [you]. I say, sacred Majesty, that it seems to me that if their Indians are removed

at one stroke they will risk their lives to save their estates; and so, in order to reward them for their services, as well as to perpetuate and pacify the land, your Majesty should order the distribution to be made effective. . . ." [7] In the same letter he added that the Audiencia had suspended certain provisions of the New Laws in order to prevent greater troubles and "notable disobedience"—probably a reference to the Metztitlán affair.

Six months later the viceroy reported that the crisis was becoming acute. "Among the Spaniards there is great discontent and poverty, and among the Indians more license and easy living than their fickleness can support. I suspect that in both these races difficulties will occur which will be hard to remedy, because the land is so full of Negroes and mestizos that they greatly exceed the number of Spaniards, and they [the Negroes] all wish to purchase their liberty at the cost of their masters' lives, and this wicked race will join with those who rebel, whether they be Spaniards or Indians. . . ." To remedy the situation he urges again the distribution of encomiendas to conquerors and settlers.

Like his predecessors, Velasco was intensely irritated by what he thought was the unjustified interference of the religious in the administration of the Indies, although he does not mention Las Casas by name. "Those who inform your Majesty that it [the land] can be supported without Spaniards with the means to defend it and with something to lose if they fail, and [who advise you] that it can be supported by the religious alone, to my way of thinking are deceiving themselves and have little knowledge of the natives, because [the latter] are not so well grounded in our Holy Catholic Faith, or so forgetful of the wicked religion which they had during their infidelity, that one should entrust a matter of such magnitude to their virtue."

The removal of forced personal services in the mines and

plantations was causing a deepening depression. "Let your Majesty not be persuaded that the mines can be worked without [the forced labor of] the Indians . . . unless the Spaniards work them with their own hands, and I doubt they will do so, even though they see themselves dying of hunger. . . . As soon as the slaves are liberated, which will be shortly, the royal treasury as well as private citizens will suffer a great loss, because there is no mine so rich that it can stand being worked by wage-earners, for it will cost twice as much as it produces." [8] The labor crisis was particularly felt in Mexico City.

The Spaniards are very resentful because the New Laws touch them all. The Council [of the Indies] has declared that it is personal service for the Indians to bring royal and private tributes to this city. Since the greater part of such tributes is in foodstuffs . . . there is much want in the city, and I find no means of provisioning it, because, if the Indians do not do it, no disposition which I or the Spaniards make will suffice to provide the city even with bread and water, and fodder for the horses, which are the strength of the country. Counting the number of people who ordinarily dwell in the city, I find that between Indians and Spaniards, mestizos and Negroes, and outsiders who come to traffic here, there are usually 200,000 mouths [to feed]. Consider, your Majesty, how they are to be fed, for there are not among them a thousand farmers and the city is surrounded by a lagoon, unless [food] be brought in from without. Carts and pack animals are not sufficient, and they have more than they can do [anyway] to provide wood and charcoal, because the Indians have been relieved of bringing it in, which they considered a great bother. The provisioning of this city with wheat and maize—as well as all the other cities in the country—cannot be done unless it be done with Indians. . . . As personal services are removed, the necessity becomes as great as that suffered by a city besieged.[9]

The reassessment of the tribute turned out to be an endless process. In general, the Audiencia was instructed to ascertain what tribute the Indians had paid in the days of their "infidelity" and to assess them accordingly. Payment in kind, a system taken over from the Aztecs, had been the universal practice before the enactment of the New Laws. It consisted of virtually everything the Indians produced, as was seen in the tribute list for Cuernavaca given in Chapter 8. The *Suma de Visitas* was probably compiled in an attempt to get at a rational basis for assessments, for tribute in kind could not be reduced to any intelligible system of accounting. A property tax had been proposed and rejected, for the Indians had no real property. It was therefore natural that the Spaniards should apply to New Spain the medieval head tax with which they were familiar, since payment in services was now forbidden by the New Laws. The matter admitted of no delay, because the rapidly shrinking Indian population was badly oppressed by the rigid rates which compelled them to pay tribute for the dead. One of the purposes of the visita of Jerónimo de Valderrama in 1564 was to determine the best method of taxing the Indians. At that time the oidor Vasco de Puga was in charge of recounting and reassessing all the provincial towns.[10]

Viceroy Martín Enríquez described the tribute system which continued to be used.

The system which has been followed, and which is still followed, in the assessment of the Indians is personal and not according to property. The highest tribute is one peso of eight reales and half a fanega of maize, and it has never risen above this point. If in some parts they pay less, and if some pay in mantas or in other things (and they are few), it is made the equivalent of one peso and half a fanega of maize. Although it does not seem that there is much justification for this [system], the [small] amount of the tribute makes us accept it, for it seems to us that those who have least are not injured and that those who have the capacity [to pay more] receive a favor. Every time that I have discussed the matter with the oidores . . . they have always held that the tribute should be a head tax and not a property tax.[11]

It is difficult to get at the truth of the effect of the tribute on native life. Commentators were divided, as usual, into two mutually contradictory camps. Certain members of the Mendicant orders cried that the tribute was the cause of the diminution of the Indian population.[12] Civil officers, like Valderrama, pretty generally thought that the Indians were getting off too easily, although they do not make out a very convincing case. For example, in 1562 the Audiencia filed a long report with the Council of the Indies based on visitas of various Crown towns carried out by corregidores. They found that the two Indian *barrios* of Mexico City (San Juan and Tlatelolco) had a net count of 18,042 tributaries who were paying an average tribute of 16,000 pesos a year. The corregidor of Hueytlalpa counted the tributaries of Huejotzingo *casa por casa y vecino por vecino* and found that they numbered 11,318. They were paying in 1560 a tribute of 11,308 pesos and 5,654 fanegas of maize. The Audiencia was particularly scandalized by the favored position of Tlaxcala, the tribute of which had been fixed in 1538 at 8,000 fanegas of maize for the whole province, "because of the services which they and their ancestors had rendered in this land," although Tlaxcala had, according to the Audiencia, 100,000 tributaries.[13]

There is little point in belaboring the Spanish Crown for imposing tribute on the Indians. If it had not done so it would have afforded an example of high-mindedness the like of which the world had never seen. Given its chronic shortage of funds, it is remarkable that it made, through the Audiencia, a conscientious and continuing effort to keep the tribute of the Crown towns adjusted to the fluctuations of population and crops. For example, the town of Huejotzingo was assessed in 1543 100 cargas of mantas worth 13 pesos each, or 1,300 pesos, and 4,000 fanegas of maize. In 1552 Diego Ramírez adjusted the tribute to 2,000 pesos and 4,000 fanegas of maize. In 1556, because of a drought, the cash tribute was reduced to 1,000 pesos, although the maize tribute was increased to 5,000 fanegas. The next year the money tribute was suspended altogether and the assessment was made in maize alone, 8,000 fanegas. In 1558 the tribute was 6,000 pesos and 6,000 fanegas. In 1560 the tribute was rationalized to one peso per tributary and half a fanega of maize, making a total of 11,308 pesos and 5,654 fanegas of maize—which, incidentally, gives a trustworthy basis for estimating the population. In 1566 the tribute was adjusted to 8,571 pesos and 4,285 ½ fanegas; in 1570, to 7,360 ½ pesos and 3,680 ¼ fanegas.[14]

We have no such positive evidence that the tributes collected by the encomenderos were subject to the same kind of rigorous adjustment. On the contrary, Alonso de Zurita, who was oidor of the Audiencia from 1555 to 1565, states flatly that the encomenderos were in the habit of padding the population counts of their villages, including "cripples, the blind, the maimed, paupers and other wretches who cannot work." [15] Although Zurita's evidence is suspect, since he belonged to the Las Casas-Fuenleal-Mendieta anti-encomendero school of thinking, it would be very odd indeed if some encomenderos did not abuse their power. On the other hand there is abundant evidence that by the period upon which we are entering the encomenderos had been sufficiently chastised and were not pushing their Indian tributaries beyond endurance. Motolinía's testimony to that effect is not to be shrugged off. Also, Francisco de Ceynos, oidor of the Audiencia from 1530 to 1546, and from 1558 to 1565, wrote a long report to the Council of the Indies in 1565 reviewing the whole history of the tribute. He ends with the following illuminating statement:

New assessments . . . are made daily, and thus it is being brought about that no person, religious, layman, or Indian, may use [the services of] the poor without compensation . . . so that when they have paid their tribute they are free of all [other] services and unpaid labor. The treatment of the Indians by the encomenderos is greatly improved, and they are the persons . . . from whom [the Indians] receive the least abuse; because, with the privilege which your Majesty has granted them in the legitimate succession, they understand that it is to continue, and they handle this matter [of the Indians] with great moderation and love. And thus in this royal Audiencia there are few cases concerning this matter, which formerly was its principal business.[16]

Three further considerations lead me to believe that Motolinía and Ceynos were essentially correct in their estimate of the improved relations between encomendero and Indian. By 1560 Crown towns and encomienda towns were so thoroughly intermingled, as a glance at the map (see chap. 12), will show, that it would have been difficult for an encomendero to collect without detection a much larger *per capita* tribute than was being paid by the Crown Indians of the next village. Moreover, many towns by that time were shared by Crown and encomendero and one assessment covered both. It may be assumed that an effective control over both was thus established and that violations of the tribute schedule could not easily have been concealed. This assumption is borne out by the records of the General Indian Court, which from 1592 to 1820 had jurisdiction over all complaints brought by Indians against Spaniards, and vice versa. It is astonishing that suits against encomenderos were exceedingly rare and that suits for abuses of the tribute by encomenderos are almost nonexistent in those records.[17] It is reasonable to believe that the encomenderos by this time had come to recognize that their real and permanent interests demanded that they keep their Indians fairly contented. After all, the Indians were their bread and butter and if mistreated had only to pack up and remove to the nearest Crown town or to that of another encomendero.

This last argument is supported by a number of interesting cases which establish rather conclusively that the encomenderos and their charges were coming to accept a paternalistic or feudal relationship, the encomendero protecting the Indians from other Spaniards in exchange for the privilege of being supported by their tributes. It should not be mistaken for philanthropy. As early as 1550 a suit was brought by a small encomendero, Gonzalo Gallego,[18] against Antonio de Godoy, alcalde mayor of Zacatula, for removing his Indians and forcing them to work in Zacatula. He complained that his Indians were thus prevented from working their lands *and from paying the tributes for which they have been assessed.* The Audiencia ordered Godoy to desist, on pain of 100 pesos fine.[19]

That the Crown was intimately concerned in this process of transformation may be gathered from a royal cédula of May 27, 1582, which ordered the governor of Guatemala, Diego García de Valverde,[20] to investigate and correct the abuses reportedly committed by encomenderos, corregidores, and alcaldes mayores against the Indians. These abuses included (1) collecting tributes on ancient population counts, when the actual number of Indians had diminished by as much as two-thirds; (2) collecting tributes for dead or absent Indians; (3) selling encomienda Indians to one another; (4) using Indians as slaves; (5) beating them; (6) loading them excessively; (7) making them sleep in the fields, where they died from the bites of poisonous reptiles; (8) mistreating them so badly that mothers killed their children rather than have them serve the Spaniards; (9) causing the Indians to starve themselves to death, or to hang themselves, for the same reason; (10) causing them generally to hate the name of Christian.

Valverde had been in Guatemala for four years, and he evidently considered the cédula an indictment of his administration, for the forty-two page report he sent to the

Council of the Indies is essentially a defense of himself.[21] Nevertheless, given his high reputation as a public servant and the eminent witnesses upon whom he drew for confirmation, it is difficult to believe that his report is erroneous in any important respect.

When he had arrived in Guatemala in 1578 he found that there had been a critical loss of population and that the encomenderos were, in fact, collecting tributes based on ancient counts. He had immediately ordered a new count and a general survey of conditions, using the priests and religious of the villages as his agents. Then he had sent out competent visitadores, who had reassessed the tributes of 150 villages and reduced them to conform to the actual count. He had further opened the Audiencia to receive direct reports from the Indians on deaths and absences— this over the opposition of the encomenderos. He had also set up a kind of department of vital statistics in the charge of the bishops and of the provincials of the Mendicant orders, to keep account of the changes in population. In the district of Comayagua, for example, the bishop and the religious had reported a loss of a third of the Indians in some encomiendas and of two-thirds in others, and the tribute rolls had been rectified accordingly.

Valverde had discovered only two cases of abuse of tamemes. Both offenders had been punished: Juan de Torres, alcalde mayor of Trinidad, had been banished and his goods confiscated; Alonso de Nava, alcalde mayor of San Salvador, was even then under arrest awaiting trial. Valverde called attention of the Council of the Indies to the difficulties of transport in a country where there were no pack animals—everyone had to use tamemes, who were paid for their services.

He brought to his support a number of depositions, some of which went well beyond his restrained defense of himself. Don Pedro de Liévano, Dean of the Cathedral of Guatemala, testified that in his twenty-two years' service in the country he had never heard of the excesses described in the cédula. "Rather, this witness knows that the Indians can look after themselves and that no one dares to abuse them, because these are no longer the times which the encomenderos once called 'golden' when they were free to abuse the Indians." He agreed that the Indians were greatly diminished, but ascribed it to "secret judgments of God beyond the knowledge of men" in the form of three or four epidemics which had come from Mexico.

Francisco González, *maestrescuela* of the cathedral school, said that the abuses enumerated in the cédula no longer existed, "for the encomenderos and other persons do not dare to abuse the Indians because . . . the said Licenciado Valverde looks after them, their conservation, and good treatment."

Fray Juan de Cija, Guardian of the Franciscan convent of Comalapa, testified to the same effect and added the remark that *"In these times the encomenderos protect the Indians against persons who abuse them,* and when it happens that some person commits some abuse he is rigorously punished by the magistrates of His Majesty."

Fray Juan Tresino, Mercedarian; Fray Mateo García, Mercedarian; Fray Juan de Santisteban, Prior of the Dominican convent of Guatemala; Fray Juan de Castro, Provincial of the Dominican order; and Diego Ramírez, Royal Accountant—all testified in detail to the accuracy of Valverde's report.

It may be that the statement of Fray Juan de Cija, just quoted, was inspired by a case which had been heard by the Audiencia of Guatemala just two years before. In it Bernal Díaz del Castillo, then in his nineties, successfully defended the Indians of his encomienda against a landgrab attempted by one Martín Ximénez and a priest, Antonio López.[22] The significant argument for us in the plea of Bernal Díaz is that

"These lands are the ones in which the Indians have their fields of maize, peppers, and cacao, *and from which they pay their tributes.*"

A case with similar implications was brought before the General Indian Court of Mexico at about the same time. Melchor de Pedraza, encomendero of the towns of Atotonilco and Zacamal (in modern Hidalgo), brought suit against the Indian governors of the same towns for forcing the Indians of his encomienda to work in their fields and in their commerce—"from which it results that, besides the harm they receive, most of the year they are occupied in this and have no time to cultivate their own fields, *from which they get their support and the payment of their tributes.*" The Court ordered that the Indians might not be used in any personal service without express permission of the viceroy.[23]

In the competition for the constantly diminishing labor supply (no labor, no tribute) it was natural that encomenderos, hacendados, corregidores, and alcaldes mayores should get in one another's way. Francisco de Solís Orduña y Barraga, encomendero of the important town of Acolman (in the modern state of Mexico), brought suit against the Indian governor, Don Buenaventura de los Reyes, a *principal* of Tlaxcala, for conniving with certain Spanish farmers of the vicinity to supply them with laborers from his encomienda. The Court ordered an investigation.[24]

A more remarkable case arising from the same motives was a suit brought by the Indian governors of the towns of Astapa, Jaguacapa, and Jalapa, in the encomienda of Lucas de Barros (in modern Tabasco), against the alcalde mayor of Tabasco. They testified that they were in the habit of working for their encomendero whenever he requested it and that he paid them for it and treated them well *de obra y palabra,* but that the alcalde mayor was molesting them and trying to prevent their so doing. The Court enjoined the alcalde mayor from interfering with them.[25] This seems to be a clear case of the Indians' accepting their encomendero as their natural ally against outsiders. Their emphasis upon his good treatment of them is refreshing, but it was probably not typical.

One last bit of evidence to illustrate the taming of the encomienda is the changing attitude of the Mendicant orders. In the latter part of the sixteenth century the only writer who mounted the ancient hobby of Las Casas was Jerónimo de Mendieta, whose *Historia eclesiástica indiana* (1596), masterpiece though it is, faithfully repeats Las Casas' oversimplified indictment. Against Mendieta must be placed the depositions of the orders canvassed by Tello de Sandoval in 1544 and the absence of other critics among them. The Mendicants were certainly not abdicating their position as defenders of the Indians, but they had switched targets from the encomenderos to the Crown. In 1594 the Franciscans made a bold attack on the mita or repartimiento system of forced labor, representing to the Council of the Indies that such services were not only contrary to natural law but were contrary to common sense.[26] It is significant that they do not mention the encomienda at all.

The danger of defending a thesis such as I have advanced is that one may be charged with playing the devil's advocate. Let me repeat, the encomenderos of New Spain were the same tough breed that had devastated the Antilles and overrun a continent. It should be clear that I am not writing a brief for them, but attempting to demonstrate that they had learned, in the course of time and by hard experience, not to destroy their very means of subsistence, and that they and their charges found themselves bound together by common interests.[27]

12.

Economic and Demographic Aspects

THE DEEPENING crisis caused by the rapid decline of the Indian population led to a systematic attempt by the Audiencia to discover what the manpower resources of the country really were. From the time of the *Suma de Visitas* (*ca.* 1544) to the end of the century a large number of estimates and actual counts were made. The decade of 1560–1570 particularly was a period of intense demographic activity when the gathering of data was put into the able hands of the oidor Dr. Vasco de Puga, the compiler of the frequently quoted *Cedulario*. Altogether, counting the *Suma,* some sixteen lists were got together, the last one being the immense petition of the encomenderos of 1597. These are the documents which S. F. Cook and myself used in our *Population of Central Mexico in the Sixteenth Century,* and for convenience in reference I shall follow the same system, designating the various sources by the letters "A" to "P." [1]

It was suggested in Chapter 10 that one of the apparent

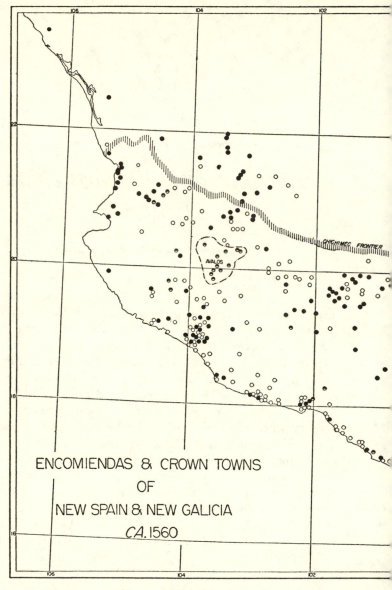

ENCOMIENDAS & CROWN TOWNS

OF

NEW SPAIN & NEW GALICIA

CA. 1560

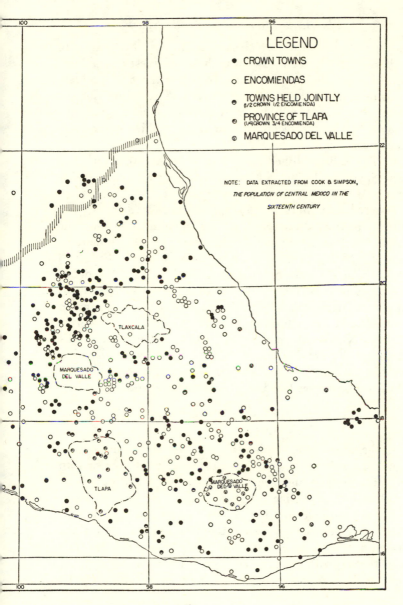

LEGEND

- • CROWN TOWNS
- ○ ENCOMIENDAS
- ◑ TOWNS HELD JOINTLY
  (1/2 CROWN 1/2 ENCOMIENDA)
- ◕ PROVINCE OF TLAPA
  (1/4 CROWN 3/4 ENCOMIENDA)
- ⊗ MARQUESADO DEL VALLE

NOTE: DATA EXTRACTED FROM COOK & SIMPSON, *THE POPULATION OF CENTRAL MEXICO IN THE SIXTEENTH CENTURY*

TLAXCALA

MARQUESADO DEL VALLE

TLAPA

MARQUESADO DEL VALLE

motives of the Crown which lay behind such humanitarian legislation as the New Laws was the reconquest of the New World from the Spanish conquerors. So the first problem (not necessarily the most important and certainly not the most interesting) will be to determine what success the Crown had in the reconquest in the last third of the sixteenth century.

Cook and I established (p. 16) that the total population of New Spain, exclusive of New Galicia, in the decade 1560–1570 was about 4,204,700, or 1,051,175 tributaries. Of the privately held tributaries 369,735 are accounted for in "B," which contains a complete list of encomiendas. But the values in "B" are consistently depressed, as is easily demonstrated. Of the 325 encomienda towns which it lists, 173 appear also in the more trustworthy "C" to "N" documents, as well as in the "P" list of 1597—which gives us ample statistical control. In "B" these 173 towns are given a total of 243,625 tributaries (i.e., pesos of tribute), whereas "C" to "N" give them 307,974. It seems justifiable to take the latter value as the true one for the 173 towns and to adjust the "B" list accordingly. Thus the adjusted value for all the encomiendas listed in "B" becomes by proportion:

$$\frac{307,974 \times 369,735}{243,625} = 467,352$$

In the same 173 encomienda towns the decline in population between 1560–1570 and 1597 was from 307,974 to 171,553, or 44.3 per cent, which we may accept as the standard rate of decline for all towns.

The Crown holdings in 1560–1570 were, by subtraction, 583,823 tributaries. Between that decade and 1597 the Crown acquired, by escheat and confiscation, 121 encomienda towns, with 78,147 tributaries (as of 1560–1570).[2] The holdings of the Crown in 1597, therefore, may be ascertained by applying this simple formula: Crown tributaries = (583,823 + 78,147) × 0.557 = 368,712.

The relative positions of Crown and encomienda holdings for the two periods are best shown in tabular form.

	1560–1570	1597
Encomiendas	467,352	215,205 [3]
Crown towns	583,823	368,712
Totals	1,051,175	583,917

Note that the net loss in the encomiendas is 252,147, or 54 per cent, whereas the net loss of the Crown is 214,911, or 37 per cent. In other words, by 1597 the Crown had made a relative gain of 17 per cent at the expense of the encomiendas.

Lest the reader get the false notion that the families of the encomenderos were suffering undue hardship, it should be mentioned at this point that the conquistadores and their offspring were not at all backward about pressing their claims for preferred treatment in the distribution of "vacant" lands. Many of them, perhaps most, became proprietors of large tracts: cattle *estancias* of one square league (6.76 sq. miles), sheep *estancias* of $\frac{4}{9}$ square league (3 sq. miles), farm sites of 1 or 1½ *caballerías* (105.4 and 158.1 acres respectively), and owners of mines, sugar, flour, and stamp mills, city lots, and inns. The incomplete records of *mercedes* in the Mexican Archives contain many hundreds of such grants. An amusing instance of the colossal effrontery of the claimants is afforded by the nephew of the old conqueror Diego de Ordaz. Young Ordaz was in Spain in 1538. Parading his uncle's record before the Council of the Indies, he got for himself the princely grant of three square leagues (about twenty square miles!) of the choicest land in the valley of Puebla. Viceroy Mendoza let him cool his heels for four years and finally let him have the stand-ard *caballería* of land near Tepapayeca, that is, a fourth of a square league.

By long odds the greatest, the richest, and the most en-during of the encomiendas of New Spain was, of course, the Marquesado del Valle de Oaxaca, granted to Cortés in 1529 along with his glittering title.[4] It was unique in that it was made a true fief in perpetuity and thus became the envy, admiration, and goal of all encomenderos. It was also an anachronism and an anomaly, and, after the initial mis-take of allowing it, the Council of the Indies made no more such grants in New Spain and bent its talents to whittling down the extravagant claims of the Marqués. His title specified that he was to have "the lands and vassals, the woods and pastures, all waters, both running and standing, and complete civil and criminal jurisdiction—all the rights, in short, which belonged to the Crown itself in the afore-said lands. . . . His entire possessions were formed into a *mayorazgo* (an entailed estate) in 1535, so that the prop-erty should pass entire to his heir and remain in the family undivided." [5]

Cortés was an empire-builder in the grand manner. Al-though the terms of his grant gave him only 23,000 tribu-taries, it was rightly suspected that the Marquesado con-tained many more than that, and the second Audiencia made a partly successful attempt to reduce it. To that ef-fort we owe our earliest knowledge of the actual extent of the Marquesado. In a petition to the Audiencia in 1532 pro-testing the removal of some of his towns, Cortés listed all his possessions, or, at least, as many as he could remember.[6] To give an idea of the colossal extent of the Marquesado, as well as to show what the Audiencia did to it, I have listed in the table below Cortés' claims as of 1532, italicizing the names of the towns which appear under other holders in the "A" to "P" documents. In the center column I give the numbers of tributaries in 1560–1570, and in the right-hand column the values in 1597.

THE MARQUESADO DEL VALLE

Towns claimed by Cortés in 1532	Tributaries 1560–1570	Values in 1597
Coyoacán and Tacubaya	5,902½	3,974
Dependencies (*sujetos*) of same:		
Tescaliacaque (?)		
Ocotepeque (?)		
Atlapulco	750	440
Xalatlaco	1,600	972
Capulhuac	587	548
Toluca	4,964	2,207
Dependencies of same:		
Metepec, Tepemachalco,		
and *Calimaya*	4,617	2,299
Tlachichilco (?)		
Zinacantepec	1,400	1,191
Tlacotepec	1,380	489
Cuernavaca	18,200	7,714½
Tepoztlán	2,718½	1,734½
Yautepec	4,973	2,337½
Oaxtepec	3,669½	2,020 [a]
Yecapixtla	6,150	3,488½
Cuilapan	7,464	3,001
Oaxaca (viejo)	1,257	617½
Etla	2,439	1,138
Tlacuilabacoya	357	60

a In "P" Oaxtepec is given the incredibly low value of 367½ tributaries which is so far out of line with the contiguous districts of Tepoztlán, Yautepec, and Yecapixtla that I ascribe it to a clerical error. The district of Oaxtepec occupied the fertile and well-watered valley of the Cuautla River, in modern Morelos, and has always been one of the garden spots of Mexico. It seems unreasonable that it should have lost *nine-tenths* of its population while its neighbors were suffering the normal decline. I have therefore adjusted its value by equating it with the values for the three districts named—which gives the following proportion:

$$\frac{7.560.5 \times 3,699.5}{13,841.5} = 2,020$$

THE MARQUESADO DEL VALLE (*Con't*)

Towns claimed by Cortés in 1532	Tributaries 1560–1570	Values in 1597
Dependencies in the Valley of Oaxaca:		
Talistaca	522	
Macuilxochitl	298	
Zimatlán and *Tepezimatlán*	1,700	
Ocotlán	1,022	
Tanquehuagay (?)		
Los Peñoles	600	
Huajolotitlán	1,361	
Cuxutepec (?)		
Tulzapotlán (?)		
Mitla	583	
Tlacolula	357	
Zapotlán (?)		
Tehuantepec [b]	3,442	
Jalapa	928½	779
La Rinconada	180	52
Cotaxtla [c]	20	34
Tuxtla	1,060	655
Tepeaca	9,400	
Totals for Marquesado	60,903 [d]	30,164

[b] The province of Tehuantepec, which occupied the valley of the Tehuantepec River, was taken over by the Crown, but Cortés was allowed a yearly compensation of 3,442 fanegas of maize and 1,527 pesos from the tributes of the Crown province of Chalco. Only the town of Jalapa in the Tehuantepec Peninsula remained in the Marquesado. (Document "E.")

[c] The province of Cotaxtla occupied the valley of the Cotaxtla River in Vera Cruz. It seems to have been almost totally depopulated early in the sixteenth century.

[d] The 1560–1570 values are taken from an inventory entitled *Relación de lo que valieron las rentas del Marques del Valle en los años de 1568 y 1569, hecha por Juan de Cigorondo, contador del dicho estado.* (*Epistolario de Nueva España*, XI, 5–60.) The occasion was the seizure of the Marquesado by the Crown during the trial of Martín Cortés for implication in it in the conspiracy of 1566. Since it was drawn up by the accountant of the estate, it must be accepted as accurate. I have made two adjustments in it in order to bring the number of tributaries into the normal pattern of one peso and half a fanega of maize per tributary. The formula for deriving the number of tributaries from the total tribute is:

$$\text{Tributaries} = \frac{\text{pesos of tribute} \times 2 + \text{number of fanegas}}{3}$$

The assessment for Cuernavaca was 27,300 pesos in mantas only. The number of tributaries, therefore, was $\frac{27,300 \times 2 + 0}{3}$, or 18,200. The assessment for Toluca was 4,467 pesos plus 5,957 fanegas. Its tributaries, therefore, numbered $\frac{4,467 \times 2 + 5,957}{3}$, or 4,964.

If we take Cortés' petition of 1532 seriously, the Marquesado was pared down by 16 towns and 29,619 tributaries (as of 1560–1570). Even so, the inventory of 1569 shows that the total income of the Marquesado from tributes alone (including cash and kind) was about 86,000 pesos a year, contributed by 60,903 tributaries. This handsome income did not, of course, represent a clear profit. Out of it were paid the salaries of a number of functionaries; it supported the missions of the Mendicant orders in many of its villages; and it paid tithes to the secular Church.[7]

The loss of tributaries in the Marquesado between 1560–1570 and 1597 is difficult to account for. Its rate of 50.5 per cent, against the general decline of 44.3 per cent, is unexpected, for we would think that the Marquesado, which occupied some of the richest territory in New Spain and which should have been free, moreover, from the endemic instability of other encomiendas, would have suffered less than they. The only plausible explanation for the discrepancy is that the 1597 report on the Marquesado may have been based on the same kind of data as the "B" list, in which case we might be justified in raising it considerably, possibly by a half.

Three other large groups of holdings are worth considering in detail because they were shared by the Crown and the encomenderos and thus give an excellent control over our statistics.

The province of Avalos, in Jalisco, was conquered, probably in 1524, by Alonso de Avalos.[8] How the Crown came to possess half of it we do not know. As Sauer surmises, the original co-holder with Avalos may have been Hernando de Saavedra, who lost his encomienda "en las minas de Michoacán" to Manuel de Guzmán, a henchman of Nuño de Guzmán, by action of the Crown officers in 1525, when Saavedra was off with Cortés in the Honduras expedition. The second Audiencia confiscated all the encomiendas granted by the first—which would explain the Crown's ownership.[9] However it was, the earliest record we have of Avalos (the *Suma de Visitas*) shows Alonso de Avalos and the Crown sharing it equally.

The Avalos towns occupy the richest part of the Bajío country and cluster around the volcanic lakes of Chapala, Tilapan, San Marcos, and Sayula. The records of this "veritable principality," as Sauer calls it, are fortunately among the most complete and consistent that we have. In view of the catastrophic decline of the population in the rest of New Spain, it is extraordinarily interesting to trace the demographic history of this smiling province in the second half of the sixteenth century. It is best shown by a table.

PROVINCE OF AVALOS

Towns	1540	1560	1570	1597
Amacueca	888		551½	467
Ajijic	598		295½	308
Atoyac	1,414		833	703
Cocula	621		651½	906
Chapala	825		290	386
Jocotepec	224		147	278
Sayula	952		1,080	1,802
Techalutla	939		738	530
Teocuitatlán	551		358	288
Tepec	250		190	189
Zacoalco	1,172		1,176	1,145
Totals	8,434 [a]	9,000 [a]	6,320½ [a]	7,002 [a]

a Sources: "A," "B," "E," and "P," respectively.

The startling fact that stands out here like a good deed in a naughty world is that, even if we use the suspiciously rounded "B" value for the second period, the province of Avalos lost only 22 per cent of its population between 1560 and 1597, but the rest of New Spain lost at more than twice that rate. If, on the other hand, we use the ordinarily trustworthy "E" list, Avalos gained more than 10 per cent! Why this should be so our records do not say. My guess is that Alonso de Avalos must have been an extraordinarily able man, strong enough to discourage the followers of

Nuño de Guzmán and others from meddling with his encomienda. Another likely factor was the rich land and the healthful environment, which made it possible for the population to resist epidemics and to recuperate its losses very quickly. It may be, also, that the presence of two rival powers in the same encomienda acted as a brake on the cupidity of both. Again, they may have stood back to back against outsiders to protect their common interests. And, finally, the Indians themselves would not be averse to taking advantage of the rivalry and playing them off against one another. Any and all of these situations would ease the circumstances of the Indians. These speculations may be tested against the history of two other groups.

The province of Tlapa, in the eastern part of the modern state of Guerrero, numbered twelve towns. It was held, one-fourth by the Crown, one-fourth by Bernaldino Vázquez de Tapia, and one-half by Beatriz de Estrada.[10] The demographic history of the province in tabular form looks like this:

PROVINCE OF TLAPA

Towns	1560	1570	1597
Tlapa		952	
Atlixtac		244	
Caltitlán		689	
Atlimaxacingo		1,093	
Igualan		454	
Ixcateopan		283	
Petlacala		198	
Chiepetlán		258	
Tenango-Tepexi		243	
Azoyú		268	
Totomixtlahuacan		383	
Cuitlapa		308	
Totals	4,000 [a]	5,373 [a]	2,908 [a]

a Sources: "B," "J," and "P," respectively. The "J" list is the most detailed and carefully compiled of any, but "C," "E," "I," and "L" all give values between 5,332 and 5,500.

In Tlapa our speculation falls flat, because the rate of decline here is 45.9 per cent, against the general rate of 44.3 per cent. Evidently the joint holders did nothing to arrest the loss in that wild and little known country. We have, however, one more test to make. Outside of Avalos and Tlapa, the Crown held a half-interest in eighteen other encomiendas for which we have complete records. Their history, in tabular form, follows.

ENCOMIENDAS HELD JOINTLY BY CROWN AND ENCOMENDEROS

Towns	1560	1570	1597
Atlahuaca (Oaxaca)	2,000	1,396	1,076
Autlán (Jalisco)	1,100	682	111
Coixtlahuaca (Oaxaca)	1,000	3,800	3,590
Coyuquilla (Guerrero)	325	200	274
Cuatinchán (Puebla)	1,500	2,568	2,918
Jicayán and Atoyac (Oaxaca)	400	380	525
Malinalco (Mexico)	1,870	2,000	2,535
Mizquiahuala (Hidalgo)	340	806	877
Piaxtla (Puebla)	1,000	710	580
Tancítaro (Michoacán)	1,000	755	714
Tenango del Valle (Mexico).	1,400	777	788
Teopantlán (Puebla)	575	555	990
Teotlalco and Centayuca (Puebla)	5,190	4,221	3,200
Tequisistlán and Totolcingo (Mexico)	420	462	553
Tiltepec (Oaxaca)	160	200	238
Tlacozautitlán (Guerrero)	2,400	2,533	1,774
Tlaquilpa (Hidalgo)	900	866	482
Zoquitlán (Puebla)	440	422	312
Totals	21,020 [a]	19,533 [a]	17,947 [a]

[a] Sources: "B," "D," and "E," and "P," respectively. I used "D" only for the small town of Zoquitlán.

It is noteworthy that this large sample represents all parts of the Central Plateau—which seems to eliminate accidents of geography from possible explanation of this aberration. If we use our ordinarily dependable "E" list we find that the net loss between the 1560–1570 decade and 1597 was only 7.1 per cent. Even if we use the larger "B" value —which might here be justifiable—the loss is still only 14.6 per cent. The situation, then, in these jointly held towns is closely parallel to that of the Avalos group. Given the magnitude and wide spread of the sample, its consistent demographic history can hardly be ascribed to chance. Disregarding the vagary presented by the relatively unimportant Tlapa towns, we can only infer that conditions in most jointly held towns were exceptionally favorable to the Indian population. If our inference is correct it may be that there was a tendency for the Indians to migrate to them—which would partly account for their stable population. The phenomenon suggests one final observation; that is, it seems remarkable that in the century-old controversy over the proper disposition of the Indians it occurred to no one that their preservation would have been more probable if they had all been placed in joint encomiendas.

Notes

Abbreviations Used in the Notes

AGI: Archivo General de Indias, Seville, Spain.

AGN: Archivo General de la Nación, Mexico.

DII: *Colección de documentos inéditos relativos al descubrimiento, conquista y organización de las antiguas posesiones españolas.* 42 vols. Ed. Pacheco, Cárdenas and Mendoza. Madrid, 1864–1889.

DIM: *Colección de documentos para la historia de México.* 2 vols. Ed. J. García Icazbalceta. Mexico, 1858–1866.

DIU: *Colección de documentos inéditos relativos al descubrimiento, conquista y organización de las antiguas posesiones españolas de ultramar.* 2ª serie. 17 vols. Madrid, 1885–1925.

HAHR: *Hispanic American Historical Review.*

Puga: Vasco de Puga, *Provisiones, cédulas, instrucciones de su Majestad. . . .* 2 vols. Mexico, 1878.

[1] Solórzano, *Política Indiana*, I, 107–116.

[2] Oviedo, *Historia General*, I, 59–61; *Las Casas, Historia de las Indias*, II, 109–110; Isabella to Fonseca, April 16, 1495 (Navarrete, *Viages de Colón*, II, 173). "From 1508 to 1516 all purely administrative matters were attended to exclusively by Bishop Fonseca and the secretary [of the Council of Castile] Lope de Conchillos, and judicial matters were in the competence of the Council of Castile. . . . The name Council of the Indies appears for the first time in a cédula of September 14, 1519." (Ernesto Schäfer, *El Consejo Real y Supremo de las Indias*, I, 26–27, 35.)

[3] "There are in that island," wrote Columbus, "mountains and valleys and meadows, and beautiful fat lands for planting and sowing, for raising cattle of all kinds, for cities and villages. The ports are such as you would not believe unless you saw them, as are the many broad rivers of sweet waters, most of which are gold-bearing. . . . The people all go about naked as their mothers bore them, save only that some of the women cover a single part with a green leaf, or with a cotton cloth made for the purpose. They have no iron or steel or arms, nor are they apt for such things, not because they are not well set up and beautiful, but because they are wonderfully timorous. . . . They are so guileless and generous with what they possess that you would not believe it without seeing it." (Columbus to Luis de Santángel, Treasurer of Aragón, February 15, 1493. Navarrete, *op. cit.*, I, 167–175.)

[4] Ferdinand and Isabella to Fonseca, Jan. 13, 1496. (*DII*, XXXVIII, 352–354. Italics mine.)

[5] Columbus to Ferdinand and Isabella, Jan. 30, 1494. (Navarrete, *op. cit.*, I, 225–241.)

[6] Las Casas, *op. cit.*, II, 180–181. The story is accepted by Juan Bautista Muñoz, who observes that Niño's action was "an imprudence which angered the sovereigns, discredited the colony, and injured the Admiral unbelievably." (*Historia del Nuevo Mundo*, I, 256.)

[7] Herrera, *Historia General*, I, 256.

[8] Ferdinand and Isabella to Pedro de Torres, *contino* in the royal household, June 20, 1500. (*DII*, XXXVIII, 439–440, and note by J. B. Muñoz.) It may be well to remind the reader that, although edicts concerning the government of the Indies were issued in the names of both monarchs, the responsibility was the Queen's alone. Ferdinand did not assume the regency of the Indies until her death, in 1504.

[9] Ferdinand and Isabella to Diego Gómez de Cervantes, Corregidor of Jerez de la Frontera, Dec. 2, 1501. (*DII*, XXXI, 104–107. See also Las Casas, *op. cit.*, II, 435–447, and Oviedo, *op. cit.*, I, 76.)

[10] Contract of the Queen with Cristóbal Guerra, July 12, 1503. (*DII*, XXI, 187–193.)

[11] Isabella to all captains going to the Indies, August, 1503. (*DII*, XXXI, 196–200.)

[12] Ferdinand and Isabella to Nicolás de Ovando, Governor of Española, Feb. 5, 1504. (*DII*, XXXI, 214–215.)

[13] The Crown may have been influenced also by the loss of revenue, for slaves paid no tribute. There was a general emancipation of Indian slaves in New Spain between 1549 and 1552. (See L. B. Simpson, *The Emancipation of the Indian Slaves and the Resettlement of the Freedmen*.)

[14] Cédulas of Ferdinand and Isabella, June 22, 1497. (*DII*, XXXVIII, 386–391. See also Navarrete, *op. cit.*, II, 207, 209, 212; and Las Casas, *op. cit.*, II, 131–132.)

[15] Columbus to the Nurse of Prince John, 1500. (Navarrete, *op. cit.*, I, 271–276.)

[16] Las Casas, *op. cit.*, II, 134.

[17] Oviedo, *op. cit.*, I, 64.

[18] Columbus to Isabella, 1498. (Las Casas, *op. cit.*, II, 348.) Herrera, *op. cit.*, I, 118, 120.

[19] The reader will note multitudes of instances, like this one, in which the early Spanish lawmakers showed a total lack of comprehension of Indian culture. The primitive peoples of the Antilles, of course, had no conception of "tribute," "land values," and the rest. Later on, when the Council of the Indies came to include men experienced in Indian affairs, native customs were accepted as a kind of common law, where they did not conflict with Spanish law.

[20] L. B. Simpson, *The Repartimiento System of Native Labor in New Spain and Guatemala.*

[21] Instructions of Ferdinand and Isabella to Fray Nicolás de Ovando, Comendador de Lares, Sept. 16, 1501. (*DII*, XXXI, 13–25.) The prohibition of Jews, Moors, and the rest is encountered frequently in the first century of Spanish occupation—which leads us to suspect that a good many of them found their way to this continent.

[22] Columbus to the Nurse of Prince John, 1500. (Cited in n. 15.)

[23] Instructions of Ferdinand and Isabella to Nicolás de Ovando, March 29, 1503. (*DII*, XXI, 156–174.) The naïve attempts to legislate for the good of the Indians, without sacrificing the interests of the Crown or those of the colonists, persisted in all the codes of the Indies, although custom and common sense bent later practice in the direction of the "good of the commonwealth." (See below, chap. 3: The Laws of Burgos.)

[24] Ferdinand and Isabella to Ovando, March 29, 1503. (*DII*, XXXI, 174–179.)

[25] "The encomienda [of Castile]," writes Chamberlain, "consisted in the temporary grant by the sovereign, of territory, cities, towns, castles, and monasteries, with the powers of government and the right to receive the revenue, or a stipulated part thereof, and the services owed to the Crown by the people of the areas concerned. . . . In its jurisdictional aspect the encomienda was a charge of government, the comendador, or encomendero (*comendero*), exercising the authority of the Crown in the area involved, and in its territorial aspect it constituted a temporary patrimony." (Robert S. Chamberlain, *Castilian Backgrounds of the Repartimiento-Encomienda*, pp. 19–66.) We shall see that

the Crown had no intention of allowing the encomienda of Castile to be duplicated in the Indies.

[26] Isabella to Ovando, Dec. 20, 1503. (*DII*, XXXI, 209–212.)

[27] *Recopilación de las leyes de Indias*, VI, x, i.

[28] For example: "Could the poor Indians," exclaims Sir Arthur Helps, "but have known what a friend to them was dying, one continued wail would have gone up to heaven from Hispaniola and all the western islands." (*Spanish Conquest in America*, I, 150.) In a more rhapsodic vein the Mexican historian, Vicente Riva Palacio, sings her praises. "Without the unbreakable energy of Isabella the Catholic, and without that gesture of noble and Christian magnanimity, without that sweet affection which she professed for those who were then called Indians, and without the powerful influence which her example exercised over all the monarchs who succeeded her, the marketplaces of Europe, Asia, Africa, and America would have been filled to overflowing with slaves brought from Mexico and Peru. . . ." (*México a través de los siglos*, II, vii.)

NOTES TO CHAPTER 2

[1] Contract of Ferdinand with Vicente Yáñez Pinzón, April 24, 1505. (*DII*, XXXI, 309–317.)

[2] Ferdinand to Ovando, Nov. 15, 1505. (*DIU*, V, 110–113.)

[3] This view is contrary to the belief of some authorities. "The marriage of Spaniards with Indian women," writes Serrano y Sanz, "was a very general fact." (*Orígenes*, p. 384.) In his support he quotes a passage of Las Casas: "There was, and I saw it myself, a village or town called Vera Paz, of sixty Spanish inhabitants, most of them hidalgos, married to the native women of that land." (*Apologética Historia*, chap. xxiv.) Serrano y Sanz also quotes the report of Rodrigo de Alburquerque, who made a redistribution of the Indians of Española in 1514, showing that encomiendas were given to sixty Spaniards who had native wives. But an analysis of Alburquerque's report shows that he distributed 692 encomiendas among the Spaniards: 63 to Spaniards with native wives, 19 to women, and the remaining 475 to single men. That is, out of 673 possibilities there were 63 mixed marriages, or less than 10 per cent, and that after twenty years of Spanish occupation. As for Las Casas' "hidalgos," every Spaniard landing in the Indies considered himself *ipso facto* an hidalgo. The impartial Manzanedo, writing in 1518, says: "Many of those married to *cacicas* . . . are persons of little esteem and consequence." (Serrano y Sanz, *op. cit.*, appendix, p. 569.) For the town of Vera Paz, Alburquerque lists forty-eight encomiendas, only six of which were held by Spaniards with native wives, against the sixty attested by Las Casas.

[4] Ferdinand to Ovando, Feb. 8, 1505. (*DIU*, V, 67–70.)

[5] Ferdinand to Ovando, Oct. 21, 1507. (*DIU*, V, 117–120.)

[6] A clue to the King's motive is provided by the report of the *juez repartidor* Alburquerque, cited in n. 3. In his redistribution of the Indians the King re-

ceived 1,430 in encomienda, and other members of the Court received 3,720. The evil of absentee ownership of encomiendas was fought by colonists and missionaries alike, but it was not definitely forbidden until 1542.

[7] Ferdinand to Ovando, April 30, 1508. (*DII*, XXXII, 5–24; *DIU*, V, 125–145.)

[8] Contract of Ferdinand with Diego de Nicuesa, June 9, 1508. (*DII*, XXXII, 29–43.) The Indians of Tierra Firme, as it turned out, were the most skillful metallurgists of the New World and were in no need of instruction.

[9] Ferdinand to Ovando, July 13, 1508. (*DIU*, V, 148–155.)

[10] Ferdinand to Ovando, May 3, 1509. (*DII*, XXXI, 424–431.)

[11] Cédula of Ferdinand, Oct. 21, 1508. (*DII*, XXXII, 55–60.)

[12] The Crown never abandoned this stand, although some concessions were made later on. The only grant made in perpetuity was that of Cortés.

[13] The clergy were not disqualified from holding encomiendas until 1542.

[14] Instructions of Ferdinand to Diego Columbus, May 3, 1509. (*DII*, XXXI, 388–409.) In Alburquerque's report of the redistribution of 1514, of the 27,000 Indians allotted only 112 were assigned to churches, hospitals, monasteries, and individual priests.

[15] The wretches from the Bahamas were not, in fact, slaves but *naborias perpetuos,* a term which was familiar to the feudal-minded Spaniards as *vassallos patrimoniales,* that is, serfs not bound to the land. The Indians of Española were considered to be simple naborias, giving approximately two-thirds of their time to their encomenderos, the remaining third being used for the cultivation of their subsistence crops. The kidnaped Indians, having no land to cultivate, naturally had no need of time for themselves and so were forced to serve their masters perpetually—hence the name. The real difference between their status and that of chattel slaves is not cleared up by any document I have discovered. The question is an idle one in any case, because the kidnaped Indians hardly lived long enough to be interested in their civil status. Of the 60,000 Indians brought to Española from the Bahamas between 1509 and 1519, according to the Dominicans, only 800 were alive at the latter date. (The Dominicans of Española to Cardinal Chièvres, Dec. 4, 1519. *DII*, XXXV, 239–250.) The *juez de residencia,* Alonso Zuazo, two years earlier, reported that of the 15,000 Indians brought from the Bahamas 13,000 had perished. (Alonso Zuazo to Cardinal Chièvres, Jan. 22, 1518. *DII*, I, 304–317.) There is an excellent discussion of the origin of the naboria in J. H. Parry, *The Audiencia of New Galicia,* pp. 56–57.

[16] Ferdinand to Diego Columbus, Aug. 14, 1509. (*DII*, XXXI, 436–439.)

[17] Ferdinand to Diego Columbus, Aug. 14, 1509. (*DII*, XXXI, 449–452.) I have found no record that any such payment was ever made to the Crown by the encomenderos. In New Spain the tribute of one gold peso a year was retained by the encomendero, or, in the Crown towns, by the Crown.

[18] Ferdinand to Diego Columbus, Nov. 12, 1509. (*DII*, XXXI, 470–476.)

[19] Ferdinand to Diego Columbus, Nov. 14, 1509. (*DII*, XXXI, 487–505.)

[20] Ferdinand to Miguel de Pasamonte, Nov. 14, 1509. (*DII*, XXXI, 513–518.)

[21] Ferdinand to Diego Columbus and the royal officers, Feb. 28, 1510. (*DIU*, V, 200–205.)

²² Ferdinand to Diego Columbus and the royal officers, June 15, 1510. (*DII,* XXXII, 79–95; *DIU,* V, 227–241.) The discrepancy between the three-fourths tax on kidnaped Indians prescribed in the cédula of Aug. 14, 1509, and the four-fifths mentioned here is not explained. I suspect that neither was ever collected.

²³ The historian's impartiality is strained beyond endurance at this point. The ghastly stories of the destruction of the Bahamas Indians circulated by Las Casas and the Dominican missionaries could very well be true if conditions were bad enough to make the incredible Ferdinand's conscience bother him. "In truth," wrote Las Casas, "one [of these slavers] told me that from the Lucayos [Bahamas], where great havoc was wrought in this manner, to Española, a distance of sixty or seventy leagues, a ship might sail without compass or chart, guiding itself solely by the trail of dead Indians who had been thrown from the ships" (*Brevissima Relación,* p. 266). The Dominican missionaries, writing thirty years before the appearance of Las Casas' book of horrors, testified: "It happened that every time that Indians were brought from their lands so many died of hunger on the way that we think that by their trail in the sea another ship might find its way to port." (The Dominican Fathers to Cardinal Chièvres, Dec. 4, 1519. *DII,* XXXV, 233.)

²⁴ Ferdinand to Pasamonte, June 5, 1511. (*DII,* XXXII, 153–163.)

²⁵ Ferdinand to Diego Columbus, June 21, 1511. (*DIU,* V, 266–267.)

²⁶ Ferdinand to Diego Columbus, June 22, 1511. (*DIU,* V, 267–269.)

²⁷ Cédula of Ferdinand, June 22, 1511. (*DIU,* V, 262–264.)

²⁸ Ferdinand to Diego Columbus and the royal officers, June 25, 1511. (*DII,* XXXII, 185–198.)

²⁹ Cédula of Ferdinand, July 3, 1511. (*DIU,* V, 258–262.)

NOTES TO CHAPTER 3

¹ It seems unlikely that the aboriginal population of Española was more than 500,000. Las Casas typically makes it 3,000,000. (*Historia de las Indias,* III, 359.)

² Las Casas, *op. cit.,* III, 372. Oviedo also attributed the destruction of the islanders partly to their wickedness: "And added to this . . . were the great, hideous, and enormous sins and abominations of this savage and bestial people." (*Historia General,* I, 72.)

³ Fonseca was Las Casas' *bête noire,* for he opposed all Las Casas' schemes for the salvation of the New World, and he is consequently given a great deal of space in the *Historia de las Indias.* Las Casas is followed by most writers for the character of Fonseca. E. G. Bourne is an exception. (*Spain in America,* pp. 221–222.) In support of Las Casas it may be pointed out that Fonseca received an encomienda of 244 Indians in Alburquerque's redistribution of 1514, although in accepting it he only followed the example of the King and all the others concerned in the government of the Indies. The interlocking interests of the Court are well shown by Alburquerque's report, in which officials and relatives are rewarded in Indians as follows (*DII,* I, 50–236):

The King	1,430
Juan de Fonseca, Bishop of Burgos	244
Lope de Conchillos, Secretary of the Council of Castile	264
Hernando de la Vega, member of the same	745
Maria de Toledo, wife of Diego Columbus	428
Diego Columbus, Admiral of the Indies	250
Ferdinand Columbus, bastard son of Christopher	206
Miguel de Pasamonte, Treasurer-General of the Indies	251
Juan Cabrero, the King's Chamberlain	424
Almanza, the King's Secretary	238
Lucas Vázquez de Ayllón, Appellate Judge of the Indies	440
Rodrigo de Alburquerque, *Juez Repartidor*	270
Total	5,250

[4] Herrera, *Historia General*, I, 244–245. For a more exhaustive treatment of the Dominican effort and its political philosophy the reader is referred to Lewis Hanke, *First Social Experiments in America,* and to Silvio Zavala, *La Encomienda Indiana,* and *Filosofía de la Conquista.*

[5] Las Casas, *op. cit.,* III, 361–453.

[6] Ferdinand was not so stricken with remorse that he refused to accept the encomienda of 1,430 Indians allotted to him shortly afterward in Alburquerque's redistribution.

[7] Roland D. Hussey, "Text of the Laws of Burgos," *HAHR,* XII, 306–321; L. B. Simpson, *The Laws of Burgos of 1512.*

[8] The congregation of scattered Indians into larger units became a fixed policy of the Crown. Toward the end of the sixteenth century the congregation of all such Indians was decreed and partly accomplished in New Spain, the methods and aims being substantially the same as those laid down in the Laws of Burgos. (L. B. Simpson, *The Civil Congregation.*)

[9] Presumably in Latin. This article and the five following are sufficient proof that the Crown intended to restrict the jurisdiction of the encomendero to that of a lay missionary. See also Art. 12.

[10] This laudable principle seems never to have been enforced. In New Spain the excessive fees charged by priests for administering the sacraments were the cause of continuous complaints in the Juzgado General de Indios until the end of the Old Regime.

[11] By giving the Franciscans the responsibility and the privilege of educating Indian boys the Crown seems to have been showing its disapproval of the agitating Dominicans. This is the only article in which either of the orders is mentioned. Serrano y Sanz advances the thesis that the Dominicans were in actual rebellion against the Crown. (*Orígenes,* p. 351.) In New Spain, later on, the Franciscans fell into equal disfavor for agitating against the notorious Nuño de Guzmán and the first Audiencia.

[12] The enforcement of all articles is put into the hands of royal inspectors or commissioners (*visitadores*).

[13] It is clear, even at this early date, that the Indian was considered to be a ward of the Crown and that, as such, he could legally be forced to work only for the public benefit. This is the premise by which all forced labor of "free" Indians was justified throughout the colonial period.

[14] All public servants above a certain category were required by Spanish law

to submit to a kind of trial (*residencia*) after the expiration of their terms in office. Charges of misconduct and claims for damages could be brought against them for a limited time, and their salaries were held back until they were cleared.

[15] A dead letter. Alburquerque paid no attention to this provision in his redistribution, and the encomenderos of New Spain (where, to be sure, there were more Indians) were originally limited only by the supply and by their standing with Cortés.

[16] Las Casas, *op. cit.*, III, 442–445.

[17] Cédula of Ferdinand, Oct. 19, 1514. (*DIU*, IX 22–23.) Ferdinand to Diego Columbus, Feb. 5, 1515. (*DIU*, IX, 52–53.) Alburquerque's redistribution shows, however, that Spaniards with Spanish wives received on the average twice as many Indians as did Spaniards with native wives. Their difference in treatment could, of course, be owing to other factors, such as difference in rank.

[18] The Dominicans of Española to Cardinal Chièvres, Dec. 4, 1519. (*DII*, XXXV, 239–250.) The document is also reproduced in Fabié, *Vida de las Casas*, II, 19–42, with the erroneous date of June 4, 1516. This letter carries much more weight than the classic of the period, Las Casas' grisly *Brevíssima Relación de la Destruyción de las Indias* which was written thirty years later.

[19] Las Casas, *Historia de las Indias*, IV, 253–255.

[20] The literature on the subject is voluminous and has lately been augmented by the publication of Las Casas' famous tract, *De Unico Vocationis Modo*, an essay in which he demonstrated his not inconsiderable legal talent and wide learning. (Ed. and translated by Agustín Millares Carlo, Antenógenes Santamaría, and Lewis Hanke. See also Hanke's *The Spanish Struggle for Justice in the Sixteenth Century*, Part III.)

Notes to Chapter 4

[1] Las Casas' account of the Jeronymite administration of the Indies shows him at his worst. It is seventy pages of glorification of himself and disparagement of his opponents. Unfortunately for the fame of the Jeronymites, the *Historia de las Indias* (IV, 277–347) has been the most accessible source for the history of their administration. Serrano y Sanz undertook a belated rectification of it in his *Orígenes de la dominación española en América* (pp. 339–450), with an abundance of corroborative testimony.

[2] Sigüenza, *Historia de la Orden de San Jerónimo*, II, 101–110.

[3] In the adjustment following the enactment of the New Laws of 1542 a number of ex-encomenderos were made corregidores of Indian towns, or were put on straight pensions paid out of tributes.

[4] Evidently a common condition among the Spanish colonists. It will be recalled that Vasco Núñez de Balboa, in order to escape his creditors, hid himself in a cask on board one of the vessels of the *Bachiller* Fernández de Enciso.

[5] Instructions of Cardinal Cisneros to the Jeronymite Fathers, Sept., 1516. (*DIU*, IX, 53–75.)

⁶ Las Casas, *Historia de las Indias*, IV, 295.

⁷ Serrano y Sanz, *Orígenes*, p. 344.

⁸ "When Diego Velázquez learned of it . . . he sent a delegate to the island of Española with a certain account which he made to the Fathers of St. Jerome, who resided there as governors of these Indies, so that they, in the name of their Majesties, . . . should give him permission to explore the said land." (Hernán Cortés, *Cartas y Relaciones*, p. 40.)

⁹ Instructions of Cardinal Cisneros to Las Casas, Sept. 16, 1516. (Las Casas, *Historia de las Indias*, IV, 316–317.)

¹⁰ Jeronymite Fathers to Cardinal Cisneros, Jan. 20, 1517. (*DII*, I, 264–281.)

¹¹ Jeronymite Fathers to Cardinal Cisneros, June 22, 1517 (extract). (*DII*, XXXIV, 199–201.)

¹² Miguel de Pasamonte to Cardinal Cisneros, July 10, 1517. (Serrano y Sanz, *Orígenes*, Appendix, p. 558.)

¹³ Interrogatory held by the Jeronymite Fathers, 1517. (*DII*, XXXIV, 201–229.)

¹⁴ Alonso Zuazo to the King, Feb. 22, 1518. (*DII*, XXXIV, 237–267.)

¹⁵ Alonso Zuazo to Cardinal Chièvres, Jan. 22, 1518. (*DII*, I, 304–332.) The Dominican missionaries, in their letter already cited, set the figure of the kidnaped Indians at 60,000, of whom, they said, only 800 were alive in December, 1519. Zuazo's figure is the more credible, given the pious rage of the missionaries.

¹⁶ The responsibility for the introduction of Negro slaves into the New World has never been fixed. In any case it was an obvious and inevitable solution of the labor problem, and was advocated by virtually all the early reformers, including Las Casas. The Empress Isabel, in a letter to the governor of Tierra Firme, directed him to suppress the rebellious Negro slaves who had been brought to the Indies "in an evil hour" at the instance of Las Casas. (The Empress to the Governor of Tierra Firme, April 4, 1531. DIU, X, 72.)

¹⁷ Jeronymite Fathers to the King, Feb. 15, 1518. (*DII*, XXXIV, 279–286.) Their estimate of the total population, therefore, is between 10,000 and 13,000, unless they were counting only householders or heads of families. In the latter case the total population would be between 40,000 and 65,000.

¹⁸ Manzanedo accurately predicted the danger from runaway Negroes (*cimarrones*) who joined rebellious native groups or set up colonies of their own in mountain fastnesses, from which they raided commerce and white and Indian settlements. Tierra Firme, because of its large number of Negro slaves, was long molested by cimarrones. "Near the town [of Nombre de Dios] the jungle begins, which is so heavily wooded that one cannot get through it except by hacking down the thick and tangled branches. The cimarrones are thus enabled to fortify themselves in it because of their skill in hiding and defending themselves, and it often happens that they slip into the city without being heard . . . and seize the Negresses whom they find there." Our informant goes on to say that the cimarrones were especially dangerous when they got into contact with the French and English, who gave them arms, and they formed themselves into military companies and attacked the pack trains crossing the

Isthmus. (Dr. Criado de Castilla, *Sumaria descripción del Reyno de Tierra Firme*, May 7, 1575. Quoted by Carlos Pereyra, *Historia de América Española*, V, 176–178.) In Guatemala, according to Thomas Gage, "What the Spaniards most fear, until they come out of the mountains, are some two or three hundred Blackmoors, Simarrones, who for too much hard usage have fled from Guatemala and other parts from their masters to these woods, and there they live and bring up their children and increase daily, so that all the power of Guatemala, nay, all the Country about (having attempted it) is not able to bring them under subjection." (*New Guide to the West-Indies*, p. 291.)

[19] Bernardino de Manzanedo to the King, 1518. (Serrano y Sanz, *Orígenes*, Appendix, pp. 567–575.)

[20] Jeronymite Fathers to the King, Jan. 10, 1519. (*DII*, I, 366–368.)

[21] The King to the Jeronymite Fathers, Aug. 22, 1518, and Dec. 9, 1518. (Serrano y Sanz, *op. cit.*, pp. 441–442.)

[22] Las Casas, *Historia de las Indias*, V, 159.

[23] Rodrigo de Figueroa to Charles V, July 6, 1520. (*DII*, I, 417–421.)

[24] Figueroa to the King, 1520. (*DII*, I, 379–385.) The King to Figueroa, May 18, 1520. (Serrano y Sanz, *op. cit.*, Appendix, pp. 605–607.)

NOTES TO CHAPTER 5

[1] Cabildo of Vera Cruz to the King, July 10, 1519. (Cortés, *Cartas*, pp. 1–34.)

[2] Hernán Cortés to Charles V, May 15, 1522. (Cortés, *Cartas*, p. 271.)

[3] There has been a good deal of confusion among writers about the meanings of these two terms but their etymology makes the distinction between them clear enough: *repartimiento* deriving from *repartir*, "to allot or distribute"; *encomienda* from *encomendar*, "to give in trust." Repartimiento was frequently used in official documents for encomienda, but the former term had several other applications, as has been brought out by F. A. Kirkpatrick. He lists three common usages of repartimiento: "1. The distribution (in fact, forcible sale) of goods to the Indians by corregidores. This use, where *repartimiento* means *repartición*, cannot be confused with the other two. 2. The allotment of groups or gangs of Indian labourers to works such as tillage, building, mining, transport; or the labour gang itself thus allotted. 3. The allotment of encomiendas (*repartimiento de encomiendas*) or the encomienda itself." (*HAHR*, XIX, 373–379.) R. S. Chamberlain, in an attempt to get around the difficulty, adopted the term "repartimiento-encomienda," which is justifiable but awkward.

[4] A reference to the famous *requerimiento*, a document concocted by the advisers of Ferdinand the Catholic which the Spanish explorers were supposed to read to the Indians before undertaking their conquest. If the Indians did not accept the message contained in it they might be subjugated by force. It is probably the most naïve document ever written and excited a humorous vein in even that solemn historian of the conquest, Sir Arthur Helps. "I confess that the comicality of the document has often cheered me in the midst of tedious research, or endless details of small battles." (*Spanish Conquest in America*, I,

383.) The first paragraph of the requerimiento will give a notion of its general tenor: "On the part of the King, Don Fernando, and of Doña Juana, his daughter, Queen of Castile and León, subduers of the barbarous nations, we their servants notify and make known to you, as best we can, that the Lord our God, Living and Eternal, created Heaven and Earth, and one man and one woman, of whom you and we, and all the men in the world, were and are descendants, and all those who come after us. But, on account of the multitude which has sprung from this man and woman in the five thousand years since the world was created, it was inevitable that some men should go one way and some another, and that they should be divided into many kingdoms and provinces, for in one alone they could not be sustained." (Lewis Hanke, "The Requerimiento and its Interpreters," in the *Revista de Historia de América*, I, 25–34. See also the same author's *The Spanish Struggle for Justice in the Conquest of America*, chap. iii.) Hanke concludes that the requerimiento, in spite of its jargon, is at least evidence that the preaching of Montesinos had "disturbed the Court" (p. 36). It undoubtedly did, but it seems to me that the requerimiento was the kind of response that might be expected from the cynical Ferdinand; it was a lawyer's way out of an uncomfortable situation.

⁵ The Council of the Indies was unacquainted with Indian hospitality. It was not always necessary to seize women. Cortes was embarrassed by the profusion of concubines pressed upon him by his hosts. The most famous was, of course, Doña Marina, who acted as his interpreter during the conquest.

⁶ Instructions of Charles V to Hernán Cortés, June 26, 1523. (*DIU*, IX, 167–181.) The main provisions had already appeared in a similar document issued to Francisco de Garay in 1521 for the "discovery" of Pánuco. (Navarrete, *Viages*, III, 147–153.)

⁷ Charles V to Cortés, Oct. 15, 1522. (*DII*, XXVI, 65–70.)

⁸ Cortés to Charles V, Oct. 15, 1524. (*DIM*, I, 470–483.)

⁹ The intrigues of Cortés are well described in Luis González Obregón, *Los Precursores de la Independencia Mexicana en el Siglo XVI.*

¹⁰ Solórzano, *Política Indiana*, II, 7–8.

¹¹ Instructions of Charles V to Luis Ponce de León, Nov. 4, 1525. (*DIU*, IX, 214–226. See also the secret instructions to the same in the "Residencia de Cortés," *Archivo Mexicano*, I, 25–28.)

¹² The usefulness of missions in stabilizing the conquest, as suggested by Cortés, was recognized by the Crown throughout the period of imperial expansion. (See discussion by C. H. Haring, *The Spanish Empire in America*, pp. 202–203.)

¹³ Cortés to Charles V, 1524. (*DII*, XII, 277–285.)

¹⁴ The four were respectively treasurer, accountant, inspector, and factor. Among their wide responsibilities they collected and forwarded the King's revenue, paid salaries, etc., and, in this case, they advised Cortés in the government. They had been appointed October 15, 1522. (*DII*, XXVI, 65–70.) For a brief description of their functions see L. E. Fisher, *Viceregal Administration in the Spanish-American Colonies*, pp. 99–101; H. I. Priestley, *José de Gálvez*, pp. 78–79.

15 The two-years dictatorship of Chirinos and Salazar is well documented. For Cortés' side see the memorial of Juan de Ortega, *et al.*, to Charles V, Feb. 20, 1526. (Cortés, *Cartas*, pp. 341–350.) Also Cortés to Charles V, Sept. 11, 1526. (*Ibid.*, pp. 369–376.) For the opposing side see Diego de Ocaña to the Council of the Indies, Sept. 17, 1526. (*Ibid.*, pp. 351–367.) Also Rodrigo de Albornoz to Charles V, Dec. 15, 1525. (*DII*, XIII, 45–84, and Appendix to this volume.)

16 There were not lacking among Cortés' enemies those who thought that Ponce's death and the earlier one of Francisco de Garay were too opportune to have been entirely accidental. The circumstances of Ponce's death looked particularly suspicious, but nothing was proved against Cortés in his residencia, which was dominated by his archenemy, Nuño de Guzmán. In any case it hardly seems necessary to attribute Ponce's death to poison; rather it would have been extraordinary if the old man had survived the long voyage across the Atlantic, with bad food and worse water. For a full account of the episode see Luis González Obregón, *Los Precursores de la Independencia Mexicana*, pp. 40–57, 108–126.

17 Alonso de Estrada to Charles V, Sept. 20, 1526. (*DII*, XIII, 84–86.)

18 Instructions of Charles V to Luis Ponce de León, Nov. 4, 1525. (*DIU* IX, 214–226.)

19 Cortés to Charles V, Sept. 11, 1526. (Cortés, *Cartas*, pp. 369–376.)

20 Ordinances of Cortés for the government of the Indians, n.d. (*DII*, XXVI, 163–170.) *Idem* for the government of the Spaniards, March 20, 1524. (*DII*, XXVI, 135–148.)

21 Instructions of Hernán Cortés to Francisco Cortés, his lieutenant in the town of Colima, 1524. (*DII*, XXVI, 149–159.)

22 Rodrigo de Albornoz to Charles V, Dec. 15, 1525. (*DII*, XIII, 45–80, and Appendix to this volume.) It should be borne in mind that Albornoz, who was a Cortés man, was writing during the administration of Chirinos and Salazar, when the Velázquez faction was having a field day looting the country.

23 Cortés to Hernando de Saavedra, his lieutenant at Truxillo and La Natividad de Nuestra Señora, 1525. (*DII*, XXVI, 185–194.)

24 Charles V to Luis Ponce de León, Nov. 9, 1526. (Puga, I, 31–33.)

To judge by the number and vigor of the instructions regarding Indian slavery, many of the conquerors had gone into the business. Juan de Torquemada, who, to be sure, is not the most trustworthy witness, remarks that the Indian children were never sent to Spain, because their parents had the notion that they were going to be sold into slavery, and they raised such an outcry that the project had to be abandoned and an explanation sent to the Empress, the author of the scheme. (*Monarquía Indiana*, III, 262.)

25 Cédula of Charles V, Nov. 17, 1526. (*DIU*, IX, 268–280.)

26 Charles V to Juan de Zumárraga, Jan. 10, 1528. (Puga, I, 227–231.)

Notes to Chapter 6

[1] Instructions of Charles V to the Audiencia of Mexico, April 5, 1528. (Puga, I, 47–53.)

[2] Charles V to the Audiencia of Mexico, April 5, 1528. (Puga, I, 54–55; Solórzano, *Política Indiana,* I, 257.)

[3] Charles V to Nuño de Guzmán, April 5, 1528. (Puga, I, 62–83.)

[4] How the Council of the Indies could have chosen a notorious adventurer and spoiler like Nuño de Guzmán for such a high post is indeed difficult to explain. It may be that he had been orally briefed before setting out; he clearly conceived his principal duty to be the destruction of Cortés. In support of this theory it may be pointed out that the misconduct of the first Audiencia did not bring about his disgrace. On the contrary, he was allowed to complete his calamitous conquest of New Galicia and to remain there as governor until 1537.

[5] Cortés was very friendly to the Franciscans and had urged that the conversion of New Spain be put in their hands. The Franciscans reciprocated and were always warm partisans of Cortés. The Dominicans were thus forced into the uncomfortable position of supporting Nuño de Guzmán, a position which they were obligated to take in any case because of their tie-in with the Council of the Indies. These important political alliances have never been properly brought out. It may be doubted, however, that Zumárraga was a henchman of Cortés. Not only was he a sturdy and incorruptible zealot, but he laid much of the blame for the factions in Mexico at the door of Cortés. (See his famous letter to Charles V of August 27, 1529, in J. García Icazbalceta, *Don Fray Juan de Zumárraga,* Appendix 3, and the extract of it translated in the Appendix to this volume. For a succinct and authoritative discussion of the important role of the Mendicant orders in New Spain, see George Kubler, *Mexican Architecture of the Sixteenth Century,* I, 1–21.)

[6] Accusation of Nuño de Guzmán against Fray Juan de Zumárraga, April 29, 1529. (*DII,* XL, 468–560.)

[7] Juan de Zumárraga to Charles V, Aug. 27, 1529. (J. García Icazbalceta, *Don Fray Juan de Zumárraga,* Appendix, pp. 1–42.) The importance of this letter is such that I have translated and abstracted the more pertinent sections of it in the Appendix.

[8] Charles V to the Audiencia of Mexico, June 5, 1528. (Puga, I, 110–112.)

[9] Charles V to all royal officers of the Indies, Sept. 19, 1528. (*DIU,* IX, 368–371.) This decree was later incorporated into the New Laws, Art. 27. (See chap. 10, below.)

[10] Charles V to the Audiencia of Mexico, the Bishops of Tlaxcala, Mexico, *et al.,* Sept. 19, 1528. (*DIU,* IX, 372–375.) Same to same, Nov. 20, 1528. (Puga, I, 116–119; *DIU,* IX, 379–383.)

[11] By Rodrigo de Albornoz, in his letter cited in chap. 5, n. 22.

[12] Charles V to the Audiencia of Mexico, *et al.,* Dec. 4, 1528. (*DIU,* IX, 386–399.)

[13] Herrera, *Historia General,* II, 148–151.

[14] *Ibid.,* II, 151.

[15] The Queen to the Audiencia of Mexico, Aug. 24, 1529. (Puga, I, 140–141.)

[16] Same to same, Aug. 10, 1529. (*DIU,* IX, 423–424.)

[17] Same to same, Aug. 10, 1529. (Puga, I, 136–137; Torquemada, *Monarquía Indiana,* III, 257; *DIU,* IX, 425–426.)

[18] Same to same, Aug. 24, 1529. (Puga, I, 139–140; Torquemada, *op. cit.,* III, 257; *DIU,* IX, 426–428.)

[19] Same to same, Aug. 24, 1529. (*DIU,* IX, 434–439.)

[20] The Queen to the royal officers of New Spain, Oct. 8, 1529. (*DIU,* IX, 439–440.)

[21] The Queen to the Audiencia of Mexico, Oct. 8, 1529. (*DIU,* IX, 444–447.)

[22] E. Schäfer, *El Consejo Real y Supremo de las Indias,* II, 7–10.

NOTES TO CHAPTER 7

[1] Audiencia of Mexico to the Empress, March 30, 1531. (Ternaux-Compans, *Voyages,* 2e série, V, 128–149.)

[2] Juan de Salmerón to the Council of the Indies, Jan. 31, 1531. (*DII,* XIII, 186–195; Aiton, *Antonio de Mendoza,* pp. 22–24.)

[3] Diego de Encinas, *Cedulario Indiano,* III, 7. (Quoted by Silvio Zavala, *La Encomienda Indiana,* pp. 63–64.)

[4] Instructions of the Queen to the corregidores of New Spain, n.d. (Puga, I, 217–219.)

[5] Instructions to governors and corregidores of the Indies, et al., July 12, 1530. (Puga, I, 203–216.)

[6] Audiencia of Mexico to the Empress, March 30, 1531. (Ternaux-Compans, *op. cit.,* V, 130.) In practice the salaries of these officers varied considerably from the published scale. In the decade of 1540–1550 corregidores were paid an average of 200 pesos a year; alguaciles, 220; chaplains, 150. By that time the jobs were much sought after. ("Memoria de los corregimientos de la Nueva España," Paso y Troncoso, *Papeles de Nueva España,* II, 23–49.)

[7] The Queen to the Audiencia of Mexico, July 12, 1530. (Puga, I, 154–185.)

[8] The Queen to all officers of the Indies, Aug. 2, 1530. (Puga, I, 231–234; *DIU,* X, 38–43.)

[9] The Queen to Zumárraga, Aug. 2, 1530. (Puga, I, 227–231.)

[10] The Queen to the Audiencia of Mexico, Apr. 20, 1533. (Puga, I, 291–302.)

[11] In a list of conquerors and settlers compiled at the time of the visita of Tello de Sandoval in 1544, eighty encomenderos are named who had lost their encomiendas by confiscation, mostly small fry. (Icaza, *Conquistadores y Pobladores de Nueva España.*) The oidor Ceynos wrote that more than two hundred encomiendas granted by the first Audiencia were annulled by the second. (Francisco de Ceynos to Philip II, 1565. *DIM,* II, 237–243.)

[12] Juan de Salmerón to the Council of the Indies, Jan. 23, 1531. (*DII,* XIII, 186–195.)

[13] For the extremely interesting history of the founding of Puebla, see François Chevalier, "Signification sociale de la fondation de Puebla de los Angeles." (*Revista de Historia de América,* No. 23, pp. 105–130.)

[14] The Audiencia of Mexico to the Empress, Mar. 30, 1531. (Ternaux-Compans, *op. cit.,* V, 128–149.) The juego de cañas was a jousting game in which two mounted teams, armed with light canes and shields, maneuvered and tossed the canes at one another. The main purpose of the game seems to have been to allow the players to display their horsemanship for the benefit of female onlookers. It was a favorite sport in colonial Mexico.

[15] Juan de Salmerón to the Council of the Indies, Mar. 30, 1531. (*DII,* XIII, 195–205.)

[16] The Audiencia of Mexico to Charles V, Aug. 14, 1531. (Ternaux-Compans, *op. cit.,* V, 150–182.)

[17] Salmerón to the Council of the Indies, Aug. 13, 1531. (Ternaux-Compans, *op. cit.,* V, 183–197.)

[18] Jerónimo López to Charles V, n.d. (*Documentos inéditos para la historia de Ibero-América,* I, 45–48.) López' whine is typical of the encomenderos and is a typical misstatement. He held in encomienda the town of Axacuba (in the modern state of Hidalgo) which at that time had 2,985 tributaries (heads of families) and yielded an income of 1,840 gold pesos a year. (Paso y Troncoso, *Papeles de Nueva España,* I, 20–21.) López was for many years a regidor of the city of Mexico and at the time of his death was a fairly wealthy man. (See his will published in the *probanza* of his son. *Publicaciones del Archivo General de la Nación,* XII, 220–331.)

[19] Jerónimo López to Charles V, July 4, 1532. (*Documentos inéditos para la historia de Ibero-América,* I, 19–21.)

[20] The Queen to the Audiencia of Mexico, Dec. 10, 1531. (Torquemada, *op. cit.,* III, 259.)

[21] The Queen to the Audiencia of Mexico, Mar. 20, 1532. (Puga, I, 252–253; *DIU,* X, 136–137.)

[22] The Queen to the Audiencia of Mexico, Mar. 20, 1532. (Puga, I, 256–274; *DIU,* X, 106–135.)

[23] The Queen to the Audiencia of Mexico, Apr. 15, 1532. (Solórzano, *op. cit.,* II, 23.)

NOTES TO CHAPTER 8

[1] The *cacao* was a standard medium of exchange among the ancient Mexicans and was adopted by the Spaniards as currency in their trade with the Indians. It was valued at 80 to 100 to the *real,* 640 to 800 to the *peso de oro común,* 30 to 38 pesos to the carga of 24,000 cacaos which in turn was divided into three *xiquipiles* of 8,000 each. (Suárez de Peralta, *Noticias Históricas de la Nueva España,* pp. 166–167.) The cacao was still used in Humboldt's time (1803). "The cacao is still made use of as a sort of inferior coin in Mexico." (*Political Essay on New Spain,* II, 26.)

[2] Audiencia of New Spain to the Empress, Apr. 19, 1532. (Ternaux-Compans, *Voyages,* V, 201–207.)

[3] Fuenleal to Charles V, Apr. 30, 1532. (*DII,* XIII, 206–224.)

[4] Fuenleal to Charles V, July 10, 1532. (*DII,* XIII, 224–230.)

[5] Fuenleal to Charles V, Sept. 18, 1532. (*DII,* XIII, 233–237.)

The Tlaxcalans continued to be the petted darlings (comparatively speaking) of the government throughout the colonial period. They were exempted from personal services as a reward for their aid in the conquest, they were made virtually autonomous, and their tribute was hardly more than a token, 8,000 fanegas of maize a year. ("Relación de los pueblos que están en la Corona Real" [*ca.* 1570]. MS, AGI, *Audiencia de México,* leg. 323 [60–3–23]).

[6] Fuenleal to Charles V, Nov. 3, 1532. (*DII,* XIII, 250–261.)

The repeated references to the slave-trade and mining complex in this period probably arose from the discovery of silver and gold deposits in Michoacán, Colima, and Jalisco. There was a regular gold rush to the west during these years, and the slave-catching gangs virtually depopulated large sections of the coast. (C. O. Sauer, *Colima of New Spain in the Sixteenth Century,* pp. 84–96.)

[7] The Audiencia of Mexico to the Queen, Nov. 3, 1532. (Ternaux-Compans, *op. cit.,* V, 208–213.)

[8] Salmerón to the Queen, Nov. 1, 1532. (Ternaux-Compans, *op. cit.,* V, 207.)

[9] Fray Martín de Valencia, *et al.,* to the Empress, Jan. 18, 1533. (Ternaux-Compans, *op. cit.,* pp. 224–228.)

[10] The Queen to the Audiencia of Mexico, Apr. 20, 1533. (Puga, I, 291–302.)

[11] The recitation in Latin of certain parts of the service was obligatory. Other measures generally thought necessary for the salvation of the Indians were monogamy, the segregation of the sexes between puberty and matrimony, and the adoption of European dress, for the missionaries were properly horrified by nakedness. It will be recalled that early missionaries to the Sandwich Islands dressed the natives in mother-hubbards. The disastrous effects of such regulation are well known. (See Peveril Meigs, 3rd, *The Dominican Mission Frontier of Lower California;* S. F. Cook, *Population Trends among the California Mission Indians.*)

[12] Opinion of the Council of the Indies on the government of the Indies, Nov. 18, 1533. (*DII,* XII, 133–142.)

[13] Charles V to the Audiencia of Mexico, Aug. 2, 1533. (Puga, I, 309–312.)

[14] It was characteristic of visitadores that their reports should reflect the wishes of their superiors. There is abundant evidence that the Marquesado was relatively well managed. Certainly the rich province of Cuernavaca was never in any danger of being "abandoned" by the Indians or anyone else. (See chap. 11, below.)

[15] Declaration of the tribute paid to Hernán Cortés by the Indians of Cuernavaca, Jan. 24, 1533. (*DII,* XIV, 142–147.)

The payment of tribute in kind, a system taken over from the Aztecs, persisted until about 1560 and made any kind of understandable bookkeeping impossible. Cortés had been granted a total of 23,000 tributaries for the Marquesado, and he was repeatedly and justly accused of concealing the actual number. (Cook and Simpson, *The Population of Central Mexico in the Sixteenth Century*, pp. 4–6.)

In the earlier *residencia* of Cortés held by Nuño de Guzmán and the first *Audiencia* he was accused of all the abuses mentioned by García and a great many more, including assorted murders, but it was so manifestly loaded against him that the Council of the Indies ignored it. The whole *residencia* may be found in the *Archivo Mexicano: Documentos para la historia de México*.

[16] Salmerón to the Council of the Indies, Aug. 13, 1531. (Ternaux-Compans, *op. cit.*, V, 196.) The Audiencia of Mexico to Charles V, Aug. 14, 1531. (Ternaux-Compans, *op. cit.*, pp. 150–182.)

[17] Charles V to all officers of the Indies, Feb. 20, 1534. (*DII*, X, 192–203.)

[18] Woodrow Borah, "The Collection of Tithes in the Bishopric of Oaxaca during the Sixteenth Century." (*HAHR*, XXI, 389.)

[19] "Relación ... de las tasaciones de los pueblos de yndios ... que están encomendados en personas particulares" (1560), MS. AGI, *Indiferente General*, leg. 1529 [145-7-8]. (It is also available, in a rather faulty transcription, in Paso y Troncoso, *Epistolario de Nueva España*, IX, 2–48.)

The royal towns are in a separate list: "Relación ... de las tasaciones de los pueblos de yndios ... que están en la Real Corona" (1560), MS. AGI, *Patronato*, leg. 181 [2-2-3], ramo 38. (It is not included in Paso y Troncoso's *Epistolario*.)

[20] Charles V to the Audiencia of Mexico, Apr. 3, 1534. (*DIU*, X, 205–206.)

[21] L. B. Simpson, *The Repartimiento System of Native Labor in New Spain and Guatemala*, pp. 82–92.

[22] Charles V to the Audiencia of Mexico, Apr. 18 and May 4, 1534. (*DIU*, X, 206–208.) Same to all officers of the Indies, May 4, 1534. (*DIU*, X, 210–211.)

[23] Schäfer, *El Consejo Real y Supremo de las Indias*, I, 70, 354.

[24] Bernal Díaz del Castillo, *Verdadera y notable relación del descubrimiento y conquista de la Nueva España y Guatemala*, II, 243–244.

NOTES TO CHAPTER 9

[1] A. S. Aiton, *Antonio de Mendoza*, p. 42, citing the *Actas del Cabildo* of Mexico City for November 12 and 13, 1535.

[2] Aiton, *op. cit.*, pp. 34–42. For the complicated functions of the viceroy see, besides Aiton, L. E. Fisher, *Viceregal Administration in the Spanish-American Colonies, passim*; C. H. Haring, *The Spanish Empire in America*, pp. 119–136; and especially Schäfer, *El Consejo Real y Supremo de las Indias*, II, chap. i.

[3] Instructions of the Queen to Antonio de Mendoza, Apr. 25, 1535. (*DIU*, X, 245–263; *DII*, XXIII, 426–445.)

[4] Mendoza to Charles V, Dec. 10, 1537. (*DII*, II, 179–211.)

The cash tribute was not established until after the middle of the century, when it was fixed at one peso de oro común for each married man, and half a fanega of maize a year. For a discussion of the origins of the tribute see José de la Peña Cámara, *El Tributo*.

[5] The Queen to Mendoza and the Audiencia of Mexico, May 31, 1535. (Puga, I, 367–368.)

[6] Charles V to Luis Ponce de León, Nov. 4, 1525. (*DIU*, IX, 214–226.)

[7] The Queen to Mendoza and the Audiencia of Mexico, May 26, 1536. (*DII*, XLI, 198–203; *DIU*, X, 322–329.)

[8] The Queen to Mendoza and the Audiencia of Mexico, Nov. 13, 1535. (Puga, I, 376.)

[9] The Queen to the Audiencia of Mexico, Feb. 16, 1536. (*DIU*, X, 316–317.)

[10] The Queen to the Bishop of Mexico, June 26, 1536. (Puga, I, 384–385.)

[11] Zumárraga to Charles V, Apr. 17, 1540. (*DII*, XLI, 161–184.)

[12] The Queen to Mendoza and the Audiencia of Mexico, July 14, 1536. (*DII*, XXIII, 454–467.) The constant repetition of these pathetic injunctions is fairly good proof that they were ignored in the main. Certainly there is no evidence that the ordinances against sexual irregularities were successfully enforced.

[13] The Queen to Mendoza and the Audiencia of Mexico, Aug. 7, 1536. (Puga, I, 390–391.) Petitions for help of this kind were extremely numerous, and uncounted *probanzas* of the merits of the conquerors clutter up the Archives of the Indies.

[14] The Queen to Mendoza and the Audiencia of Mexico, Nov. 20, 1536. (Puga, I, 394–395; Torquemada, *Monarquía Indiana*, III, 261.)

[15] The Queen to the Audiencia of Mexico, Sept. 12, 1537. (*DIU*, X, 381–382.)

[16] The Queen to Mendoza, Sept. 20, 1537. (Puga, I, 404.)

[17] Charles V to Mendoza and the Audiencia of Mexico, Nov. 18, 1537. (*DIU*, X, 385–386.)

[18] He evidently intended that the alcalde mayor should be a true governor, above the encomenderos and corregidores. Actually there was little difference between the functions of the corregidor and those of an alcalde mayor; the former governed a town and the latter a *provincia*. But a large town with its supporting territory might be much more important than the territory of an alcalde mayor. The duties of the two officers were essentially the same and are so treated in the *Recopilación* (Lib. V, Tit. II).

[19] His advice was not heeded, and the primitive tribes of the remote west were all but annihilated by the hardened troops of Nuño de Guzmán. The best modern account of the conquest of New Galicia is that of José López-Portillo y Weber, *La Conquista de la Nueva Galicia*.

[20] Mendoza could hardly have been serious in this proposal, because the Crown was not in the habit of paying for the conquest of new provinces and was not likely to begin it at that late date.

[21] Mendoza was correct. Silk culture became an important and profitable activity, particularly in Oaxaca, and lasted until the China trade gradually suffocated it. (Woodrow Borah, *Silk Raising in Colonial Mexico*.)

[22] Mendoza to Charles V, Dec. 10, 1537. (*DII*, II, 179–211.)

[23] The immense increase in the business of the Council owing to the conquest of Peru may account for its neglect of New Spain. The administration of the Indies was getting more and more complex, and the consequent lack of supervision of Indian law (Las Casas had returned to Spain in 1539 and was com-

plaining loudly of the treatment of the Indians) made it imperative to organize that body more efficiently. The result of the agitation was the *Ordenanzas para la administración del Consejo de las Indias*, promulgated at Barcelona, Nov. 20, 1542. (Schäfer, *op. cit.*, I, 61–70.)

Notes to Chapter 10

1 The violence of the feeling against Las Casas during the crisis caused by the New Laws almost passes belief. The most bitter, as well as the most respectable, denunciation of him is the letter written by the saintly Fray Toribio de Benavente (Motolinía) to Charles V, extracted in the Appendix to this volume.

2 There is a voluminous literature on this tragic episode: Las Casas, *Historia de las Indias*, V, 165–199. Las Casas is closely followed by Mendieta, *Historia Eclesiástica Indiana*, I, 41–57; Helps, *The Spanish Conquest in America*, II, 116–142; Fabié, *Vida de las Casas*, pp. 107–122; MacNutt, *Bartholomew de las Casas*, pp. 112–173. An original account is in the testimony of Miguel de Castellanos, accountant with the Las Casas expedition to Cumaná (*DII*, VII, 109–116). A more critical treatment will be found in Serrano y Sanz, *Orígenes de la Dominación española en América*, pp. 426–435. Oviedo, of course, scoffed at the Cumaná expedition, but his judgment is one with which the modern reader will agree: "He who would be a captain cannot become one by chance, but must be experienced in war, and because he [Las Casas] knew nothing of it and trusted only to his good intentions, he failed." (*Historia General*, I, 599–602.) A more sympathetic view is given at length by Lewis Hanke (*The Spanish Struggle for Justice*, pp. 47–71). Hanke shows that the Crown was sufficiently convinced of the practicability of founding free, self-governing Indian communities to undertake one more experiment in Cuba. This model settlement dragged out a miserable existence from 1531 to 1535 and finally succumbed to Indian indifference and Spanish skepticism.

3 Remesal, *Historia de Chiapa*, p. 103; Puga, I, 231–234.

4 Oviedo, *Historia General*, I, 157–158. The Queen to the Audiencia of Santo Domingo, July 4, 1532. (*DII*, I, 482–485.) Contract of Captain Barrionuevo with the Audiencia of Santo Domingo, March, 1533. (*DII*, I, 487–505.)

5 Alonso de Maldonado to Charles V, Oct. 16, 1539. (Quoted by Remesal, *Historia de Guatemala*, pp. 121–124.) Motolinía, who was unwilling to admit anything good about Las Casas, sneered: "Then he went to the kingdom called Vera Paz, which is said to be such a great matter. This land is near Guatemala, and I have visited and taught near there . . . and it is not one-tenth what has been claimed for it." (Motolinía to Charles V, Jan. 2, 1555. In Appendix to this volume.) It is curious that Thomas Gage, himself a Dominican, although a renegade at the time of his writing, should have spent upward of ten years in Guatemala without having learned of, or, at least, without mentioning Las Casas' connection with Vera Paz. "The *Vera Paz* is so called for the *Indians* of that Country, hearing how the *Spaniards* had conquered *Guatemala* and did

conquer the Country round about, wheresoever they came, yielded themselves up peaceably and without any resistance unto the Government of Spain. . . . All this Country as yet is not subdued by the *Spaniards,* who have now and then some strong encounters with the barbarous and heathen people which lie between this Country and *Yucatan.*" (Thomas Gage, *New Survey of the West-Indies,* p. 304.) In Gage's time Vera Paz had long since been reconquered by the Indians, in 1556. (Hanke, *The Spanish Struggle for Justice,* p. 81.) Vera Paz was not occupied in the conventional way until the campaign of 1692–1699, conducted by Jacinto Barrios Leal, operating from Guatemala, and Martín de Ursúa y Arismendi, operating from Yucatan. (Villagutierre Soto-Mayor, *Historia de la conquista de el Itza,* pp. xii–xxv.)

6 Lewis Hanke, in his excellent chapter on the genesis of the New Laws, gives more weight to the influence of Las Casas than I am inclined to accept, and ends with the somewhat unexpected asseveration that "the Dominican friar Bartolomé de las Casas had set in motion as revolutionary a change in American society and in the administration of Spain's great empire overseas as his contemporary Nicolaus Copernicus achieved in astronomical circles with his *De revolutionibus orbium coelestium,* printed in the same year as the New Laws" (*op. cit.,* 95).

7 Francisco de Vitoria, *De Indis,* pp. 115–187. That Vitoria was under no illusion about the efficacy of his argument in changing the laws of the Indies may be surmised by his curious aside: "It might seem at first sight that all this discussion is useless and idle."

8 Silvio Zavala, *La Encomienda Indiana,* pp. 89–95.
The importance of the Valladolid council is evident from the roster of its members: García de Loaisa, President of the Council of the Indies; Sebastián Ramírez de Fuenleal, President of the Audiencia of Valladolid; Juan de Zúñiga, tutor of Prince Philip; Francisco de los Cobos, Secretary of the Council of the Indies; García Fernández Manrique, member of the same (and also serving as alternate for President Loaisa); Hernando de Guevara, of the Council of Castile; Juan de Figueroa, *idem;* Jacobo González de Artiaga, of the Council of Orders; Bernal Díaz de Luco, of the Council of the Indies; Gutierre Velázquez de Luco, *idem;* Juan de Salmerón, *idem;* Gregorio López, appointed to the Council of the Indies in 1543. (Schäfer, *El Consejo Real y Supremo de las Indias,* I, Appendix I.)

9 *DII,* XVI, 376–406; Stevens and Lucas, eds., *The New Laws of the Indies.* (Italics mine.)

10 Cortés to Charles V, 1542. (Ed. by H. Stevens.)

11 There are many accounts of this episode: Helps, *Spanish Conquest,* IV, 105–106; Bancroft, *History of Mexico,* II, 524–529; Aiton, *Antonio de Mendoza,* p. 163; Priestley, *The Mexican Nation,* pp. 66–68; Zavala, *La Encomienda Indiana,* p. 102. For the revolt of the encomenderos of Nicaragua under the romantic leadership of Rodrigo de Contreras and its suppression by Pedro de la Gasca, see Lozoya, *Vida del segoviano Rodrigo de Contreras, gobernador de Nicaragua.*

12 Opinion of the friars of the Order of St. Dominic of New Spain on the

encomienda, May 5, 1544. (*DII*, VII, 532–542.) It is signed by Diego de la Cruz, Prior; Domingo de Betanzos, Prior; Hernando de Oviedo; Tomás de San Juan; Francisco Aguilar; Didacus de la Cruz; Gundisalvus de Santo Domingo; Jordán de Bustillo; Alonso de Santiago; Juan de la Magdalena; Joannes Lupus; Dominicus de Anunciatione.

[13] H. H. Bancroft, in his zeal for debunking the Church, ascribes the clergy's opposition to the abolition of the encomienda to considerations of material interest. "The reason is readily understood. There were many advantages to the church connected with the encomienda system; besides, Bishop Zumárraga was the owner of the important town and encomienda of Acuituco [Ocuituco, in the modern state of Morelos], and the Austin friars controlled Tezcuco, at the time the largest encomienda in New Spain." (*History of Mexico*, II, 524.) Bancroft is wrong in one important respect: a few encomiendas were granted in New Spain before 1542 for the support of religious houses and charitable institutions, but not to individual clergyman. Hence Zumárraga could not have been the "owner" of Ocuituco, which had been assigned to the cathedral chapter of Mexico for the support of the Hospital del Amor de Dios. All such grants were canceled by the New Laws, over the protests, to be sure, of the clergy. The *Suma de Visitas* (*ca.* 1544) shows both Ocuituco and Texcoco as Crown towns. (J. García Icazbalceta, *Don Fray Juan de Zumárraga*, p. 226; Paso y Troncoso, *Papeles de Nueva España*, I, Nos. 421 and 776.)

[14] Antequera was established as a Spanish town near the Indian town of Oaxaca. By "the same thing" Zárate evidently means that the two places were contiguous. Antequera became the modern city of Oaxaca; the other is Oaxaca Viejo.

[15] Don Juan de Zárate, Bishop of Antequera, to Prince Philip, May 30, 1544. (*DII*, VII, 542–552.) The Mixteca town mentioned by Zárate could well have been Teposcolula, one of the earliest and most productive silk centers. At the time of his writing it was paying 900 pesos tribute, but by 1568 it had risen to 5,026 pesos. Teposcolula belonged to the Crown. ("Relación de las tasaciones," above cited in chap. 8, n. 19. The Mixteca was beginning its silk boom, and raw silk was selling at 1½ pesos a pound. (Borah, *Silk Raising in Colonial Mexico*, pp. 24–31.)

[16] The congregation of the convent of St. Francis of Mexico City to Charles V, June 1, 1544. (*Nueva Colección de documentos para la historia de México*, II, 187–192.)

Francisco de Terrazas to Charles V, June 1, 1544. (*Documentos inéditos para la historia de Ibero-América*, I, 113–123.)

Gómez Maraver to Charles V, June 1, 1544. (*DII*, VIII, 199–212.) Among the clergy Maraver was perhaps the most enthusiastic advocate of the encomenderos. He achieved notoriety by recommending the continuance of Indian slavery, for he saw no way to protect the peaceful Indians and the settlers of New Galicia from the warlike tribes except by fire, sword, and slavery. He had recently been through the ferocious Mixtón War and had an understandable fear of its repetition. In New Galicia, which was still suffering from the barbarous effects of Nuño de Guzmán's conquest, as well as from the Mixtón War, the administration of the New Laws was extraordinarily difficult. Tello de Sandoval, in obedience to his instructions, sent the oidor Lorenzo de Tejada to Guadalajara to proclaim them, but Tejada observed great caution in their execution. He removed the illegal encomiendas of Nuño de Guzmán and Coronado, but did little to disturb the rest. In his report to the Council of the Indies Tejada admitted his helplessness in the face of the hostility of the encomenderos and advised the establishment of a royal audiencia as the only agency competent to carry out the Crown's intent. (J. H. Parry, *The Audiencia of New Galicia in the Sixteenth Century*, pp. 29–31.)

[17] Petition of the delegates of New Spain to the King, June, 1545. (*Historical Documents relating to New Mexico*, I, 126–145.)

[18] Opinion of Hernán López of the Council of the Indies on the matter of perpetuity, 1545. (*Historical Documents relating to New Mexico*, I, 150–155.) The editors of the New Mexico series may have mistaken the name. There was no Hernán López on the Council of the Indies at that time. There was, however, a Gregorio López. (E. Schäfer, *op. cit.*, I, 354.)

[19] Cédula of Charles V, Oct. 20, 1545. (Puga, I, 472–475; *Recopilación*, Lib. VI, Tit. VIII, Ley iiii.)

[20] Bernal Díaz del Castillo to the Council of the Indies, Feb. 1, 1549. (L. B. Simpson, *The Emancipation of the Indian Slaves*, Appendix, pp. 32–36.)

[21] The Queen to the Audiencia of Mexico, Feb. 14, 1549. (Puga, II, 8–14.)

[22] R. S. Chamberlain, *The Conquest and Colonization of Yucatan*, Chap. 15.

[23] The Queen to the Audiencia of Mexico, Jan. 7, 1549, and Feb. 22, 1549. (Puga, II, 7–8, 14–18.)

[24] Mendoza to the Council of the Indies, n.d. (*DII*, XLI, 149–160.)

[25] The Queen to the Audiencia of Mexico, June 1, 1549. (Puga, II, 20–24.)

[26] Charles V to Mendoza, Mar. 11, 1550. (Puga, II, 60–61.)

[27] Charles V to the viceroy and Audiencia of New Spain, Apr. 16, 1550. (*DII*, XXIII, 520–547.) The reader is, of course, appalled by the repetitiousness of such instructions, which by that very fact show that they were not rigidly enforced, as, indeed, many of them could not be. No adequate machinery was set up for the hearing of Indian complaints until 1573, when Viceroy Enríquez established the *Juzgado General de Indios*.

[28] Charles V to the Audiencia of Mexico, Apr. 16, 1550, and May 6, 1550. (Puga, II, 67–68, 83–84.)

[29] Torquemada, *Monarquia Indiana*, II, 254.

[30] Simpson, *The Repartimiento System*, *passim*.

NOTES TO CHAPTER 11

[1] I shall not go into the legal history of the last stage of the encomienda which was mainly concerned with the right of inheritance. The matter has been exhaustively explored by Silvio Zavala in his *La Encomienda Indiana* (pp. 185–223), to which the reader is referred.

[2] The most readable account of the tragic conspiracy of the Avila brothers (1564–1566) is that of Luis González Obregón, *Los Precursores de la Independencia Mexicana en el Siglo XVI.* See also my *Many Mexicos*, chap. xi: "The Second Generation."

[3] The extraordinary bitterness of the feud, as early as 1625, is best described in the words of the acute and malicious Thomas Gage: "In all the Dominions of the King of Spain in America there are two sorts of *Spaniards* more opposite one to another than in *Europe* the *Spaniard* is opposite to the *French,* or to the *Hollander,* or to the *Portugal;* to wit, they that are born in any parts of *Spain* and go thither, and they that are born of *Spanish* Parents, whom the *Spaniards,* to distinguish them from themselves, term *Criollos,* signifying the Natives of that Country. This hatred is so great that I dare say nothing might be more advantageous than this to any other nation that would conquer *America* [p. 20]. . . . But they [the Creole friars] being natives and born in that Country discovered presently unto us that inveterate spight and hatred which they bare to such as came from Spain; they told us plainly that they and the true *Spaniards* born did never agree, and that they knew their Superiors would be unwilling to admit of us; yet furthermore they informed us that they thought we might be entertained in the Province of Guaxaca, where half the Fryers were of *Spain* and half Criolians and Natives; but in case we should not speed there, they would warrant us we should be welcome to the Province of *Guatemala,* where almost all the Fryers were of *Spain* [p. 184] . . . [There was] no place I so desired to live in . . . as in Guaxaca, which I had attempted as I travelled by it, had I not understood that the Creole or native Fryers were many and as deadly enemies unto those that came from *Spain* as were the Mexicans." (*A New Survey of the West Indies,* pp. 192–193.)

[4] Charles V to Diego Ramírez, May 22, 1550. (Paso y Troncoso, *Epistolario de Nueva España,* VI, 11–15.)

[5] The province of Metztitlán had been granted originally to Andrés de Barrios and Alonso de Mérida. The former's half share fell to Diego de Guevara, probably through his having married the widow of Barrios—a common practice since the Law of Succession of 1536. I have not been able to discover what Barrios and Mérida did to deserve this rich prize. In 1560 the encomienda was yielding an admitted tribute of 13,500 *pesos de oro común.* (*Relación de las tasaciones,* Paso y Troncoso, *op. cit.,* IX.)

[6] The most detailed account of the Ramírez episode and description of the whole apparatus of provincial visitas is that of W. V. Scholes, *The Ramírez Visita.* The experiences of the visitadores Lebrón de Quiñones, Contreras, and De la Marcha in New Galicia closely paralleled that of Ramírez. (J. H. Parry, *The Audiencia of New Galicia in the Sixteenth Century,* chap. iii.)

[7] Luis de Velasco to Charles V, Nov. 22, 1552. MS, Archivo Histórico Nacional, Madrid, *Cartas de Indias.* (Quoted by Silvio Zavala, *La Encomienda Indiana,* p. 134.)

[8] Velasco was writing just before the introduction of the quicksilver amalgam process, which revolutionized the economy of New Spain, turning it away from agriculture to silver mining. It became, in fact, immensely profitable to work

silver mines with paid labor, instead of with the traditional slave gangs and repartimientos. (Simpson, *The Repartimiento System*, pp. 44–66.) Gold mining, which was still limited in the main to river bed placers, seems to have been harder hit. "For many years gold mines have not been worked . . . because, when the Indians [slaves] were removed, all [the mines] were ruined on account of the high cost of working them. Except in a few rivers nothing is extracted, and even that in a very small amount." (Viceroy Martín Enríquez to Philip II, April 28, 1572. *Cartas de Indias*, pp. 280–289.)

[9] Luis de Velasco to Charles V, May 4, 1553. (*Cartas de Indias*, pp. 263–269.)

[10] Luis de Velasco to Philip II, Feb. 26, 1564. (*Cartas de Indias*, pp. 276–279.)

[11] Martín Enríquez to Philip II, September 23, 1575. (*Cartas de Indias*, pp. 305–314.)

[12] They were not unanimous. Motolinía, in his letter of January 2, 1555, which I have so frequently quoted, wrote: "Know, your Majesty, that the Indians of this New Spain are well treated and that they pay less tribute than do the farmers of old Spain, each in his way. I mean almost all the Indians, because there are some few towns whose assessment was made before the great epidemic and whose tributes have not been adjusted. . . . Today the Indians know and understand very well their assessments and will not give a *tomín* more in any circumstances; nor does the encomendero dare to demand a cacao more than the assessment, for [if he does] his confessor will not absolve him, and the justice will punish him when he learns of it."

[13] "Pareceres del virrey, arzobispo, y audiencia de Nueva España sobre la manera de tributar de los indios" (1561–1562), MS, AGI, *Patronato*, leg. 182 [2–2–3], ramo 2. (See also Cook and Simpson, *Population of Central Mexico in the Sixteenth Century*, Appendix 1.)

[14] "Relación de las tasaciones ... de los pueblos que están en la Corona Real" (1571), MS, AGI, *Patronato*, leg. 182 [2–2–3], ramo 40. (See also Cook and Simpson, *op. cit.*, Appendix 1.)

[15] Alonso de Zurita, *Breve relación de los señores de la Nueva España*, pp. 120–121. (*DII*, II, 1–126.)

[16] Francisco de Ceynos to Charles V, 1565. (*DIM*, II, 237–243.)

[17] The records of the Juzgado General de Indios in the Archivo General de la Nación of Mexico are badly scattered, the main body being in the *Ramo de Indios*. Its seventy-seven volumes are, nevertheless, a large enough sample to justify this generalization. Actually, of the small number of suits brought against encomenderos, *qua* encomenderos, only four are for extortion or excessive tribute: *Indios* II, No. 925, Tlápam, 1583; VII, Nos. 65 and 66, Acaxuchitlán, 1616; X, pt. 3, No. 54, Villa Alta, 1632; and XXIII, No. 289, Huazalingo, 1659.

[18] Gallego held the town of Huixtlán (in modern Guerrero). According to the *Suma de Visitas* (No. 857), it had 87 tributaries, and in 1560 it was yielding a tribute of 130 pesos.

[19] Decree of Antonio de Mendoza, May 2, 1550. (MS, AGN, *Mercedes*, III.)

[20] Valverde was an experienced and trusted Crown officer. He was appointed oidor of the Audiencia of Quito in 1564; president of the same Audiencia in 1572; oidor of the Audiencia of Lima in 1573; president of the Audiencia

of Guatemala in 1577; president of the Audiencia of Guadalajara in 1587. He died before taking this last post. (Schäfer, *El Consejo Real y Supremo de las Indias*, pp. 473, 480, 492, 503.)

[21] "Información hecha por mandado del muy ilustre señor licenciado García de Valverde ... sobre lo que pasava ... cerca de los tributos demasiados que pagavan los yndios y malos tratamientos que se les hazían" (1582), MS, Archivo Colonial de Guatemala, Leg. 1, No. 1.

[22] "Autos de Martín Ximénez estante en esta corte sobre las quatro cauallerías de tierra que pide en terminos del pueblo de Yzquintepeque, las quales tienen contradichas Francisco de Valverde e los yndios de los pueblos de Huanagaçapa e los de Hueymango," (1579–1580), (MS, Archivo Colonial de Guatemala, 55 fols. See also L. B. Simpson, "Bernal Díaz del Castillo, Encomendero." *HAHR*, XVII, 100–106.)

[23] Decree of Lorenzo Suárez de Mendoza, May 8, 1583. (MS, AGN, *Indios*, II, No. 772.)

[24] Decree of the Marqués de Guadalcázar, Dec. 5, 1619. (MS, AGN, *Indios*, VII, No. 439.)

[25] Decree of Lope Díez de Armendáriz, Nov. 16, 1639. (MS, AGN, *Indios*, XI, No. 371.)

[26] "Parecer del Padre Provincial y otros religiosos teólogos del orden de San Francisco, dado en México a 8 de Marzo de 1594, acerca de los yndios que se dan en repartimiento a los españoles," MS, AGN, *Historia*, XIV.

[27] There is an impressive number of cases in Silvio Zavala's *Fuentes para la historia del trabajo en Nueva España*, running from 1579 to 1617, in which the encomenderos protect their Indians against various abuses by corregidores, Spanish farmers, Indian officers, and press gangs. The student will find them in Vols. II, 203, 207, 363, 391; III, 29, 34, 42, 76, 113; IV, 324, 411; V, 91, 211; VI, 5, 102, 187, 190, 301.

NOTES TO CHAPTER 12

[1] "A." *Suma de Visitas. Papeles de Nueva España*, Vol. 1. Ed. Francisco del Paso y Troncoso (Madrid, 1905).

"B." *Relación de las tasaciones de los pueblos de yndios ... que están encomendados en personas particulares*. 1560. *Epistolario de Nueva España*, Vol. 9, 2–48. Ed. Francisco del Paso y Troncoso (Mexico, 1940). (Corrected against the MS.)

"Relación de las tasaciones de los pueblos de yndios ... que están en la Real Corona." 1560. MS, AGI, *Patronato*, leg. 181. (Note: These two *relaciones* are two parts of the same one.)

"C." "Relación de las tasaciones que se han hecho en los pueblos que están en la Corona Real en esta Nueva España." 1571. MS, AGI, *Patronato*, leg. 182.

"D." *Relación del distrito y pueblos del Obispado de Tlaxcala*. Por Alonso Pérez de Andrada, Vicario General. Ca. 1570. *Epistolario de Nueva España*, Vol. 14, 70–101.

"E." "Relación de los pueblos que están en la Corona Real . . ." *Ca.* 1570. MS, AGI, *Audiencia de México*, leg. 323.

"F." "Relación de los tributos de los pueblos del Obispado de Tlaxcala." 1570. MS, AGI, *Audiencia de México*, leg. 270.

"G." "Relación de todos los conventos y beneficios que ai en esta provincia de la Guasteca de Pánuco . . ." *Ca.* 1570. MS, AGI, *Audiencia de México*, leg. 1841.

"H." "Relación de los pueblos de la Nueva España cuya doctrina estaba a cargo de los padres agustinos." 1569–1571. MS, AGI, *Indiferente general*, leg. 1529.

"I." "Relación de los pueblos de yndios que los religiosos de Sant Agustín tienen a su cargo . . ." Por Fray Juan Adrián, Provincial. 1572. MS, AGI, *Patronato*, leg. 182.

"J." *Cartas de religiosos.* 1565–1570. *Relación de los obispados de Tlaxcala, Michoacán, Oaxaca y otros lugares.* Ed. Luis García Pimentel (México, 1904), pp. 97–153.

"K." *Descripción del Arzobispado de México,* hecha en 1570. Ed. Luis García Pimentel (México, 1897).

"L." *Lista de los pueblos de indios encomendados en personas particulares.* 1565–1570. (In same volume as "J," pp. 153–188.)

"M." *Relación de los obispados . . . 1565–1570. (Ibid.)*

"N." *Geografía y descripción universal de las Indias.* Por Juan López de Velasco. Ed. Justo Zaragoza (Mexico, 1894).

"O." "Relaciones geográficas de la Nueva España." 1579–1584. MS, Academia de la Historia, Madrid, 12–18–3. (Published in part in *Papeles de Nueva España*, Vols. 3–7.)

"P." *Información ... sobre el estado en que se encontraba la sucesión de indios. . . .* 1597. *Epistolario de Nueva España*, Vol. 13, 3–165. (Corrected against the MS.)

(A critical discussion of these documents will be found in Cook and Simpson, *The Population of Central Mexico in the Sixteenth Century*, pp. 1–9.)

[2] This value was established by computing the number of tributaries in 121 encomienda towns which appear in the 1560–1570 lists but which do not appear in the "P" list of 1597. Some were confiscated at the time of the 1566 conspiracy (e.g., Coeneo and Carandacho, in Michoacán; Cuautitlán, in Mexico; and Olinalá, Papalutla, and Zirándiro, in Guerrero, with an aggregate of 9,744 tributaries. Document "C"). It must be assumed that the rest, since they did not disappear, also escheated to the Crown.

[3] "P" actually lists only 213,553 tributaries, but I have added a correction of 1,652 for the district of Oaxtepec which I shall explain when I discuss the Marquesado del Valle.

[4] Cédula of Charles V, July 6, 1529. (Puga, I, 129–134.)

[5] G. M. McBride, *Land Systems of Mexico*, pp. 47–48.

[6] Hernán Cortés to the Audiencia of Mexico, Oct. 21, 1532. (*DII*, XII, 554–563.)

[7] Computed probably on the basis of the "B" list, in which the Marquesado

acknowledged a cash income from tributes of 34,797 pesos. This against the real income from tributes of 69,605 pesos, as shown in the inventory of 1569.

8 C. O. Sauer, *Colima of New Spain in the Sixteenth Century*, pp. 26–27.

9 Sauer, *op. cit.*, p. 28; J. García Icazbalceta, *Don Fray Juan de Zumárraga*, App. 14. Also, Cortés to Hernando de Saavedra, 1525. (*DII*, XXVI, 185–194.)

10 The Crown's share had been granted originally to Francisco de Ribadeo and escheated at his death. (Icaza, *Conquistadores y Pobladores de Nueva España*, pp. 141–142.) The half share of Beatriz de Estrada had belonged to her husband, Francisco Vázquez de Coronado, who seems to have got it from his wife's father, the royal treasurer Alonso de Estrada. Bernaldino Vázquez de Tapia's share was probably part of this interlocking family arrangement.

Appendices

Appendix 1

Title to an encomienda granted by Francisco de Montejo, Governor of Yucatan, to Antonio de Vergara, May 7, 1544. (From facsimile reproduction in the frontispiece.)

Don Francisco de Montejo, Adelantado and Governor and Captain-General for his Majesty in the jurisdiction of Yucatan and Cozumel and Higueras and Honduras, and of their lands and provinces, by these presents, in his Royal Name, I give in encomienda and repartimiento to you, Antonio de Vergara, citizen of the Villa de Santa María of the Valley of Comayagua, the town of Taxica, which lies within the boundaries of the said Villa, with all its lords and caciques and nobles, and all the divisions and subject villages of the said town, so that you may use and profit by them in your estates and commerce, provided that you indoctrinate them and teach them in the things of our Holy Catholic Faith, and treat them according to the Royal Ordinances which have been issued, or which may be issued, for the good and increase of the said Indians; and in this I charge your conscience and discharge that of his Majesty and mine; and I command any and all magistrates to put you in possession of the said Indians and to protect you in it; and if anyone should do the contrary I condemn him to pay a fine of fifty pesos of good gold for the King's treasury and exchequer; and in his Royal Name I give it you in remuneration for your services and hardships and expenditures, and for the services which you have rendered his Majesty in the conquest and pacification of the jurisdiction of Higueras and Honduras.

Done in this city of Gracias a Dios, the seventh day of May, 1544. The said repartimiento and encomienda I grant unto the said Antonio de Vergara without prejudice to any third party.

[signed] El Adelantado, Don Francisco de Montejo

By command of his Lordship [signature of notary] [1]

[1] "Probanza de Antonio de Vergara." 1543. MS, Archivo Colonial de Guatemala.

Appendix 2

Rodrigo de Albornoz, Accountant of New Spain, to Charles V, December 15, 1525.[1]

This unique document is included for its bearing on conditions in New Spain during the dictatorship of Chirinos and Salazar, while Cortés was absent on the Honduras expedition. It is particularly enlightening on the slaving activities of the conquistadores. Albornoz, although himself a royal officer, argues for the perpetual encomienda. His letter is mainly an indictment of Chirinos and Salazar.

[Albornoz gives an account of the Honduras expedition, which was undertaken against his advice, and of the death of Cortés and all his men, which he has taken great pains to verify. He urges the Emperor at once to appoint a governor and an audiencia. He complains of the rebellious attitude of the Cortés party. He advises that many more Franciscan friars from the convent of San Gabriel be sent to New Spain, as they have been instrumental in pacifying the turbulent factions among the Spaniards and have converted a great number of Indians.]

As your Majesty has been informed, the people of these parts eat human flesh, not only because it was the custom of their ancestors and because of the scarcity of cattle in these parts, but also because, being accustomed to human flesh, they find it sweeter than that of the fowl and game which they have and raise. Since the country has been under the administration of your Majesty, with the friendship and association of the Christians, they have been eating the fowl of Castile, and pork, and mutton, and veal, and beef, and the other flesh which they see the Christians eating, and they prefer the wine of Castile to the *pulque* which they use for wine and which resembles beer, although it is not.

And, as they are a reasonable people and do a great trade in buying and selling everything in which they can earn a living, by selling to the Christians, raising Spanish fowl, and setting out gardens and attending to them, and raising

[1] (*DII*, XIII, 45–84.)

cattle, being as much given to it as are the farmers of Spain, and being much more subtle and quick, it is fitting for the service of your Majesty and the settlement and increase of these parts that the officers of Española, San Juan, and Cuba permit the free shipment of cattle, cows, mares, sheep, and rams to this country, because there is an abundance there and a lack here. . . .

If your Caesarean Majesty should order the Indians to be given in perpetuity, either in encomienda or of their own free will, or in any way which your Majesty may be pleased to order, it will be for the good of your service that those to whom Indians are given, either in perpetuity or for a period, be obliged to sow a certain quantity of land with Spanish wheat, so that the people who are here and those who are coming will settle and take root and decide to remain in this land, which is as fertile as Spain and resembles it. There is wheat already growing here where the Indians plant it. And let them [the settlers] plant a certain number of vines and trees and grains and vegetables of Spain. And let it be obligatory upon each to plant them within a year or a year and a half after being granted his Indians, and [to raise] a certain number of cows and sheep and mares, and to keep a horse and arms according to the number of Indians he has, and [to do this] in the sight of, and at the discretion of, the governor and officers of your Majesty. Thus, since the land is so fertile and so like Spain, they will cultivate it and the people will remain in it, Christians as well as Indians, and your Majesty will receive a much greater tribute from it, and the people will not be so ready, as they are now, to leave it and go back to Spain, and to strip the Indians because they have no security in their possession. This is the cause of the ruin of your Majesty's islands and of the increase and settlement of those of Portugal, for the Portuguese are great colonizers.

[Albornoz begs his Majesty to order all ships coming to New Spain to bring plants and grains from Castile.]

As your Caesarean Majesty has learned, and as those of your high council have learned, the Indians of these parts are very intelligent and peaceful and accustomed to work, and are as used to paying tribute to Montezuma and their overlords as are the farmers of Castile. Since they are already living in the way and manner of the latter, and since your Majesty has ordered us to bring this about as the best and surest means for the increase of your revenue, I have attempted to encourage them to continue in their adoption of the manners and customs of the vassals of Castile. And, although several [Spaniards] have interfered with me, moved by their private interests, as your Majesty must know, I came to an understanding with the cacique of Zacatula, which is on the coast of the South Sea where two Spanish ships are being built; and I sent an officer of mine to him . . . and we agreed on what he was to contribute to your Majesty every four months. It was that he should give two cups of gold and two bars, and maize and cacao beans, which are like almonds and which they use here for money and for their beverage. When the four months were up he came with it at the very time he had agreed upon. And in the same manner we reached an agreement with the lords of Zascatecla [*sic*] and with those of this city of Temixtitán [Mexico] about ordinary tributes. And thus the same would have been done with all the provinces and towns of this New Spain if we had not been interfered with by some persons known to your Majesty.

[Albornoz will have all the natives paying tribute within the year if he is allowed to carry out his plan. He begs the King to send to New Spain a competent person as governor.]

And your Majesty may believe that if, for this purpose and for the relief of the country, since God has disposed of Hernán Cortés, you do not send a governor who will be of age, authority, and wisdom, and free from cupidity, and one who will believe that he is coming only to serve your Majesty, this country will be ruined and nothing will ever be done for the good of your Majesty's service. These lands are so far removed from the presence of your royal Majesty, and the remedies for the evils committed are so late in coming, that many bad servants are raised up and we all stretch our consciences, and some never think that your Majesty will remember to punish those who are disserving you here and who so shamelessly go against your service.

In this country, as your Majesty knows, there have been, with licenses procured there [at Court], expeditions into provinces and tribes to take slaves, on the pretext that they have refused to render obedience to your Majesty. These licenses were procured by delegates who have gone there [to Court] in the name of this country, although they generally go only to do what is in the interest of those in power. Your Majesty has ordered that demands first be made of the Indians before a notary, with the help of interpreters who were to give them to understand that they were to come under the dominion of your Majesty, and that if they refused to do so they would be captured and made slaves. If, most Catholic Lord, in this case all the precautions had been taken which they gave your Majesty to understand [would be taken] and which are fitting for the service of God and your Majesty . . . it would be very well and proper; but . . . it should not have been done with tricks and frauds, or for the sake of robbing them or making them slaves, but by inducing them with words and practices to adopt our Faith and the service of your Majesty.

As I have learned, it has often happened that when the Indians of some province went to offer their obedience, and in peace, the Christians fell upon them and made those who were following understand that they did not wish to be friends, but to kill them. They did not wish the Indians to offer them obedience, so that they might rob them and make them slaves. Thus great havoc has been wrought and will be wrought in this country, and its people ruined, together with those who might have come under the dominion of your Majesty, unless you order the remedy immediately.

In no wise should this [slave-taking] be allowed without great cause, for it is a heavy charge on one's conscience. Your Majesty gave permission to the people of this country to buy from the Indians the slaves they had among them-

selves, but much abomination and cruelty is also practiced
against them. Your Majesty was given to understand that
the Spaniards would buy them, but they are rarely bought.
The Christian demands gold of the cacique, and if he says
he has none, or if he has it and gives it to him, he is required
to give a hundred or two slaves besides. And if perhaps the
cacique has not so many, for the sake of obeying he gives
others of his vassals who are not slaves. And the Christian,
in order to content his employer, forces them to say they are
slaves, although they are not. If their cacique demands it of
them they will suffer death rather than admit they are not
slaves, for they are very obedient to their lords. Thus great
harm will come to the land if your Majesty does not order
this remedied and if you do not inform yourself about those
who go there [to Spain and who should have] greater zeal
and less greed.

And in order that your Majesty may provide for the good
of your service I shall tell the advantages and disadvantages
which there seem to be in this business. The advantage which
there is in the said slaves is that, if there are many of them
in the power of the Christians, more gangs of slaves will
be sent to the mines, and more gold and silver and other
metals will be produced, and the revenues and fifths of your
Majesty will be increased, and the Christians will establish
more plantations with them. And, since they are in the
power of the Christians, they, and especially their children,
will become Christians, and some of the Christians will
teach them in the Faith, although few of us do as much as we
should.

The harm, Catholic Majesty, that is done the Indians by
making them slaves and branding so many is that the greatest service and aid that the Indian lords have for settling
and cultivating the land and for paying tribute to the Christians by whom they are held in encomienda, is in having
slaves. . . . In the second place, since the Christians demand of them much more [tribute] than they can give, in
order to satisfy the Christians, with ten slaves that they send
them, they send six others who are not, and sometimes these

are branded as slaves, because they themselves say they are slaves just to satisfy their lords. In the third place, when the caciques have not enough vassals [to give as slaves] they bring some of their own children and sell them to one another, for some of the Indians have from ten to twenty wives, especially the chiefs, and it happens that one man will have twenty or thirty children, and it seems that they use them in their commerce, just as the Christians use animals. In the fourth place, the Indians make slaves of one another for very slight matters: some are purchased from their parents for ten or twelve measures of grain; another is purchased from his father for seven or eight blankets, which they use for clothing; another, because he was fed while a child for half a year or a year. And thus for very slight reasons and in jest they make slaves of one another, and for such frivolous reasons that while I was present examining slaves one said that he was not a slave. Asked whether his parents were, he said they were not, but that one day while they were at their *areytos*, which is their feast day, someone had a drum which they use in their fiestas like the people of Spain, and he took a notion to beat upon it; and as its owner would not let him beat upon it without pay, and as he had nothing to give, he said he would be his slave. So the other let him beat the drum that day, and thenceforth he was his slave, and afterward he had been sold three or four times in their *tiangues*, or fairs, which they hold daily. Thus even musicians are sold, which is a laughable thing and very harmful for the conscience as well as for the service of your Majesty.

Moreover, if great moderation and care are not exercised, the slaves will diminish daily, although the land is well peopled, because the slaves taken in the cold provinces and brought to the mines in the hot country die and diminish from the labor as well as from the heat, and the same holds true for those brought from the hot country to the cold, although not so much. . . .

Some, Caesarean Majesty, who have been in these parts

and had experience here, say that the reason for their destruction and diminution is that they [the Spaniards],
great or humble, have no care for anything but to get rich
and make enough money to go back to Spain. Thus they
exploit the country and take what they can and flay the
Indians, and when they think they are going to get a great
deal more out of them, there is no more, and they are
finished. . . .

The Indians, most Puissant Lord, as your Majesty has
been informed many times, are many and able, strong, of
great stature and fond of war, and so intelligent that they
need only to be drilled and to have arms in the manner of the
Christians. Being so quickwitted, they are becoming used
to them, and they see that horses and Christians die from a
blow or a lance-thrust like themselves, whereas they formerly thought they were immortal, and two or three
hundred would fly from one or two on horseback. So now
it happens that an Indian will make a stand against a Christian on foot, a thing which they would not have done before,
and ten or twelve Indians will attack a horseman on one
side, and as many more on the other, and seize him by the
legs. Then seeing how the Christians fight and arm themselves, they do the same and secretly try to collect arms and
swords. And they can make pikes with the gold they give
the Christians, because in the quarrels which the Christians
have among themselves . . . they have used the Indians
against one another.[2] This is a bad thing and worthy of
rigorous punishment by your Majesty. Besides, they teach
the Indians to fight, so that one day when they have the
opportunity or the equipment they will not leave a single
Christian [alive]. . . .

Moreover, in order that this country may be perpetuated
it seems to those who have had experience here that your
Majesty should see to its settlement and grant privileges

[2] The passage is obscure. The sense seems to be that the Christians hire the
Indians in their private wars and that the Indians could arm themselves with the
proceeds.

to those who are here and to those who are to come. They hold that your Majesty, in order to perpetuate the land and to be served more loyally than heretofore, should not fail to give Indians to those to whom you have granted [promised?] Indians in perpetuity, because those who have governed here, even for three days, give Indians, and thus they are better obeyed than if they were lords of the land. And, since they give them without your Majesty's authority, they seek present rewards rather than their duty. . . .

If in any of your domains, Caesarean Majesty, it was ever necessary to prescribe the manner of life of your subjects and vassals, here it is even more necessary, for, since the land is rich in food and in gold and silver mines, and since everyone becomes swollen with the desire to spend and possess, by the end of a year and a half he who is a miner, or a farmer, or a swineherd, no longer wishes to be so, but wishes to be given Indians, and so he tries to spend everything he has on ornaments and silks, and the same holds for his wife, if he has one. And in the same fashion the other mechanics cease from pursuing their trades and incur excessive expense and do not work or extract gold or silver from the mines, thinking that the Indians . . . will serve them and support their families and their gentility and mine gold for them. . . . I have heard many times from those who have been a long time in these islands that in the days when silks and brocades were not brought in, the people were busy in the mines, and the best man in the land enjoyed going to them, and the least had six or seven thousand pesos in bars and was trying to send them to Castile to his family or relatives. But now that all are gentlemen and will not apply themselves to gold mining, although there is the best equipment for it that was ever in any land yet discovered, because of the many slaves and the numerous population, the one who ought to have most in this country is in debt, and thus everything is ruined and daily is getting worse. . . . I certify to your Majesty that the wives of mechanics and public women wear more silks than does the wife of a gentleman in Castile, and thus all are poor and ruined, and they destroy the poor Indians, who are the best servants in the world. . . .

From this great city of Temixtitlán, December 15, 1525, your Caesarean and Catholic Majesty's very humble vassal and servant who kisses your royal feet and hands.

Rodrigo de Albornoz

Appendix 3

The Bishop-elect of Mexico, Don Fray Juan de Zumárraga, to Charles V, August 27, 1529.[1]

It would be difficult to name a more important figure in the early history of New Spain than Bishop Zumárraga, and it would be equally difficult to name a more important document than this letter of his exposing the corruption of the first Audiencia. It was instrumental in bringing about the disgrace of Nuño de Guzmán and it brought home to the Council of the Indies the danger of entrusting the government of New Spain to any but men of the highest integrity. Zumárraga shows himself to be a strong advocate of the perpetual encomienda and repeats the standard arguments in favor of it. His plea for greater powers for himself as Protector of the Indians was ignored by the Council, which abolished that ambiguous office shortly afterward.

†

I.H.S.

Sacred Caesarean Catholic Majesty: May the grace, peace, and mercy of Our Lord Jesus Christ be with your Majesty.

I beg your Majesty, with all the respect that I owe you, to condescend to read all of this my letter, which is true and exact, written with the sincere and loyal purpose of serving God and your Majesty, free from all passion, being what your Majesty has most desired from this country. In it will be found the universal remedy for the Spaniards and natives here, and for their physical relief and help, and for the relief of your Majesty's royal conscience. Since your Majesty ordered me to do so and I accepted it as a cross and a martyrdom, I shall tell you what is happening, although in so doing I shall risk nothing less than my life, in case this letter is taken by those who would spare no pains to get it, as I have been warned, but it would be well spent in my duty to God and your Majesty and my fellow men, and any persecution that I may suffer, although it is not desired, will be blessed

[1] (J. García Icazbalceta, *Don Fray Juan de Zumárraga*, Appendix, pp. 1–42; *DII*, XIII, 104–179.)

214

by that Judge who judges with equity and whom no one can deceive.

[Zumárraga reviews the history of the feud between the Cortés and Velázquez factions in Mexico City; the imbroglio during the absence of Cortés in Honduras; the usurpation of the government by the factor Salazar; the return of Cortés; the arrival and death of the juez de residencia, Luis Ponce de León; the coming of the first Audiencia under Nuño de Guzmán; their jealousy of Cortés; their conspiracy with Salazar and their persecution of the Cortés men; their seizure of encomiendas and abuse of the Indians; their connivance with the interpreter Pilar.[2]]

And so, with the advice of the factor and the machination of this Pilar the interpreter, the president and oidores sent messengers throughout the peaceful part of the country and to all the lords and principal persons, commanding them to appear before him [Pilar], and when they arrived the said Pilar made them long speeches in the house of the president, in secret, and I believe and certify that it was not for the purpose of baptizing them and that they did not come empty-handed. Nor were they [Guzmán and the oidores] displeased with their coming and their offering, for no one was left without his present. With these gifts their greed was awakened, and, forgetful of everything contained in your Majesty's instructions, they took this [enriching of themselves] as their special care. . . . I certify to your Majesty that it is the opinion of those who live in this country, and mine, that the president and oidores have used, and are still using and profiting by them, Indians in a greater number than 100,000, for they are using the Indians [tributaries] reserved for your Majesty and those of Don Hernando Cortés, and especially those of this great city and the towns of the lagoon, and those of the city of Coyoacán, Chalco, Tlamanalco with its subjects, and the city of Texcoco with its subjects. They demand of them

---

[2] García del Pilar was a trusted henchman of Nuño de Guzmán and accompanied him as interpreter in the conquest of New Galicia. He is the author of one of the relaciones of that conquest. (*DIM*, II, 248–261.)

provisions and clothing and other things in such quantity that they have built warehouses for maize and textiles to store the excess beyond what they need for their households and what they give to their friends and servants. . . .

These Indians serve them in public for their maintenance, and as many others serve them in the mines, supplying the gangs of slaves who mine gold for the president and oidores and their servants; and other [Indians] are building great palaces for them of many rooms and living quarters, and beautiful houses, sumptuous and pleasant, and they are [also] building for them near this city, mills and other properties of great value. Not twenty days ago the mills of the president were finished which are in the center of an Indian town called Tacubaya . . . six millwheels altogether, surrounded by a garden which the lord of that village had. The Indians receive not a little grief and sadness from them, not only because they have been deprived of what is theirs, but because their town has suffered such damage that they will be forced to find a new site for it. Worse yet, the water which the poor Indians used for irrigation is now taken by the mills, and without it they can by no means live. . . .

Likewise, since the Audiencia came, they have declared vacant many and very good encomiendas of Indians, more than thirty of them, either by exiling those who held them, or by confiscation. Although there are many conquerors who are without them and who have well deserved them—these are the ones whom your Majesty expressly commanded to be provided for—they have not been given a single Indian; rather [the president and oidores], in order to strengthen themselves with their favorites and protect themselves from opposition, have distributed them in the following manner: [Zumárraga lists the encomiendas distributed by the Audiencia].

And with all this abundance there has never been the least provision made for one conqueror among the many who are daily crying out to them for help. These are married men and settlers who are suffering great want, and it is necessary for your royal conscience that these be provided for before the others.

[All public offices have been distributed in like manner among the friends of Guzmán and the oidores.]

Because I think that nothing should be concealed from your Majesty I say that the lords of Tlatelolco of this city came to me weeping so bitterly that I was struck with pity for them; and they complained to me saying that the president and oidores were demanding of them their good-looking daughters, sisters, and female relatives. And another lord told me that Pilar had demanded of him eight handsome girls for the president. I answered . . . that they should not give them, and for this reason, it is said, one of these lords was threatened with hanging.

[Zumárraga is threatened by Guzmán; the latter's impious conduct; the president and oidores are ruled by their concubines, who are the real government of New Spain; the president and oidores force open the convent school at Texcoco and carry off two pretty Indian girls; Zumárraga is disturbed by the razing of the leper hospital which was built by Cortés; Guzmán building several sumptuous dwellings on the site.]

Innumerable Indians are still working on them, being forced to work like slaves, without holidays and without a handful of maize being given them to eat. They have to carry all the materials on their heads and to supply the materials themselves. I have been told by trustworthy persons that on Corpus Christi Day several died in this work. . . .

[Guzmán and the oidores have also persecuted and robbed Pedro de Alvarado and all those who were against the factor Salazar.]

As soon as I came to this country, most Puissant Lord, I was informed that the province of Pánuco, of which Nuño de Guzmán is governor, had been destroyed and devastated, because the said Nuño de Guzmán had taken from it a great number of its free natives and had branded them and sold them in the islands. And, since I wished to learn more about the business—for it seemed to me very harmful and contrary to your Majesty's royal purpose—I have learned and verified that as soon as Nuño de Guzmán was received in that province he gave a general license to all its inhabitants [Spaniards] to take twenty or thirty slaves [each] for the islands, and this was done. When this trade came to the attention of the merchants and traders of the islands and they saw that it was profitable, they came to the province of Pánuco in their own interest, and because Guzmán called them, and he himself sent to have ships fitted out for it. And things have come to such a pass that the whole province is dissipated and destroyed. Nine or ten thousand souls have been removed, branded as slaves, and sent to the islands. And truly I think there were more, because above twenty-one ships have sailed from there laden [with slaves]. . . .

For this reason so much harm has come to that province, and such has been the astonishment and terror of the natives, that they have decided to adopt as their best remedy, and it has been so ordered by their chiefs, to abandon their villages and fly to the wilderness, and that no one should have intercourse with his wife, so as not to have children to be made slaves of before their eyes and carried away from their country. . . .

All that is known of the fate of the poor Indian vassals of your Majesty who have been taken from this country is that three shiploads of them have sunk, and others have thrown themselves into the sea and drowned; and so would others do if they were not watched and guarded and kept in prison by the Spaniards so that they will not kill themselves. Those who reach the islands, being very weak from hunger and thirst . . . and afflicted by the narrowness of their quarters, upon arriving at a land so foreign to their nature, catch diseases and pestilences, and all die. This [slaving] has been done on the pretext that license for it has been procured from your Majesty, so that merchants may engage in this trade with better will. And, if it is true that

your Majesty issued such licenses, for the reverence of God
do very great penance for it!

From this evil custom and the diabolical daring that
Nuño de Guzmán brought with him from that province, it
happened that as soon as he entered this city as president
and found himself lord of the land, he secretly caused to be
brought together, by means of the interpreter Pilar, a great
number of Indians of this province, and he sent them to
Pánuco so that they might be branded there and sent to
the islands with the rest. Hence it has happened that the
president and oidores, after having assigned the vacant encomiendas to their relatives and servants, and to those of
the factor . . . are giving to their footmen and others
of lesser quality, in lieu of wages, licenses to buy slaves. And
they sell the licenses and gamble with them publicly, and
those who buy them buy [the slaves], and thus many free
Indians lose their liberty. Things are in such a bad state that
if your Majesty does not remedy them, soon there will be
no remedy, because the country is being ruined at a rapid
rate. I am sending your Majesty a deposition of witnesses
in this matter, made secretly before a notary, and by it you
will learn what is happening, and so I shall dwell no further
upon it. . . .

And now, most Puissant Lord, I wish to give your
Majesty, as briefly as I can, an account of what has happened to me with regard to the charge which your Majesty
gave me so urgently as protector and defender of the Indian
natives of these parts, for it is well that you should know
how your royal commands are being executed.

I arrived with the four oidores, as I have said, at the port
of New Spain, and in a very short time it was published
throughout the land among Spaniards and natives that I
was coming as protector and defender of the Indians, appointed by your Majesty's hand, and that your Majesty had
chosen me for it because of the special regard I had for them.
And immediately I set out for this great city of Mexico,
which is seventy-five leagues from the port. And when it

was known among the Indians, who are as quick-witted as your Majesty has been informed, and they learned that I was coming, many lords of the country came to receive me on my way, bringing gifts, for they are accustomed not to come empty-handed. These gifts I would not accept, nor any part of what they were bringing, and they showed great joy and great rejoicing at my coming, thinking that I was coming from your Majesty to remedy their ills and give them justice for the wrongs they had received. I always gave them hope of it, making clear to them the intention of your Majesty and the love you have for them. And I told them to go to the city of Mexico, and there I should speak with them and inform myself further, and with this I dismissed them. And after I arrived at this city and took lodgings in the monastery of San Francisco, a great number of lords and chief men of the country gathered together and came to see me and to learn what your Majesty commanded of them. I spoke to them through a Flemish religious, Fray Pedro de Gante, a good interpreter, and told them that your Majesty had been informed that the lords of New Spain were very loyal vassals of your Majesty and have served you very well, especially those of the provinces of Huejotzingo, Tlaxcala, and other provinces, and that for this reason and because they are vassals of your Majesty, you are not pleased that any harm or mistreatment come to them; rather, that you wish them to be defended and maintained in peace and justice and that no one is to take from them what is theirs, so that they may live and dwell securely in their houses and towns, and that if anyone should harm them he is to be punished for it according to your Majesty's laws; and that if heretofore anyone harmed them it had been against your Majesty's wishes and without your Majesty's knowledge; and that, since your Highness loves them a great deal as your vassals, you had sent me here as their protector and defender; and that they were to believe that I was to do exactly as your Majesty commanded, for I should not dare to do otherwise so long as they were good; but, if they were bad your Majesty commanded them to be punished. . . .

I made this speech to all the lords of this city and the surrounding country and to others of many other places, and it became known to all the rest, and as the poor Indians have suffered so many robberies and so much violence and ill treatment, and had heard that I was coming to them by command of your Majesty, they began to come to me with many complaints of devilish and abominable crimes. And when I began to exercise my office, taking depositions against the delinquents, and the factor Salazar saw it, he advised the president and oidores that if they consented to it they were lost, because they would not have the authority to rob the country, and the lords of it would not come at their call, and that if they should come they would give them nothing, but would look to me as judge. . . .

This [advice] seemed so good to the president and oidores that they decided to go against your Majesty's ordinance, holding their own interest as more important; and they sent to command me that I was not to have authority in anything concerning the Indians, in hearing their complaints, directly or indirectly, because such was the pleasure of the royal Audiencia, with a certain penalty, because I was not an elected [bishop], but only presented or nominated, and that I was of no greater authority than any friar among my companions; nor would they allow me [to do] anything else, but that as such I might teach them [the Indians] if I wished, without any further authority.

[Zumárraga offers to show the Audiencia his orders again, and he warns the members that he will carry out his instructions even at the cost of his life.]

When they saw my reply and determination they again sent a public notary to me with witnesses, and he notified me of another command, that I was not to exercise my office as protector and defender of the Indians, or to have anything to do with them . . . on pain of loss of my benefice and deportation, and that, in addition, they would proceed against my person, for I was not elected, but only presented, as I have said.

I answered as best I could, because in all this land there is not a lawyer who dares to advise me, or to come to my house, or to receive me in his. Even when the president was in the cabildo with the regidores, as is his habit, it was suggested that guards and spies be posted to see who should enter my house or speak to me, so as to punish him. Thus by his command it was published in the Audiencia, the president and oidores being in that tribunal of your Majesty, that no Spaniard should come to me on any business concerning the Indians, on pain of losing them; and the Indians were commanded through the interpreter Pilar not to come to me with complaints, on pain of hanging. Pilar notified them of this and published it, with the additions and glosses which he usually makes, and so it was soon known throughout the country. The natives were frightened and the Spaniards astounded, and no one dared to speak to me, any more than to an excommunicate. I am sending this order to your Majesty with the reply I made, so that your Majesty may read it. . . .

At the time this was going on some Indians came to me with so many complaints against Spaniards that it was a wonderful thing, and I was astonished that they could stand the ill treatment as well as the robberies which the visitadores commit wherever they go, and of which I am sending your Majesty a deposition made secretly. One Spaniard I have heard of had such a diabolical spirit that he put a lord on a cross with three nails, like Christ, because he was not given all the gold he had demanded, and in this manner other Diocletian cruelties. Another killed and hanged Indians, because they did not give him what he demanded. I went to see the president about it, and he paid no attention; nor did he do a thing regarding the Indians, although he sees that they are being killed.

The lords of the province of Huejotzingo also came secretly to me to complain. At the time they were in the encomienda of Don Hernando Cortés and they said they served Don Hernando as his majordomo commanded them, and that they gave the tributes agreed upon. Some time before [they said] the president and oidores had put another tribute upon them, and they considered it a worse one, for they were obliged to bring to the house of each oidor every day for his maintenance, seven chickens, many quail, and sixty eggs, not counting the tribute they had to give to Pilar, or the wood and charcoal and other small matters, and a great quantity of maize; and they have paid it up to now but can stand it no longer, for it is a distance of eighteen leagues over a snow-covered pass, and many persons are needed in this daily service; and for this reason they have used men, pregnant women, and children as carriers, and a hundred and thirteen of their number have died. And they begged me to aid them; otherwise they would make off into the wilderness, for they had no other recourse.

I made answer as best I could, telling them that such was not the will of your Majesty and offering them a speedy remedy, and so they went secretly away consoled. I spoke to the president and the oidores . . . telling them that some fathers had written this to me from Huejotzingo, so that they might not know that the Indians had come and complained to me. And I told them that your Majesty had commanded me to protect the Indians and that I could not ignore it, but must remedy it, although I knew I might lose my life. In short [I told them] that they should moderate their demands to what was just, for many other towns served them, and to give me a memorandum of the tribute and that I should have it brought in, while attempting to avoid these deaths. The president answered that they [the Indians] had to do what the Audiencia commanded, whether they died or not, and that if I meddled with defending them, they would punish me as the Bishop of Zamora had been punished; [3] and that they were not going

---

[3] The trial and execution of Don Antonio Acuña, Bishop of Zamora and one of the leaders of the revolt of the *comuneros,* was one of the most shocking episodes of the time. His trial lasted five years. Despairing of acquittal, he plotted to break prison and in the attempt murdered one of his guards. He was barbarously tortured, but refused to confess, and was garroted March 23, 1526.

to moderate their demands or live under anyone's authority but their own, and that they would command me and take account of me, because they were my superiors, and that they were going to provide the Church with chaplains [seculars] and pay them out of the tithes, because I could dispose of only a part of them and not more.

A few days later the president and oidores learned that the lords of Huejotzingo had come and complained to me, and they immediately sent an alguacil to arrest them. I learned of it and that they had threatened to execute them, and I sent word to them to put themselves in safety, and so they did, entering a monastery of religious in the same town.

[Zumárraga goes to Huejotzingo and calls together a council of the principal friars and guardians.]

When they had gathered there and the matter had been communicated to them, they passed a resolution unanimously, after prayers and discipline, at which I assisted, that the best remedy was that one of the religious of praiseworthy life and doctrine, a good man of law, should come to the monastery of San Francisco in this city [of Mexico] and at the end of his sermon tell them [the friars] what they [Guzmán and the oidores] had said, so that they might fulfill their obligations, and that he should, after the example of Jesus Christ, tell them that through the goodness of God they had not broken their vows or the precepts of their rule, as the president and the oidores had said.[4]

It happened that it was the day of the Holy Spirit and that the sermon was delivered in the main church, while the Bishop of Tlaxcala officiated at the Mass, dressed in his pontifical robes. When the preacher had finished his sermon, and while he was still in the pulpit, he began to speak with great modesty, gentleness, and benignity, saying that he was now going to defend their good name, so that their doctrine might not be despised [as it would be if] the lives

---

[4] Zumárraga is referring to a libel circulated by Guzmán which was so bad that he could not bring himself to repeat it to the King.

of the preachers were as bad as had been said, and that the least thing could not be proved or verified, and that each one should examine his own conscience.

The president commanded him to desist and to say something else or get down from the pulpit. The preacher answered, begging them to listen for charity's sake, as he would say only what he was obliged to say and what was fitting for them [to hear]. And the oidor Delgadillo ordered an alguacil to throw him out of the pulpit; and so the alguacil and others of the followers of the factor who were with him, shouting insults and giving him the lie, took the preaching friar by the arms and habit and threw him down from the pulpit, and it was a thing of great scandal and tumult, and so they were excommunicated from the Mass.

Another day, the day after Resurrection, as the provisor would not allow Mass to be said in the church until they should be absolved, they commanded him by formal decree and sentence to be exiled from this country and from all the dominions of your Majesty, and refused to admit an appeal, although in your Majesty's name he demanded it. They said that he was not a provisor, any more than I was an elected [bishop], and that your Majesty could not elect me, and that there was a great deal to be said about the validity of the election. And they ordered an alguacil to take him at once and put him on a mule and bring him to the port and put him on board a ship. But he refused to leave the great altar of the church . . . and so the alguaciles were posted at the doors and it was proclaimed that no one was to bring him food, on pain of death, either to him or to the priests who were with him.

[Zumárraga hastens to "throw water on the fire" by granting absolution to Guzmán and the oidores. They burn the libel as their part of the bargain. Zumárraga tells the King again that the only solution for things is to send over a governor and an Audiencia who will be morally above reproach. He urges the removal of the present Audiencia, the confiscation of the property which they have acquired illegally, and, of course, the taking of their residencia.]

It is a very necessary thing, one without which there can be no peace in New Spain, that your Majesty do the Indians and the Spaniards the favor of granting the encomiendas in perpetuity. . . . And let the conquerors have the preference, and successively those who have best served in this country. . . . From it many advantages would ensue: the Indians, who are now confused, seeing that they change masters daily, have no peace or love [for us], nor do they wish to serve those who have them in encomienda, thinking to keep what they have for their next master. For this reason they receive much mistreatment, and in order to avoid serving they make off into the wilderness. They would not do so if they knew they had a perpetual master, and without doubt they would settle down. And if those who govern are absolute rulers, with the power to give and remove Indians—the Indians being the good and wealth of this country—they work their will against justice and with less opposition than your Majesty does in those kingdoms [of Spain]. The Spanish vassals are so oppressed that they dare not speak, and I swear that they are more downtrodden than in any place I have seen. This would not be true if they held their Indians in perpetuity, for they would love them and relieve them of work in order to prevent their running away, and for the sake of preserving [the heritage of] their children. And in their encomiendas they would plant vineyards and olive groves, and they would make other improvements in order to relieve their vassals of tribute and to allow them to live as they do in Spain. . . . But now everything is ruined and no one dares to plant a single thing, thinking that the next day it will be taken from him. . . .

[Zumárraga pleads for greater power for the protector.]

Let your Majesty expressly command that those who are chosen as distributors of the Indians be not allowed to have Indians in encomienda [either openly], or secretly, as the president and oidores do now. . . .

Silks are so common here that mechanics and servants of people of the lower classes, and women of the same, and mistresses and spinsters go about covered with silks, capes and smocks and skirts and kerchiefs, and great harm comes to the country from it, for the inhabitants waste and ruin themselves and become poor and indebted, and the only ones to profit are the merchants. The worst of it is that in order to keep up this silk they flay the Indians of their encomiendas and keep everything at high prices. Let your Majesty command that this be prohibited; and if it cannot be done entirely, let it be done in part, and let it be announced who may wear silks, putting at the top the conquerors and persons of quality, in the most moderate manner your Majesty thinks may be fitting, and let such as these be not forbidden to wear them. . . .

The Indians are very badly used by Spanish travelers, who take them laden wherever they wish to go, like pack animals, without even feeding them, and for this reason they suffer great harm and even die on the road. This harm is principally among those who mine gold, because, in order to maintain the slaves they have in the mines they load their encomienda Indians and send them laden thirty, or forty, or fifty leagues, more or less, and many die on the way. I have in mind a province called Tepeaca, which is now held in encomienda by the *veedor* Pero Almíndez [Chirinos] and from which they say more than 3,000 free men . . . have died on the road from carrying supplies to the mines. And in all the other places there are larger or smaller numbers of deaths, and those who have been in this country since the beginning swear that there are only half as many natives as there were. I do not say that all have died because they have been used as carriers, for they are accustomed to carry burdens since before the Spaniards came, but I do say that this immoderate loading is diminishing them very rapidly. And it is necessary that your Majesty remedy it, because otherwise the end of this country will soon be seen, like that of the islands of Española, Cuba, and others, for this loading was the principal cause of their ruin. . . .

These Indians are so submissive that they have an ancient custom of giving food to the Spaniards who come to their towns, and to the Indians who come with them, all the time they are there, and thus many vagabonds wander about from place to place with nothing to do, with two or even three Indian mistresses and as many Indians to serve them. These who thus wander about are the ones who principally do violence and robbery in the Indian towns, as has been seen daily. It is even worse, for the Indians do not dare complain of the Spaniards who live thus. Your Majesty should order that no Spaniard having Indians in encomienda may send to his town any Spaniard whatever without his being examined first by the protectors and defenders of the Indians, who will take his bond that he will not harm them. . . .

I was warned, by letters from Fray Martín de Valencia and other religious, that the natives were planning to rebel, for they had been told by their Indian disciples that arms were being made in the country; and I was shocked, expecting that as soon as these men should go off on this fine war with the flower of the land [5] they would fall upon us and kill us, and your Majesty would lose this good land and the devil would regain the mastery of the land he had lost. So I went to the lodgings of the Licenciate Matienzo and told him what was going on, petitioning him in the name of God and your Majesty to remedy it, for I did not dare to reprehend him publicly. But I did tell him that I should advise your Majesty of it [the war] even though they raised up against me more witnesses than before, and that the matter was very urgent and that the war should be stopped, for I had been informed that it was going to be carried to the conquered provinces that are already serving your Majesty, and that he was going to rob the caciques of all the gold and silver they had, especially the Cazonzi of Michoacán. . . . For the reverence of God let your Majesty remedy it, because everything is rolling toward the abyss.

I shall take it upon myself to write always about this and about other things that happen, so that the service of God and your Majesty may not perish in this land, where it

[5] Nuño de Guzmán was recruiting his army for the conquest of New Galicia.

is more fitting that it flourish than in all the others of the world.

Unconquered Caesar, may God Our Lord guard and preserve the life and most royal person and most Catholic state of your Majesty for long years, with the increase of as many more kingdoms and dominions as your royal heart may desire.

From this great city of Temixtitlán Mexico, August 27, 1529. Your Sacred Caesarean Catholic Majesty's faithful servant and chaplain,

Fray Juan de Zumárraga, Bishop-elect of Mexico.

Appendix 4

The City Council of Guatemala to Charles V, September 19, 1543 [1]

It is difficult to choose from among the vast outpouring of protests against the New Laws which deluged the Council of the Indies one which will best convey the feeling of the conquistadores. The one I have extracted here is typical and is also interesting for its patently sincere expression of grievance. There is no way to assess the impact of these protests on the Crown. It may have been great, but I rather suspect that the violent and costly rebellions in Peru and Panama were more effective in softening the harsher measures.

Your Majesty's most loyal vassals, the citizens of Guatemala, kiss your Majesty's feet and hands.

In reply to certain reports which have come to this province . . . we say that . . . we cannot believe them, and that we are as shocked as if you had ordered our heads to be cut off. If the reports are true it is as much as saying clearly that all of us here are bad Christians and traitors to our God and to your Majesty, whom we have served with our lives and our estates. . . .

According to this report, Catholic Caesar, we must abandon the hope that our children will enjoy the rewards which we their fathers enjoy and possess in the name of your Majesty. We are stunned and out of our senses, because we do not see how our sins could have been grave enough to deserve such a rigorous and merciless punishment. . . .

It is affirmed by some that the source of this cruel sentence is one Fray Bartolomé de las Casas. We are greatly astonished, unconquered Prince, that a matter of such antiquity, initiated by your grandparents, weighed by so many hands, considered by such good and clear minds so well versed in law and so abundant in good will, should be reversed by a friar unread in law, unholy, envious, vainglorious, unquiet, not free from cupidity (for all of which clear proof can be offered), and, above all else, a trouble-maker,

---

[1] "Libro de Consultas a su Magestad." MS, Municipalidad de Guatemala.

so much so that there is no part of the Indies from which he has not been expelled; nor can he be suffered in any monastery; nor is he given to obeying anyone; and for this reason he never tarries. . . .

[They beg his Majesty not to condemn them without a hearing] . . . unless that religious is a prophet or has learned what he knows through inspiration—which he has not, or even through experience. He says that he has been in these parts thirty-odd years; but thirty of them he spent in Española and Cuba, where the Indians were soon finished, and where he did his share in finishing them, and he might have told the truth about what happened [there]. . . . We say this not to speak evil of him; we say it because he is not competent to give testimony about the Indies, which are New Spain (for the rest are not called Indies), and in this New Spain, which he saw [only] from the roads over which he passed, there is much doctrine among the natives, and knowledge of God and the King, and, for the time they have been taught in the doctrine, they greatly exceed all the kingdoms and seigneuries of your Majesty. We are astounded to hear such things from that religious.

[They argue that the only way in which the two aims of his Majesty can be accomplished, that is, the salvation of the Indians and increase of the royal revenues, is by assuring the stability of the conquerors in the possession of their encomiendas.]

Your Majesty may be certain that if what is rumored in the streets is true, neither the one nor the other purpose will be attained. . . . The father religious deceives himself (may God forgive him!), for there are others here who know as much as he, and somewhat more!, and who with holy zeal and without passion have considered and studied the matter, and who desire nothing but the salvation of your Majesty, their own, and that of these poor people . . . and they are competent to see to it that the towns of the Spaniards are not destroyed or their inhabitants left to wander in the streets crying out to God and your Majesty for justice. . . .

What was your Majesty's purpose in commanding us expressly to marry? And now that we are married and burdened with children, what recourse have we except to die in despair if what we have said is carried out? For we shall lack the patience and charity to see the sons whom we leave behind reduced to beggary, or our daughters ruined, in the land which their fathers won for them. The worst of it is that this land [in that event] will never be filled with Christians, or with the Faith, or with good customs. The religious deceives himself. There are other means to bring this land to God and to your Majesty without destroying the poor people who have won it. Let your Majesty hear all sides . . . for we only desire and demand justice, and that we be measured with the same stick with which your ancestors measured the vassals who won for them their kingdoms and seigneuries. . . .

And we beg your Majesty to consider the sudden, great, and cruel punishment which God visited upon us for our sins when He destroyed the greater part of this city,[2] and the heavy expenditures which cannot be measured that we incurred in the rebuilding of it. How, Catholic Caesar, can we endure or suffer this if your Majesty does not stretch out your imperial hand and grant large favors to this city? For you owe more [favors] to it than to all [the cities] of these Indies for its great services and for the aid which the neighboring provinces have received from it. If the kingdoms of Peru, where so much treasure has been got, are under your Majesty's yoke and rule, what was the cause of it? It was the knights, horses, and arms that this city sent and sends each day, as is notorious.[3] Pay us, your Majesty, what you owe us, and reward us, as we humbly beg on our knees before your Majesty, and have pity on us who are exiled forever from our native land, because for this alone we should be

[2] The first capital of Guatemala, now Ciudad Vieja, was almost totally destroyed by earthquake and flood in 1541.

[3] Pedro de Alvarado organized and equipped a small army which he led to Peru, thinking to take part in the conquest. He sold out to Pizarro for 100,000 pesos and returned alone to Guatemala.

given what is here and nothing should be withheld from us, especially since everything we demand and desire will be spent in your royal service.

May Almighty God make many the days of your Majesty, for the protection of His Church and the increase of His Faith.

From this city of Santiago de Guatemala, September 10, 1543.

Appendix 5

Father Fray Toribio de Motolinía to Charles V, January 2, 1555 [1]

The intense hatred which Las Casas evoked is usually ascribed to the interested reaction of those who had most to lose, namely, the encomenderos. The matter was, however, much more complex than that, as I explained in Chapter 10. It is noteworthy that the missionaries, no less than the encomenderos, felt themselves threatened by the propaganda of Las Casas. This bitter philippic of the saintly Franciscan Motolinía, one of the famous "Twelve Apostles" who came to New Spain in 1524, reveals the depth of the split between the realists of New Spain, who believed that the Spaniards and Indians could be brought into a common and workable social system, and the enthusiasts of the type of Las Casas, who would have made it impossible for Spanish laymen to exploit the conquest in any way. It is an amazing thing that the Council of the Indies should have considered, even for a brief moment, that the conquerors of the New World, with whom the missionaries were now identified, might be prevailed upon quietly to yield up their gains—after fifty years!

Sacred Caesarean Catholic Majesty: May the grace and mercy and peace a Deo Patre Nostro et Domino Jesuchristo [be with you].

Three things principally move me to write this letter to your Majesty which I believe will be the means of removing some of the scruples which Las Casas, bishop-that-was of Chiapa, has imposed upon your Majesty and upon those of your councils.

[The first two are descriptions of the civilization and religion of the Mexicans before the conquest and the success of the missionaries in bringing them to Christianity.]

The third thing is to beg your Majesty to command the men of law of your councils and the universities to consider whether the conquerors and encomenderos and merchants of this New Spain may receive the sacrament of absolution and the other sacraments without their having to execute a public instrument under oath. Las Casas affirms that without this and other measures they cannot be absolved, and he imposes so many scruples on the confessors that nothing is

[1] (*DIM*, I, 253–277; *DII*, XX, 175–213.)

lacking save to send them to hell. So it is necessary that this matter be taken up with the Pope, because it would profit some of us who have baptized more than 300,000, and married and buried as many more, and confessed a great multitude besides, to know whether we are to go to hell because we have confessed ten or twelve of these conquerors.

Las Casas says that everything the Spaniards have here is ill-gotten, even though they have obtained it by trade, and even though there are [among them] many farmers and mechanics and others who have earned a living by their sweat and industry. And, that it may be the better understood, your Majesty should know that five or six years ago, as he says, I was ordered by your Majesty and your Council of the Indies to collect certain MS *confesionarios* that Las Casas had left here in the Indies; and I gave them to Don Antonio de Mendoza, your viceroy, and he burned them, because they contained false and scandalous statements. Now in the last ships that have arrived in New Spain the said *confesionarios* have come printed and have caused no little uproar and scandal in this country, because many times in them he calls the conquerors and encomenderos and merchants, tyrants, robbers, violators, rapers, and bullies. He says that they have always tyrannized and today are still tyrannizing over the Indians. He also says that all the tributes of the Indians are and have been taken unjustly and tyrannically. If such is the case your Majesty's conscience were in a pretty state, for your Majesty has half or the majority of all the more important provinces and towns of New Spain, and the encomenderos and conquerors have only what your Majesty will give them. And [he says] that all the Indians they have should be assessed moderately and that they should be well treated and cared for—as, by the grace of God, almost all are today—and that they should be taught doctrine and given justice—and so it is done. But, nevertheless, Las Casas says all the above and more, so that his principal insults are directed against your Majesty; and he condemns all the men of law of your council, calling them many times unjust and tyrannical. He also insults and condemns all those who are or have been in New Spain, ecclesiastics as well as laymen, and the presidents and audiencias of your Majesty. Certainly the Marqués del Valle and Bishop Don Sebastián Ramírez and Don Antonio de Mendoza and Don Luis de Velasco, who is governing now with the oidores, have ruled and governed and are governing very well both Spaniards and Indians.

Truly, for the few canons that Las Casas has studied, he presumes a great deal, and his disorder seems very great and his humility small, and he thinks that everyone is wrong and that he alone is right, for he says the following words literally: "All the conquerors have been robbers and rapers, and most of them more notorious for evil and cruelty than ever men were, as is now manifest to all the world."

"All the conquerors," he says, without excepting any. Now your Majesty knows the instructions and commands carried by those who go on conquests, and that they labor to keep them, and that they are of as good a life and conscience as Las Casas, and of greater rectitude and piety. I am astonished that your Majesty and those of your councils have been able so long to suffer such an ill-humored, unquiet, importunate, noisy, trouble-making fellow, as turbulent in his religious habit as he is ill-mannered, insulting, harmful, and restless. I have known Las Casas since fifteen years before he came to this country. Once he started out for the land of Peru but, unable to reach his destination, he stopped in Nicaragua, staying there for only a short time. Thence he went to Guatemala, and stayed there even less; and afterward he was in the province of Oaxaca, and did not stay there either, as elsewhere. Then, when he came to Mexico he stopped at the monastery of the Dominicans and immediately tired of it, and again took to wandering and going about in his trouble-makings, always writing accusations and [writing about] other peoples' lives, seeking out the evils and cruelties that the Spaniards had committed throughout this land so as to exaggerate and magnify the evils and sins that have been committed. And in all this he was more zealous and just than the other Christians, and more than the religious, and here he hardly concerned himself with religion!

Once he was talking with some friars and told them that what they were doing was too little, that they had not suffered or shed their blood, although the least of them was a much better servant of God than he, and served Him better, and watched over more souls, and [was of greater] religion and virtue than he, for all his importance. All his dealings have been with a few malcontents to make them tell him things to write in support of his passionate hatred of the Spaniards, and to show them that he loves the Indians a great deal and that he alone wishes to defend and favor them more than anyone. In this he busied himself a short while here, save when he was using them as carriers and abusing them.

Las Casas came as a simple friar and arrived at the city of Tlaxcala with twenty-seven or thirty-seven Indian carriers, called tamemes. At that time certain bishops and prelates were examining a bull of Pope Paul [III] which concerned marriage and baptism, and they silenced us, saying that we should not baptize adult Indians. And an Indian had come three or four days' journey to be baptized, and had asked for baptism many times and was very well prepared, catechized and taught. Then I, with many friars, begged Las Casas to baptize that Indian who had come from afar and, after we had beseeched him many times to do so, he made many conditions for the baptism, as if he alone knew more than all, and truly the Indian was well prepared. And, since he said that he would baptize him, he put on his surplice and stole, and three or four of us religious went with him to the door of the church, where the Indian was kneeling, and I know not what vagary struck him, but he refused to baptize the Indian and left us and went away. I then said to Las Casas: "So, Father, all the zeal and love which you say you have for the Indians ends with using them as carriers, and with going about writing of the Spaniards and abusing the Indians! Why, you alone use more Indian carriers than twenty friars; and, since you will not baptize or teach a single Indian, it would be well if you paid all those tired carriers of yours!"

At that time, as I have said, he had twenty-seven or thirty-seven carriers with him—I do not recall the exact number—and the greatest part of what they were carrying was accusations against the Spaniards and other rubbish. And when he went to Spain and came back a bishop he brought a hundred and twenty Indian carriers, without paying them anything; and now he is trying to have your Majesty and the Council of the Indies provide that no Spaniard may use Indian carriers, even by paying them well, as now they are well paid everywhere, and the only ones now used are three or four to carry bedding and food; besides, these things cannot be had on the road.

Afterward he always went about restlessly on the business of important people, and what he obtained in Spain was to have himself made Bishop of Chiapa. And, since he did not do what he had promised to negotiate, Father Fray Domingo de Betanzos, who was well acquainted with the matter, wrote him a long letter very publicly in which he described to him his life and disturbances and trouble-making, and the harm and damage which he had done with his indiscreet zeal and the information he had sent [to Spain] wherever he went. And even now where he is he does not cease from doing the same, pretending that he is doing so from the zeal he has for the Indians. And he shows your Majesty or your council a letter someone writes from here, and not always true, and by a memorandum which he writes he has a general cédula issued, and thus he upsets and destroys the government and the state here; and this is what all his zeal amounts to.

When he came as Bishop of Chiapa, which is the head of his bishopric, the people of that city received him, because your Majesty had sent him, with great love and humility, and they established him in his church with the pallium, and lent him money with which to pay the debts he had incurred in Spain. And a few days later he excommunicates them and imposes on them fifteen or sixteen rules and laws for the confession, and leaves them and goes away. Betanzos wrote him about this [saying], that he had made rams of his sheep and had put the cart before the oxen.

Then he went to a kingdom called Vera Paz,[2] which he says is such a great matter; and I have visited and taught thereabout, and it is not so great by one-tenth as is said there [in Spain]. There is one monastery in Mexico that teaches and visits ten times as many people as there are in the whole kingdom of Vera Paz, and the Bishop of Guatemala is a good witness of it. I saw the people, and they are of less consequence than any other. . . .

Time was when the Spaniards did not wish to see friars or priests in their towns, but for some time past they have been getting friars, and their Indians have been building monasteries, and the encomenderos have been providing food, vestments, and ornaments for the friars. It is not odd that Las Casas does not know this, because he never tried to learn anything but the evil, and not the good. He was restless in New Spain and did not learn any Indian tongue; nor did he humble himself to teach them. His occupation was to write charges on every hand, and of the sins that the Spaniards have committed, and in it he exaggerates a great deal. And truly this one activity ought not to take him to heaven, because what he writes is not all true or well substantiated. . . .

He has been trying to have himself made attorney at Court and to have it appear that the Indians are demanding him as their protector; and when the letter in which this was ordered was read in a congregation of Franciscans they all burst out laughing and could say nothing about such nonsense. He did not show at Court the letters from the chapter or congregation of Franciscans! Moreover, he induces people here to send him money and commissions. Such activities may be approved of by some, but I believe that your Majesty will abhor them, because it is clearly a temptation of our adversary to trouble your Majesty and others.

[2] Motolinía's chronology is confused. Las Casas was in Vera Paz in 1532 and came as Bishop to Chiapa in 1547.

Your Majesty should have him locked up in a monastery so that he may not cause greater evils, for otherwise I am afraid that he will go to Rome and be a cause of disturbance in the Roman court. . . .

With respect to the granting of lands, your Majesty might give the excess unoccupied and uncultivated lands to Spanish settlers who might wish to devote themselves to working them, and to others born here who ought to have something. In the past ten years the Indians have suffered a heavy mortality from pestilences, and so there is a great scarcity of people. In the places where there is the least scarcity they are reduced by two-thirds; in others by four-fifths; in others by seven-eighths.[3] For this reason there is a great plenty of land everywhere, besides the uncultivated lands and warlike territories that were not planted.

Cattle have been removed from every place where they did any damage, especially the larger herds, not because of a scarcity of lands, but because they were kept without guards and . . . overran a great deal of land and did damage. For summer pasturage they have been assigned certain dates to enter and leave, under penalties, because here, by the goodness of God, there is someone to remedy [the evil], and also someone to watch over it, like Las Casas.[4]

Since many Indians are now using horses, it would not be ill for your Majesty to forbid issuing licenses for them, except to the principal chiefs, for if the Indians become accustomed to them, many will learn to ride and will wish to set themselves up as the equals of the Spaniards. The ad-

[3] Although Motolinía exaggerates the loss of population, nevertheless the loss had been enormous since the conquest, being about one-half at the time of his writing. The effect of depopulation has not been properly studied, but it seems reasonably clear that the growth of *latifundia*, and especially the vast increase in cattle-farming, was directly owing to the vacating of agricultural lands. It may be argued that the change-over into larger units of cultivation was necessary in order to feed the cities. Even so, famines in Mexico City were of frequent occurrence in the seventeenth century.

[4] Motolinía's optimism leads him astray. Damage to crop lands by cattle was one of the most prolific sources of friction in New Spain. The records of the General Indian Court are replete with suits for damage from cattle to the very end of the colonial régime.

vantage of horses and cannon is very necessary for this country, because it gives to the few, force and advantage against the many. All this New Spain, your Majesty, is deserted and defenseless and without any fort or fortress . . . and [it should be fortified] if only because we are in a strange land and because the Negroes are so numerous that several times they have plotted to rise and kill the Spaniards. The city of Los Angeles [Puebla] has a better situation for the erection of a fortress than any other town of New Spain. It could be built there for less cost because of the many and good materials there, and it would be a security for the whole country. . . . So much for temporal matters. . . .

The central church of Mexico, which is the Metropolitan, is very poor, old, and patched, for it was flimsily built twenty-nine years ago. . . . Your Majesty should order that this church, as well as the other cathedrals, be given a town [in encomienda] as formerly, for no encomienda in all New Spain will be so well employed. They have great need of these towns for the repair, roofing, cleaning, and adorning of the churches and the houses of the bishops, for all [the bishops] are poor and in debt. Shoemakers and blacksmiths have encomiendas, but the churches have much greater need of them, for they have no rents, or what they have is very little.

I say all this with the desire of serving your Majesty and informing you of what I think of this country and what I have seen in the thirty years since we came here by command of your Majesty. . . . And of the twelve of us [Franciscans] who came at the beginning of the conversion of this people there are but two living.

Receive this letter, your Majesty, in the spirit in which I write it, and let it not have more weight than is reasonable, just, and right. And I remain the least of your chaplains, praying God that His Grace will always dwell in the blessed soul of your Majesty so that you will always do His holy will. Amen.

[Motolinía adds a ten-page postscript in which he returns to the fray with Las Casas, accusing him of malice, ignorance, etc. He is particularly incensed by Las Casas' description of slaving in New Spain and the treatment of the slaves.]

As for their treatment—I speak of New Spain, where almost all have been set free—according to my information in all New Spain there may be a thousand slaves yet to be freed, and these are being freed daily, and by the end of the year hardly an Indian slave will remain in the land. In liberating them your Majesty did your duty and even more, for you ordered those who possessed slaves to ascertain whether they were really slaves—practically an impossibility, the contrary being according to law. What you ordered was right, because the minority of them had been justly taken. He [Las Casas] says that in all the Indies there was never a just cause for making a slave—this he knows who did not leave Mexico City or its vicinity, and so it is no wonder he knows so little.

Las Casas was in this country a matter of seven years and, as they say, he spent five of them in the streets. There have been friars in New Spain who have walked from Mexico City to Nicaragua, four hundred leagues, and there are not two towns in the whole distance in which they did not preach and say Mass, and teach and baptize children and adults, few or many. And the friars here have seen and learned a little more than Las Casas about the good treatment of the slaves. The officers of the government, as well as the preaching friars and confessors—for from the beginning there have been Franciscans, and afterward came those of other orders—always took as their special care to see that the Indians, the slaves above all, were well treated and taught in all doctrine and in Christianity and God, who is the principal doer of all good. Then the Spaniards began to bring their slaves to church to be baptized, taught, and married, and those who did not do so were not given absolution. . . . It is not just for Las Casas to say that the service of the Christians oppresses them unbearably, and that the Spaniards think less of the Indians than they do of their beasts, and even less than the dung of the town square. . . .

The branding-iron called *de rescate* [for branding slaves acquired by purchase] was brought to New Spain in the year twenty-four, in the middle of May. As soon as Captain Don Hernando Cortés arrived at Mexico City, which he was governing at the time, he had a meeting in the convent of San Francisco with the friars and men of law who were in the city, and I was present. And I saw that the governor was troubled by the iron and spoke against its use, and, since he could do nothing else, he greatly limited the license which he had for the branding of slaves; and those who were branded in excess of his limitation were branded during his absence in Honduras. And the works of some who murmur at the Marqués del Valle, whom God cherish!, and who wish to blacken and obscure his deeds, I believe before God are not as acceptable as his. . . . By means of this captain God opened the door for us to preach His Holy Gospel, and he it was who forced the Indians to have reverence for the holy sacraments and for the ministers of the Holy Church. And so I have written at such length somewhat to defend his life, for he is now dead.

May the grace of the Holy Spirit abide always in the soul of your Majesty. Amen.

From Tlaxcala, January 2, 1555.

The most humble servant and least chaplain of your Majesty,

Fray Toribio Motolinía.

Appendix 6

A Seventeenth-Century Encomienda: Chimaltenango, Guatemala

Reprinted by permission from *The Americas*, vol. XV, No. 4, April, 1959, pp. 393–402. (Condensed).

Captain Francisco Antonio de Fuentes y Guzmán, whose proud boast it was (as he never tires of repeating) that he was the great-great-grandson of Bernal Díaz del Castillo, in his erratic, rambling, and frequently delightful *Recordación Florida* (c. 1690), has this to say about the ancient town that will be the subject of this article:

Three smooth and pleasant leagues north of this City of Goathemala [Antigua], on a road thickly studded with villages and tile yards, upon a high eminence in the midst of a wide and marvelous plain, but so accessible and gently sloping that, despite the many carts, the journey can be made quite comfortably in a carriage, lies the town of Chimaltenango (called by the Indians, *Bocco*). This broad and smiling plain is always clothed with pleasant and fertile meadows, and with rich and extensive cornfields. It is more than sixteen leagues in circumference, of rich and very fecund soil, and produces in abundance corn, chickpeas, beans, capons, and chickens, as well as other things. . . . The Indians of the district do not cultivate other crops, but maintain themselves with what it yields, so that the people of its villages are plentifully supplied with everything, according to their way of living, and have no need to seek food elsewhere. . . . On the contrary, the people from other villages come to their market to buy whatever they lack . . . , so that for three leagues roundabout (the distance to which their commerce extends) there is as much provender as one finds in the abundant markets of Goathemala City.

The principal town of this valley is Santa Ana Chimaltenango (from which the whole valley takes its name), of admirable plan, noble buildings, and many inhabitants, whose number passes 3,000 Indians,[1] industrious, peaceful, and excellent natives. Its

---

[1] That is to say, 3,000 *indios tributarios*, or heads of families, which gives a population of 12,000, according to the one-to-four ratio that Fuentes y Guzmán invariably employs.

square is level and spacious, and in its center they are building a fountain modeled after that in the square of Chiapa de
Indios.[2]

The Indians of the town of Chimaltenango, several Spaniards,
and the natives of the villages of San Lorenzo, San Sebastián, and
San Miguel del Tejar, operate many tile yards, with great profit
and utility, because the tile and brick made from the clay of this
district of Chimaltenango are the best and strongest . . . manu-
factured anywhere in the vicinity of Goathemala . . . , selling
at five pesos a thousand more than those made . . . in other
places. The workmen also make pots called *ollas de salineros*
(saltmakers' pots), for the saltmakers go clear to the shore of the
South Sea to make this necessary and useful condiment, which
they do with excessive and immense labor (almost unimaginable
in a human being), for they must work naked in the burning
sun and the heat of the ovens. . . .[3]

At the time Fuentes y Guzmán was writing, Chimaltenango was the largest of the six towns of an encomienda
held by Don Luis Nieto de Silva, who had inherited it from
his mother, Doña María Magdalena Ruiz de Contreras, Condesa de Alba de Yeltes. At her death, in 1686, the resident
administrator, Captain Joseph Aguilar Rebolledo, made an
accounting of his 22 years of stewardship and had a true
copy made for himself, which, preserved by some miracle,
is the basic document of this article.[4]

The encomienda of the Condesa de Alba comprised six
towns: Santa Ana Chimaltenango and San Sebastián del Tejar, already described; San Pedro Aguacatepeque and Santa
María Malacatepeque, two villages on the south slope of the
Volcán de Fuego, according to a sketch map in the *Recorda-*

[2] The fountain was completed and is today the main attraction of Chimaltenango for tourists.

[3] Francisco Antonio de Fuentes y Guzmán, *Recordación Florida: Discurso
historial y demostración natural, material, militar y política del Reyno de
Goathemala*, I, 343–345. 3 vols. (Guatemala, 1932–1933).

[4] *Una cuenta dada por el Capitán Don Joseph de Aguilar Rebolledo, vezino
desta Ziudad de Santiago de Goathemala en las Yndias, a la Señora Doña
María Magdalena Ruiz de Contreras, Condesa de Alba, de lo prozedido de la
encomienda que en indios vacos de la dicha Ziudad y su Provincia tenía dicha
señora de tres mill ducados cada año.* May 14, 1689. MS, 44 ff., in the private
collection of Mr. John Galvin of Santa Barbara, California, who generously
placed it at my disposal.

ción Florida (II, 75); Sacualpa (or Zacualpa, Tzacualpa, or Tezacualpa, depending on the map maker's whim); Espíritu Santo, "of the Corregimiento of Tecpan-Atitlán," now in the Department of El Quiché, about 30 miles north of Chimaltenango; Santiago Zambo, "of the Alcaldía Mayor of Suchitepéquez," unidentified.

Tributes were collected twice a year, at the end of the *tercio de San Juan* (June 29), and at the end of the *tercio de Navidad* (Christmas). The unit of value, to which all tributes were reduced, and in which Aguilar kept his accounts, was the *tostón de plata,* with its fractions, the *real de vellón,* and the *maravedí,* a fictitious unit used for calculating the value of all coins. Four *reales de vellón* equalled one *tostón* (½ *peso*); 34 *maravedís* equalled one *real de vellón.* Two other units used by Aguilar were the *escudo* (11 *reales,* or 2¾ *tostones*), and the silver *peso* (8 *reales* or 2 *tostones*). These values will be conventionally indicated by *tostones/reales/maravedís;* e. g., 10/2/17.

Total tribute, in money and kind,[5] 1664–1686:

Chimaltenango	168,384/1/11
San Sebastián del Tejar	12,153/0/0
San Pedro Aguacatepeque	6,290/1/0
Santa María Magdalena Malacatepeque	2,372/2/0
Sacualpa Espíritu Santo	26,102/0/0
Santiago Zambo	35,392/0/0
	250,694/4/19[6]
Less Administrator's commission of 10 per cent [7]	24,809/2/0
Net Debit	225,885/2/19

[5] "Kind" was collected in maize, chili, beans, chickens, and cacao.

[6] For the years 1661–1663 Aguilar notes that the arrears were collected "with great difficulty." "There occurred in the years 1661, '62, and '63, darkening the sun and filling all the element of the air, an incomparable plague of locusts, which devoured and destroyed fields and crops" (*Recordación Florida,* II, 23). The "great difficulty" in collecting arrears was met by casting the Indian officers into prison until they made up the deficit.

[7] The apparent discrepancy in the commission is owing to 2,599/0/0 turned over to Aguilar by his predecessor.

Credits:

Paid into the Royal Treasury of Guatemala for *escudería* [8] (22 years, 72 days) ...	8,102/0/0
Paid into same for wine and oil for the Dominican and Franciscan Orders	4,388/0/0
Same for Mercedarian Order	2,261/2/20
Alms for building the Cathedral Church of Guatemala	280/0/0
Sales tax (*alcabala*) to City of Guatemala	465/2/0
Tax for Windward Fleet (*derecho de barlovento*)	114/0/0
Scriveners' fees	3,787/3/27
To Dominican convent and religious of the City of Guatemala, for administering the sacraments and teaching the doctrine at Chimaltenango and Tejar	27,829/2/0
To parish priest of Chimaltenango, for same	5,151/3/6
To Dominican convent and religious, for same at Tejar	399/2/0
To syndic of the Franciscan convent, for same at Aguacatepeque and Malacatepeque	2,089/2/0
To secular priests of Santiago Zambo	2,397/2/0
For medical care of Indians of Chimaltenango in the *peste* of 1667 [9]	700/0/0

[8] A law of Philip II of 1571 provided that an encomendero, upon absenting himself from his district, must pay into the hand of the viceroy or governor, money with which to employ a substitute (*escudero*) to assume his functions. *Recopilación*, Lib. VI, Tit. IX, Ley vi. 2d ed., 1756.

[9] "I had to send to the said town the *curandero* Francisco de Vargas, to whom I paid 300 *tostones* for his labor in curing the Indians, which occupied him 47 days. I also reimbursed Diego González de Padilla, administrator of the tributes of the said town, for a considerable quantity of medicines, such as sirups (*jarabes*), electuaries (*lamedores*), cañafistula, sugar, and tamarind; and I gave him an order to deliver to the said Francisco de Vargas food for the sick Indians, with meat and tortillas, and the necessary number of chickens (the whole being paid for out of their tribute account), in the amount of 400 *tostones* (although I spent more than 600) . . . , a total of 700 *tostones*. I state further that I performed this service, not only because it was my duty, but because I was ordered to do so by the President [of the Audiencia], Don Fernando de Escobedo."

It is interesting to note that the *curandero* (an uncertified physician) had official status.

For miscellaneous small items (powers of attorney, dispatches, notices, etc.)	800/0/0
For transport of chickens [10]	792/2/0
Remittances to Spain, 1666–1685, in silver *tostones*	116,000/0/0
Freight charges to Vera Cruz, fees of royal silver commissioner, sacking, crating, and inspection [11]	7,237/0/0
Freight charges on 3 shipments of cacao and chocolate (700 lbs.)	1,050/0/0
Delivered, by order of the Condesa de Alba, to Capt. Joseph Varón de Veriesa	7,000/0/0
Delivered, by order of the Condesa, to the Maestre de Campo Joseph Augustín de Estrada, of Guatemala, 2,000 *escudos* ..	5,500/0/0
To Domingo de Zurrain Irigoyen, for making this accounting, with a clean copy .	350/0/0
Total Credits	196,502/2/29
Total Debits	225,885/2/19
Difference owed by Administrator	29,382/3/24

That the Indians were pushed to the limit of their capacity to pay is pretty clear. When they were pushed beyond that limit, as in the years 1684–1686, they resorted to the simple expedient of running away, as was their universal practice throughout the old régime. They might have borne up under the encomienda tribute if the Crown had not imposed additional burdens, such as the tax of a *tostón* a year (the *real servicio*) levied since 1591 to pay for the Invincible Armada and never lifted, as was the way with special taxes. They raised this tax money by forced labor in the salt pans of the south coast (salt was a royal monop-

---

[10] That is, from Chimaltenango, Tejar, Aguacatepeque, and Malacatepeque, to Guatemala City: 50,598 chickens at 1 *real* for each 20; from Sacualpa, 6,404 chickens at 2 *reales* for each 20, "because it is more distant from this city."

[11] There were no freight charges on the shipment of 12,000 *tostones* in 1683, because the silver was boxed in dyewood (*tinta*) and consigned to one Don Fulgencio Panesi, at Cadiz, who remitted the silver to the Condesa de Alba and recovered the freight and other charges from the sale of the boxes.

oly), at the cost of immense hardship and sickness. Fuentes y Guzmán describes at length the process of extracting salt from the tidal pools and mud at Ixtapa (Nahuatl *Ixtapan*, place of salt), and ends with this illuminating comment:

The truth is that this activity is a frightful scourge for the poor wretches who, bent under the heavy loads they carry, not being very strong besides, and oppressed by an intolerable number of "obligations," as their own officers call them, groan under the yoke of personal services and taxes, defenceless and voiceless. Their misery is not seen because their words are not heard.[12]

Although Chimaltenango shows a slow growth between 1664 and 1686, its population, following the vast general decline in New Spain, was most likely very much smaller than it was at the time of the *visita* of 1549 made by the *licenciados* Ramírez, Cerrato, and Rogel.[13] It was then in the encomienda of a certain Antonio Ruiz, and the assessment of 1549 shows it to have been a large and productive community.

To sum up, the encomienda of Chimaltenango in 1690 is an example of the "tamed encomienda" I described in Chapter 11 above. It had degenerated into a device for pensioning off descendants of the conquistadores or influential people at court. An astonishing part of its gross income went to the support of religious activities of all kinds, over 53,000 *tostones* (including the tithe on tribute in kind), or better

---

[12] *Recordación Florida*, II, 102–104. Fuentes y Guzmán's indignation over the pitiable lot of the Indians is not to be taken quite literally. He is writing as a good *criollo* (white American). In the seventeenth century the Spanish Empire was staggering under an ever-increasing pyramid of taxes . . . and the *criollos* were extremely unhappy about it. The Indians, to be sure, bore the ultimate and heaviest burden, and then, as the Crown absorbed more and more labor in the salt pans and elsewhere, it reduced the labor supply upon which Fuentes y Guzmán and the rest depended.

[13] *Relación y forma que el licenciado Palacio, oydor en la Real Audiencia de Guathemala, hizo para los que obieren de bisitar, contar, tassar, y rrepartir en las provincias deste Districto.* . . . (AGI, *Aud. Guat.*, leg. 128 [64–6–1], 413 ff.).

than 20%! It is a fair guess that this contribution reflected, not so much the religious enthusiasm of the encomendero, as the great power of the Orders in Guatemala.
The civil taxes were, by comparison, insignificant, about
9,000 *tostones*. The net income of the encomienda was
about 162,000 *tostones* for the 22 years, or about 7,300
tostones a year, or about 2,700 *ducados*, not far short of the
3,000 *ducados* of the grant.

Bibliography

(Note.—The archival materials are not included in the bibliography because they are fully described in the notes.)

ACOSTA, JOSE DE. *Historia natural y moral de las Indias.* Ed. Edmundo O'Gorman (Mexico, 1940).

AITON, A. S. *Antonio de Mendoza, First Viceroy of New Spain* (Durham, N. C., 1927).

Archivo Mexicano: Documentos para la historia de México. 2 vols. (Mexico, 1852–1853).

ARREGUI, DOMINGO LAZARO DE. *Descripción de la Nueva Galicia.* Ed. François Chevalier (Seville, 1946).

BANCROFT, H. H. *History of Central America.* 3 vols. (San Francisco, 1883–1888).

————. *History of Mexico.* 6 vols. (San Francisco, 1883–1888).

BORAH, WOODROW. *Silk Raising in Colonial Mexico.* Ibero-Americana, No. 20 (Berkeley, California, 1943).

————. "The Collection of Tithes in the Bishopric of Oaxaca during the Sixteenth Century," *HAHR*, XXI, 389–409.

————. "Tithe Collection in the Bishopric of Oaxaca, 1601–1867," *HAHR*, XXIX, 498–517.

BOURNE, E. G. *Spain in America, 1450–1580* (New York, 1904).

CARRANZA, BALTASAR DORANTES DE. *Sumaria relación de las cosas de la Nueva España* (Mexico, 1902).

Cartas de Indias (Madrid, 1877).

CHAMBERLAIN, R. S. *The Conquest and Colonization of Yucatan* (Washington, D. C., 1948).

————. *Castilian Backgrounds of the Repartimiento-Encomienda.* Carnegie Institution Publications, No. 509, 15–66 (Washington, D. C., 1939).

CHEVALIER, FRANÇOIS. "Signification sociale de la fondation de Puebla de los Angeles," *Revista de Historia de America*, No. 23, 105–130.

Colección de documentos inéditos para la historia de Ibero-América. 3 vols. (Madrid, 1927–1928).

Colección de documentos inéditos relativos al descubrimiento, conquista y organización de las antiguas posesiones españolas de ultramar. Segunda serie. 17 vols. (Madrid, 1885–1925).

COOK, SHERBURNE F. *Population Trends among the California Mission Indians.* Ibero-Americana, No. 17 (Berkeley, California, 1940).

Cook, Sherburne F. and L. B. Simpson. *The Population of Central Mexico in the Sixteenth Century.* Ibero-Americana, No. 31 (Berkeley, California, 1948).

Cortes, Hernan. *Cartas.* Ed. Pascual Gayangos (Paris, 1866).

———. *Cartas y otros documentos.* Ed. Mariano Cuevas (Seville, 1915).

———. *Cartas y relaciones.* Ed. Nicolás Coronado (Buenos Aires, 1946).

Cuevas, Mariano. (Ed.) *Documentos inéditos del siglo XVI para la historia de México* (Mexico, 1914).

———. *Historia de la Iglesia en México.* 5 vols. (Mexico, 1921–1928).

Cunningham, C. H. *The Audiencia in the Spanish Colonies* (Berkeley, California, 1919).

Diaz del Castillo, Bernal. *Verdadera y Notable Relación del descubrimiento y conquista de la Nueva España y Guatemala.* 2 vols. (Guatemala, C. A., 1933–1934).

Encinas, Diego de. *Provisiones, cédulas, capítulos de ordenanzas, instrucciones y cartas tocantes al buen gobierno de las Indias* . . . 4 vols. (Madrid [1596] 1943).

Esquivel Obregon, T. *Hernán Cortés y el derecho internacional en el siglo XVI* (Mexico, 1939).

Fabie, Antonio Maria. *Vida de Fray Bartolomé de las Casas.* 2 vols. (Madrid, 1879).

———. *Ensayo histórico de la legislación española en sus estados de ultramar* (Madrid, 1896).

Fisher, L. E. *Viceregal Administration in the Spanish-American Colonies* (Berkeley, California, 1926).

Gage, Thomas. *A New Survey of the West-Indies* (London [1648] 1699).

Garcia, Genaro. *Carácter de la conquista española en América y en México, según los textos de los historiadores primitivos* (Mexico, 1901).

Garcia Icazbalceta, J. *Don Fray Juan de Zumárraga, primer obispo y arzobispo de México* (Mexico, 1881).

———. (Ed.) *Colección de documentos para la historia de México.* 2 vols. (Mexico, 1858–1866.) (Cited in the notes as *DIM.*)

———. (Ed.) *Nueva colección de documentos para la historia de México.* 5 vols. (Mexico, 1886–1892).

Gonzalez Obregon, Luis. *Los precursores de la independencia mexicana en el siglo XVI* (Paris, 1906).

Gruening, Ernest. *Mexico and Its Heritage* (New York, 1928).

GUTIERREZ, CARLOS. *Fray Bartolomé de las Casas* . . . (Madrid, 1878).

HACKETT, C. W. (Ed.) *Historical Documents Relating to New Mexico, Nueva Viscaya, and Approaches Thereto, to 1773.* Collected by Adolph F. A. and Fanny Bandelier (Washington, D. C., 1923–1926).

HANKE, LEWIS. "The Requerimiento and its Interpreters," *Revista de Historia de América,* No. 1, 25–34.

——. *The First Social Experiments in America* (Cambridge, Mass., 1935).

——. *The Spanish Struggle for Justice in the Conquest of America* (Philadelphia, 1949).

HARING, C. H. *The Spanish Empire in America* (New York, 1947).

HELPS, SIR ARTHUR. *The Life of Las Casas, the Apostle of the Indies* (London [1867] 1896).

——. *The Spanish Conquest in America and its Relation to the History of Slavery and to the Government of Colonies.* 4 vols. (London [1855–1861] 1900–1904).

HERRERA Y TORDESILLAS, ANTONIO DE. *Historia general de los hechos de los castellanos en las islas y tierra firme del mar Océano.* 4 vols. (Madrid, 1601).

HUMBOLDT, ALEXANDER VON. *Political Essay on the Kingdom of New Spain.* Translated by John Black. 4 vols. (London, 1811).

HUSSEY, R. D. "Text of the Laws of Burgos," *HAHR,* XII, 306–321.

ICAZA, FRANCISCO DE. *Conquistadores y pobladores de Nueva España.* 2 vols. (Madrid, 1923).

Instrucciones que los virreyes de la Nueva España dejaron a sus sucesores (Mexico, 1867).

JUDERIAS, JULIAN. *La leyenda negra* (Madrid, 1914).

KIRKPATRICK, F. A. "Repartimiento-Encomienda," *HAHR,* XIX, 372–379.

——. "The Landless Encomienda," *HAHR,* XXII, 765–774.

KUBLER, GEORGE. *Mexican Architecture of the Sixteenth Century.* 2 vols. (New Haven, Conn., 1948).

LAS CASAS, BARTOLOME DE LAS. *Apologética historia de las Indias.* M. Serrano y Sanz, ed. (Madrid, 1909).

——. *Brevíssima relación de la destruyción de las Indias* (Seville, 1552). (In Appendix to Fabié, *Vida de las Casas.*)

——. *Del único modo de atraer a todos los pueblos a la verdadera*

Religión. Translated from the Latin by Atenógenes Santa-María. Ed. by Agustín Millares Carlos and Lewis Hanke (Mexico, 1942).

————. *Historia de las Indias.* 5 vols. (Madrid, 1875).

LEA, H. C. *A History of the Inquisition of Spain.* 4 vols. (New York, 1906–1907).

————. *The Inquisition in the Spanish Dependencies* (New York, 1908).

————. "The Indian Policy of Spain," *Yale Review,* VIII, 119–155.

LEON, ANTONIO DE. *Tratado de confirmaciones reales de encomiendas* . . . (Madrid, 1630).

LLORENTE, JUAN ANTONIO. *Oeuvres de Las Casas* . . . *précédées de sa vie* . . . 2 vols. (Paris, 1822).

LOPEZ-PORTILLO Y WEBER, JOSE. *La conquista de la Nueva Galicia* (Mexico, 1935).

————. *La rebelión de Nueva Galicia* (Mexico, 1939).

LOPEZ DE VELASCO, JUAN. *Geografía y descripción universal de las Indias desde 1571 a 1574.* Justo Zaragoza, ed. (Madrid, 1894).

LOZOYA, JUAN CONTRERAS DE. *Vida del segoviano Rodrigo de Contreras, gobernador de Nicaragua (1534–1544).* (Toledo, 1920).

MCBRIDE, G. M. *Land Systems of Mexico* (New York, 1923).

MACNUTT, F. A. *Bartholomew de Las Casas, His Life, His Apostolate and His Writings* (New York, 1909).

MEIGS, PEVERIL. *The Dominican Mission Frontier of Lower California* (Berkeley, California, 1935).

MENDIETA, GERONIMO DE. *Historia eclesiástica indiana.* 4 vols. (Mexico, 1946).

MOTOLINIA (TORIBIO DE BENAVENTE). *Historia de los indios de la Nueva España.* DIM, I, 1–249.

————. *Memoriales de fray Toribio de Motolinía.* Luis García Pimentel, ed. (Mexico, 1903).

MUÑOZ, JUAN BAUTISTA. *Historia del Nuevo Mundo.* 2 vols. (Madrid, 1793). (The second volume was never published; a MS copy is in the Bancroft Library of the University of California.)

NAVARRETE, MARTIN FERNANDEZ DE. *Colección de los viages y descubrimiento que hicieron por mar los españoles* . . . (Commonly known as *Los Viages de Colón*) 5 vols. (Madrid, 1825–1837).

OBREGON, BALTASAR DE. *Historia de los descubrimientos antiguos y modernos de la Nueva España.* Mariano Cuevas, ed. (Mexico [1584] 1924).

OROZCO Y BERRA, MANUEL. *Historia de la dominación española en México.* 4 vols. (Mexico [1849] 1938).

————. *Apuntes para la historia de la geografía en México* (Mexico, 1881).

OVIEDO Y VALDES, GONZALO FERNANDEZ DE. *Historia general y natural de las Indias, islas y tierra firme del mar Océano.* 4 vols. (Madrid, 1851–1855).

PACHECO, J. F., CARDENAS, F. DE, TORRES DE MENDOZA, L. *Colección de documentos inéditos relativos al descubrimiento, conquista y organización de las antiguas posesiones españolas.* 42 vols. (Madrid, 1864–1889).

PARRY, J. H. *The Audiencia of New Galicia in the Sixteenth Century* (Cambridge, England, 1948).

PASO Y TRONCOSO, FRANCISCO DEL. *Epistolario de Nueva España.* 16 vols. (Mexico, 1939–1942).

————. *Papeles de Nueva España.* 7 vols. (Mexico, 1905–1945).

PEÑA CAMARA, JUAN DE LA. *El tributo—sus orígenes, su implantación en Nueva España* (Seville, 1934).

PEREYRA, CARLOS. *Historia de America Española.* 8 vols. (Madrid, 1920).

PEREZ BUSTAMANTE, CIRIACO. *Don Antonio de Mendoza* (Santiago de Compostela, 1928).

PRIESTLEY, H. I. *José de Gálvez, Visitor-General of New Spain* (Berkeley, California, 1916).

PUGA, VASCO DE. *Provisiones, cédulas, instrucciones de su Majestad . . . desde el año de 1525 hasta éste de 1563.* 2 vols. (Mexico [1563] 1878).

Recopilación de leyes de los reynos de las Indias. 4 vols. (Madrid [1681], 1756).

REMESAL, ANTONIO DE. *Historia general . . . de Chiapa y Guatemala.* 2 vols. ([Madrid, 1619], Guatemala, 1932).

RICARD, ROBERT. *La conquête spirituelle du Méxique* (Paris, 1933).

RIVA PALACIO, V. (Ed., and author of vol. 2). *México a través de los siglos.* 5 vols. (Barcelona, 1888–1889).

SAUER, C. O. *Colima of New Spain in the Sixteenth Century.* Ibero-Americana, No. 29 (Berkeley, California, 1948).

SCHAEFER, E. *El Consejo Real y Supremo de las Indias.* 2 vols. (Seville, 1935–1947).

SCHOLES, W. V. *The Diego Ramírez Visita* (Columbia, Missouri, 1946).

SERRANO Y SANZ, M. *Orígenes de la dominación española en América* (Madrid, 1918).

SIGUENZA, JOSE DE. *Historia de la orden de San Jerónimo*. 2 vols. (Madrid [1605] 1909).

SIMPSON, L. B. *Studies in the Administration of the Indians in New Spain: I, The Laws of Burgos of 1512; II, The Civil Congregation; III, The Repartimiento System of forced native labor in New Spain and Guatemala; IV, The Emancipation of the Indian slaves and the resettlement of the Freedmen, 1548–1553*. Ibero-Americana, Nos. 7, 13, 16 (Berkeley, California, 1934–1940).

———. "Bernal Díaz del Castillo, Encomendero," *HAHR*, XVII, 100–106.

———. *Many Mexicos* (Berkeley and Los Angeles, 4th Ed., 1966).

SOLORZANO Y PEREYRA, JUAN DE. *Política Indiana*. 5 vols. (Madrid [1629–1639] 1930).

STEVENS, H., and LUCAS, F. W. (Eds.) *The New Laws of the Indies for the Good Treatment and Preservation of the Indians*. . . . Translated, with a facsimile reprint of the 1543 edition (London, 1892).

SUAREZ DE PERALTA, JUAN. *Noticias históricas de la Nueva España* (1589–90). Ed. Justo Zaragoza (Madrid, 1878).

TELLO, ANTONIO. *Historia de la Nueva Galicia*. DIM, II, 343–438.

TERNAUX-COMPANS, HENRI. *Voyages, relations et mémoires originaux pour servir à l'histoire de la découverte de l'Amérique*. 2ᵉ Série. 8 vols. (Paris, 1894).

TORQUEMADA, JUAN DE. *Monarquía Indiana*. 3 vols. (Seville [1615] 1723).

VILLAGUTIERRE SOTO-MAYOR, JUAN DE. *Historia de la conquista de la provincia de El Itza* ([Madrid, 1701] Guatemala, 1933).

VITORIA, FRANCISCO DE. *De Indis et de iure belli relectiones*. Ed. Ernest Nys (Washington, D. C., 1917).

YAÑEZ, AGUSTIN. *Fray Bartolomé de las Casas—Doctrina* (Mexico, 1941).

ZAVALA, SILVIO. *De Encomiendas y propiedad territorial en algunas regiones de la América Española* (Mexico, 1940).

———. *Contribución a la historia de las instituciones coloniales en Guatemala*. Jornadas, No. 36 (Mexico, 1945).

———. *New Viewpoints on the Spanish Colonization of America* (Philadelphia, 1943).

—————. *Las instituciones jurídicas en la conquista de América* (Madrid, 1935).

—————. *La Encomienda indiana* (Madrid, 1935).

—————. "Los trabajadores antillanos en el siglo XVI," *Revista de Historia de América*, No. 2, 31–67; No. 3, 64–88; No. 4, 211–216.

—————, and CASTELO, MARIA. (Eds.) *Fuentes para la historia del trabajo en Nueva España*. 8 vols. (Mexico, 1939–1945).

ZURITA, ALONSO DE. *Breve y sumaria relación de los señores y maneras y diferencias que había de ellos en la Nueva España. Nueva colección de documentos para la historia de México*, Vol. 3.

Index